DAGESTAN

DAGESTAN

Russian Hegemony and Islamic Resistance in the North Caucasus

Robert Bruce Ware and Enver Kisriev

Routledge
Taylor & Francis Group

LONDON AND NEW YORK

First published 2010 by M.E. Sharpe

Published 2015 by Routledge
2 Park Square, Milton Park, Abingdon, Oxon OX14 4RN
711 Third Avenue, New York, NY 10017, USA

Routledge is an imprint of the Taylor & Francis Group, an informa business

Copyright © 2010 Taylor & Francis. All rights reserved

Library of Congress Cataloging-in-Publication Data

Ware, Robert Bruce.
    Dagestan : Russian hegemony and Islamic resistance in the North Caucasus / by Robert
Bruce Ware and Enver Kisriev.
    p. cm.
    Includes index.
    ISBN 978-0-7656-2028-6 (cloth : alk. paper)— ISBN 978-0-7656-2029-3 (pbk. : alk. paper)
        1. Dagestan (Russia)—Ethnic relations—Political aspects. 2. Dagestan (Russia)—
Relations—Russia. 3. Caucasus, Northern (Russia)—Relations—Russia.
4. Russia—Relations—Russia (Federation)—Dagestan. 5. Russia—Relations—Russia
(Federation)—Caucasus, Northern. 6. Dagestan (Russia)—History. 7. Caucasus,
Northern (Russia)—History. 8. Islam—Russia (Federation)—Dagestan. 9. Islam—Russia
(Federation)—Caucasus, Northern. 10. Muslims—Russia (Federation)—Dagestan.
I. Kisriev, E. F. II. Title.

DK511.D2W37 2009
947.5'2—dc22   2008047517

ISBN 13: 9780765620293 (pbk)
ISBN 13: 9780765620286 (hbk)

Dedicated to Frid and Magiyat Kisriev

and

to all the Peoples of Dagestan

Contents

Acknowledgments

One must not approach the mountains without humility,
nor remain among them without reverence.

I am grateful for support from the National Council for Eurasian and East European Research, the National Research Council, the International Research and Exchanges Board, and Southern Illinois University, Edwardsville.

I am also grateful to the many colleagues who have helped me through the years. In addition to my coauthor, Enver Kisriev, special mention must go to Tatiana Chubrikova, John Colarusso, Ralph Davis, Michael Reynolds, Edward Walker, and above all, Zulfia Kisrieva-Ware. The editors and reviewers of the journals *Central Asian Survey*, *Eastern European Constitutional Review*, *Europe-Asia Studies*, *Middle Eastern Studies*, *Nationalities Papers*, *Post-Soviet Affairs,* and *Problems* of *Post-Communism* contributed to the development and improvement of our work as we shaped the building blocks of this book. Artur Tsutsiev graciously permitted us to adapt two of the maps from his *Atlas etnopoliticheskoi istorii Kavkaza* (1774–2004) (Moscow: Evropa, 2006). At M.E. Sharpe, I am grateful to Patricia Kolb, Makiko Parsons, and Ana Erlić.

Robert Bruce Ware
St. Louis, Missouri

Federal State borders
Administrative boundaries
Break-away territories

4. Republic of Abkhazia, including
 4a. territories controlled by authorities of Abkhazia (2004)
 4b. territories controlled by authorities of Georgia (2004)

5. Republic of South Ossetia, including
 5a. territories controlled by authorities of South Ossetia
 5b. territories controlled by authorities of Georgia (2004)

6. Nagorno-Karabakh republic, including
 6a. territories controlled by authorities of Nagorno-Karabakh
 6b. territories controlled by authorities of Azerbaijan
 6c. Shaumianovskii raion disputed by Nagorno-Karabakh

7. Territories of Azerbaijan occupied by Nagorno-Karabakh forces

8. Territories of Azerbaijan annexed by Armenia

9. Territories of Armenia annexed by Azerbaijan

Elista

Republic of Kalmykia

Budennovsk

FEDERATION

Kizlar

Caspian Sea

Republic of Ingushetia

Nazran Groznyy Gudermes Khasavurt

Nal'chik

Beslan

Nazran

Republic of North Ossetia

Vladikavkaz

Chechen Republic

Makhachkala

Buynaksk

Republic of South Ossetia

Republic of Dagestan

Tskhinvali

Derbent

GEORGIA

Tbilisi

ARMENIA

AZERBAIJAN

Baku

Yerevan

Nagorno-Karabakh

Stepanakert

Nakhichevan Autonomous Republic

Nakhichevan

IRAN

Aguls

Cherkess

Etnicheskaia karta

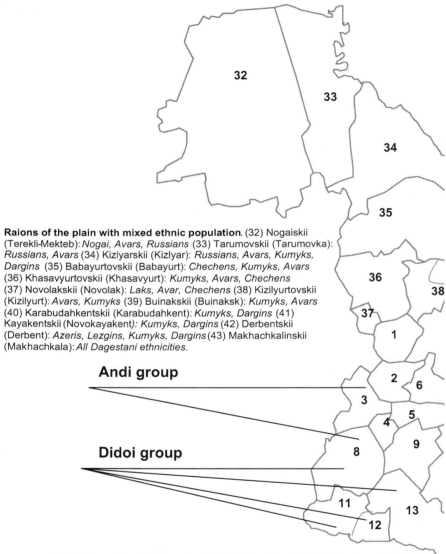

Raions of the plain with mixed ethnic population. (32) Nogaiskii (Terekli-Mekteb): *Nogai, Avars, Russians* (33) Tarumovskii (Tarumovka): *Russians, Avars* (34) Kizlyarskii (Kizlyar): *Russians, Avars, Kumyks, Dargins* (35) Babayurtovskii (Babayurt): *Chechens, Kumyks, Avars* (36) Khasavyurtovskii (Khasavyurt): *Kumyks, Avars, Chechens* (37) Novolakskii (Novolak): *Laks, Avar, Chechens* (38) Kizilyurtovskii (Kizilyurt): *Avars, Kumyks* (39) Buinakskii (Buinaksk): *Kumyks, Avars* (40) Karabudahkentskii (Karabudahkent): *Kumyks, Dargins* (41) Kayakentskii (Novokayakent): *Kumyks, Dargins* (42) Derbentskii (Derbent): *Azeris, Lezgins, Kumyks, Dargins* (43) Makhachkalinskii (Makhachkala): *All Dagestani ethnicities.*

Andi group

Didoi group

Ethnicities of Lezgin group: 1. *Rutuls* and *Tsak hurs* in Rutulskii raion; 2. *Aguls* in Agulskii raion; 3. *Tabasarans* in Tabasaranskii and Khivskii raions.

Minor Avar groups: 1. *Andi group* in Botlikhskii and Tsumadinskii raions, 2. *Didoi* group in Tsumadinskii, Tsuntinskii, Bezhtinskii and Tlyaratinskii raions.

Ethnic Map of Dagestan by Administrative Raions
(and Administrative City for Each Raion)

Avar raions: (1) Kazbekovskii (Dylym), (2) Gumbetovskii (Mekhelta), (3) Botlikhskii (Botlikh), (4) Akhvakhskii (Karata), (5) Khunzakhskii (Khunzakh), (6) Untsukulskii (Untsukul), (7) Gergebilskii (Gergebil), (8) Tsumadinskii (Agvali), (9) Shamilskii (Khebda), (10) Gunibskii (Gunib), (11) Tsuntinskii (Kidero), (12) Bezhtinskii (Bezhta), (13) Tlyaratinskii (Tlyarata), (14) Charodinskii (Tsurib)

Lezgin raions: (15) Rutulskii (Rutul), (16) Agulskii (Agul), (17) Kurakhskii (Kurakh), (18) Akhynskii (Akhti), (19) Dokuzparinskii (Usuhchai), (20) Suleiman-Stalskii (Kasunkent), (21) Magarankentskii Magaramkent), (22) Tabasaranskii (Huchni), (23) Khivskii (Khiv)

Lak raions: (24) Lakskii (Kumukh), (25) Kulinskii (Vachi)

Dargin raions: (26) Levashinskii (Levashi), (27) Akushinskii (Akusha), (28) Sergokalinskii (Sergokala), (29) Dahadaevskii (Urkarakh), (30) Kaitagskii (Madzhalis)

Kumyk raion: (31) Kumtorkalinskii (Korkmaskala).

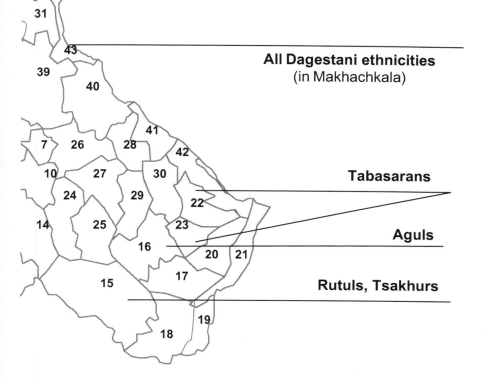

All Dagestani ethnicities
(in Makhachkala)

Tabasarans

Aguls

Rutuls, Tsakhurs

DAGESTAN

1

Introduction

Where Mountains Rise

Vertical versus Horizontal

Shortly after beginning his first term in the spring of 2000, Russia's president Vladimir Putin embarked upon a program of government recentralization. The program was presented as a necessary antidote to constitutional, administrative, and security issues arising from the period of sometimes chaotic decentralization that began in the final years of the Soviet Union and extended through the administration of Boris Yeltsin. On September 13, 2004, President Putin dramatically advanced this agenda with his announcement of sweeping electoral reforms culminating in the centralized appointment of regional governors.

These proposals were presented by President Putin in response to the Beslan school tragedy, as a means for reducing corruption and increasing security throughout the Russian Federation. In fact, it appeared that these proposals had been long in the making, but their presentation as a response to a hostage crisis in the North Caucasus served to sharpen questions about their efficacy and propriety in connection with regional problems of extremism and terrorism.

It is plausible that Russian decentralization was carried too far in the 1990s. Certainly the corrupt and self-serving regimes that it produced in the North Caucasus did little to address chronic problems of economic stagnation, infrastructural decay, environmental degradation, infectious disease, and organized crime that together contributed to alienation, radicalism, and terrorism in the region. Hence, it appeared that President Putin was correct in his premise that the problems of this region required political transformation. Yet the diminished political access and local accountability that resulted from renewed centralization led to increased levels of corruption, alienation, radicalism, and terrorism in this volatile region.

Few would fault the Kremlin for attempting to reconcile the federal constitution with its local counterparts or deny that local potentates have contributed to Russian administrative and security problems. Yet in assessing tradeoffs among corruption, economic disparity, accountability, and security it may be helpful to consider Russia's recentralization within a broader historical framework.

3

Russia's program of recentralization is the latest chapter in a series of struggles that have constituted the history of the North Caucasus over at least the past two millennia, and it bears similarities to much that has preceded it.

Historically, conflicts in the North Caucasus have derived from two competing approaches to social organization. On the one hand, the alpine geography of this region has given rise to a particularist approach to social organization based upon traditional North Caucasian values of parochialism, kinship, egalitarianism, and self-determination. On the other hand, a series of universalist approaches have been imported by civilizations that have attempted to incorporate this region into systems of expansive socioeconomic organization, commonly described as empires. Due to the demands of their geographical expanse, each of these empires has involved hierarchical systems of administration incompatible with traditional North Caucasian values.

Ironically, the expansion of these empires horizontally, across the lowlands, necessitates their organization within vertical hierarchies of social control. Conversely, the vertical terrain of the mountains sustains the egalitarianism, self-determination, and horizontal social organization of societies localized within the alpine valleys. In other words, the vertical-hierarchical organization of these empires was necessary for their successful geographical expansion, but when that expansion brought them to the foothills of the Caucasus Mountains it rendered them fundamentally incompatible with the horizontally egalitarian values of the societies that it encountered therein. At an elementary level, the series of great conflicts[1] that historically have beset this region may be seen as involving systems of lowland social administration that were organized vertically-hierarchically in order to facilitate horizontal expansion, spreading successfully until they bumped up against incompatibly parochial and horizontally egalitarian systems, which were no less a product of their vertically alpine geography.

In the past two millennia, the region has been visited by Arab, Mongol, Persian, Ottoman, and Russian empires, among others. It must be emphasized that each of these empires brought a unique culture and organizational structure. Yet all of them involved similar contrasts to indigenous social structures, all of them encountered similar problems, and all of them produced accounts that described the local populations in similar terms.

The Arrival of Islam

The Islamic expansion reached the North Caucasus soon after it began in the seventh century. Mohammad died in 632, and by 642 Suraqa bin 'Amr had led a contingent of Arabs to the gates of Derbent, in what is now southern Dagestan. After rapidly overrunning the Persian Empire, the Arabs pushed up the western shore of the Caspian Sea to the threshold of Eurasia. There they stood beneath the walls of Derbent, which span those three strategic kilometers that separate the eastern reach of the Caucasus Mountains from the Caspian shore. Recognizing the importance of the city to their northward expansion, and to virtually any other regional strategy, they proclaimed that the ancient city[2] had been established by the angel Gabriel, and declared its conquest to be divinely prescribed with divine absolution as a recompense for all who joined the struggle.[3]

Yet while they clearly recognized the strategic significance of the city, and while they had so recently overrun Persia, the Arab army proved incapable of controlling either Derbent or its environs. In 652, the Dagestanis decisively defeated the Arabs on the battlefield, and then rededicated themselves to their relentless and devastating raids against the Muslims. Though the Arabs periodically made punitive forays up the rugged slopes that they called "language mountain" as a homage to Dagestan's linguistic heterogeneity, and though they eventually managed to convert a few local potentates, they found themselves incapable of securing their own boundaries, let alone deterring constant harassment from the highlanders.[4] Ironically, the Eurasian antecedents of contemporary Russians were spared from Muslim conquest by the fierce resistance with which Dagestani parochialism met imperial expansion from the south. As Michael Reynolds puts it:

> Dagestan, in short, proved to be a difficult place to rule: geographically isolated, topographically rugged, and unrelentingly hostile. The Arabs and their chroniclers repeatedly expressed exasperation with the warlike North Caucasian infidels. Suraqa bin Amr described the torment of fighting the mountaineers in verse, and al-Masudi's angry description of a local Dagestani chieftain as a "host of robbers, brigands, and malefactors" hints at the Muslims' frustrations.[5]

Though the Muslims finally took Derbent in 686, they were never able to control Dagestan's interior. Yet if the Arabs never conquered Dagestan, they planted the seeds of its conversion when Derbent's population gradually adopted Islam. In the hills and mountains outside the walls of Derbent, the Lezgins were among the first of the Dagestani groups to come into contact with Islam at the end of the seventh century. The tradition of Islamic mysticism known as Sufism appeared in Dagestan in the eighth century, at the early stages of its development. Al-Farabi[6] and Al-Ghazali[7] are often credited with the elements of Sufism, yet its principles were also elaborated in a manuscript titled "Raihan al-Hakaik va bustan ad-Dakaik"[8] by an eleventh-century thinker from Derbent, known as el-Derbendy.

By this time Sufism was becoming the dominant form of Islam in Dagestan, which continued to nourish significant traditions of Sufi scholarship through the nineteenth century. Dagestan's localized social order and rugged terrain provided fertile ground for Sufism, which has sometimes shown antiestablishment tendencies. Followers of the Qadiri tariqah[9] appeared in Dagestan in the eleventh century, while the Naqshbandi tariqah arrived from eastern Anatolia in the fifteenth century, acquiring adherents especially among the Avar, Dargin, and Kumyk ethnicities. The Naqshbandi tariqah has acquired contemporary prominence in Dagestan through the influence of Sheikh Sayid-Efendi Cherkeevskii, but the Shazilya tariqah is also represented.

The *tariqah* is the Sufi path to God. The term is also used to identify the brotherhood with which an adherent walks that path. Each of these brotherhoods consists of a *sheikh* (teacher) and his *murids* (disciples). While all Muslims are on a path toward God, to whom they will draw closer after death, Sufism offers a mystical path toward a living union with God through the power of suffering and love. Sufis do not focus upon legalistic praxis, which they deem the "outward" manifestations of Islam. Rather, they are concerned with the "inner" meaning of the sacred texts (Koran and hadith). As a result, many orthodox/legalistic or puritanical believers have accused the Sufis of not being Muslims at all.

By the eleventh century, Derbent had become a center of Sofi practice at the northern boundary of the Muslim world. There locals were educated as *gazi* or holy warriors, and dispatched toward the highland heart of Dagestan on military marches that aimed to bring Islam to the fierce mountaineers. Because of the ceaseless resistance that the latter encountered from the locals, the spread of Islam from Derbent to central Dagestan was measured in centuries. Indeed, the indigenous Muslims of Derbent were no less beleaguered than the Arabs. In 971, for example, Christian attackers from Sarir, who may have been the ancestors of the modern Avars, overran Derbent's Muslim defenders.[10] Derbent's Muslim *amir* was occasionally driven to seek military support from the northern Slavs who were raiding Dagestan's Caspian coast from the tenth century on.[11]

Yet by the fourteenth century, Islam had reached Dagestan's largest ethnic group, the Avars. By the end of the fifteenth century, most Dagestanis had subscribed to the Shafi'i *madhab* or school of Sunni Islam.[12] Among Dagestan's numerous ethnic groups, Islam struck its deepest chords among the Avars, Dargins, and Kumyks.[13] In the fifteenth and sixteenth centuries, Islam spread to the Chechens and Ingushis, though it was not well established among these Vainakh peoples until the eighteenth century. Yet if the Vainakhs were among the region's youngest Muslims, they were also among its most zealous.

The Arabs may have failed to conquer Dagestan in the name of Allah, but Allah eventually triumphed over the next 1,000 years. And if the Dagestanis would not yield to the Arabs' imperial organization, they eventually learned to wield the faith of the Arabs as a weapon against another imperial expansion that would impinge upon them from the north at the end of that millennium. Reynolds concludes that:

> From the records left by the Arabs, we can already identify a number of factors that have distinguished the dynamics of the conflict in the Caucasus ever since. The first is the strategic nature of the region as a gateway between the Near East and the Eurasian steppes. The second is the rugged nature of its topography, which impeded the maneuver, command, and control of large fighting forces. Third, and perhaps most significant, is the equally rugged and fierce nature of the region's inhabitants. These latter two factors combined to exact a forbidding cost upon every power that has attempted to subdue the North Caucasus. The Arabs, who had overrun the Persian Empire in a mere ten years and would go on to phenomenal conquests elsewhere, were stunned by the truculence of the mountaineers. Their propensity for raids and banditry further infuriated the original Muslims. Finally, the linguistic and ethnic complexity of the region also impressed the Arabs. All of these traits would impress the later, non-Muslim conquerors as well.[14]

A History of Imperial Failures

In the thirteenth century, the Mongols arrived on the next wave of imperial expansion to strike the Caucasus. They swept down from the northeast along the Caspian shore, and occupied Derbent in 1233. Yet the Mongols had no more success than the Arabs in subduing the Dagestani highlanders, who seemed to have regarded these newest invaders essentially as "fresh meat." Eventually, the Mongols were compelled to pay tributes in order to stop the mountaineers from raiding them.[15]

Timurlenk (Tamerlane) occupied Dagestan in 1395–96; yet he moved on to the southern side of the mountains without establishing a lasting presence in the North Caucasus. In the sixteenth and seventeenth centuries, the Ottoman and Safavid empires made incursions into the northeast Caucasus without consolidating their control. Dagestani leaders successfully played the Ottomans against the Safavids, and occasionally even the Russians, in order to preserve a measure of independence.

Beginning in the eighteenth century, the Safavids met growing resistance in Dagestan. When a local Muslim leader named Hadji-Daud announced that he had been called by Allah to liberate Dagestan's Sunni population from southern Shiite oppression, he won support from Surhai-Khan, the sovereign of Kazi-Kumukh, as well as from Akhmed-Khan of Kaitag. In 1712 Surhai-Khan liberated the town of Shamakhi from the Safavid Persians. By 1721, this movement succeeded in expelling the Persians from Dagestan and northern Azerbaijan.

After he was encouraged by military successes elsewhere in his southern empire, the Persian ruler Nadir Shah vowed to reestablish the Persian presence in Dagestan in 1742. Yet just three years later, he too was forced to withdraw from Dagestan, and died soon after. Relentlessly, the Dagestanis resumed their raids into Safavid territory. As Reynolds remarks:

> The patterns first observed during the Arab invasions of the region thus repeated themselves in the period leading up to the Russian conquest. The mountaineers vigorously opposed all attempts by outsiders to impose their rule and proved to be indomitable . . . the difficult terrain, the mountaineers' pugnacity, and the lack of a central government—put a decisive stamp on the form of conflict in the North Caucasus. . . . The geography, in addition to sheltering the mountaineers from outside rule by raising the costs and lowering the benefits of intervention, also fostered the development of a culture that prized such attributes as athletic prowess, physical courage, and self-reliance; that is, martial virtues.[16]

While geographical theories of cultural determinism are often controversial, the influence of the rugged terrain upon regional character types is mentioned anecdotally by the people of this region, and has figured historically in the accounts of outside observers. For example, the Ottoman historian Ahmed Cevdet Pasha connected the region's topography to the egalitarian traditions of its natives in his conclusion that: "Since their land is steep and difficult, they do not submit to a government."[17] At the beginning of the twentieth century, John Baddeley wrote that, "The people of the Caucasus owe it not only their salient characteristics, but their very existence. It may be said without exaggeration that the mountains made the men."[18] Reynolds remarks that the geographical obstacles of the region were compounded by their cultural counterparts, rendering the mountaineers

> allergic to central control. These same factors acted to block local sovereigns as much as outside hegemons from uniting and centralizing the region. Because ad-hoc coalitions of local leaders proved sufficient for withstanding outside invasions, up until the nineteenth century there was neither much incentive nor a sociocultural basis for the formation of a state or other political-administrative structure that would embrace the North Caucasus as a whole.[19]

Nevertheless, Reynolds observes that Sunni Islam provided the North Caucasus with a "conceptual foundation for nation building." In contrast with some world religions, for example, Buddhism or Christianity, Sunni Islam is geared intrinsically toward political activity. Indeed, it would be misleading to suggest that Islam joins theology with politics, for in Islam these are not two distinct spheres of life.[20] This is because the Prophet Mohammed was, among many other things, a military and political leader.[21] He sought to offer his followers a comprehensive set of guidelines for most aspects of human life, including political affairs. For centuries, his life has been taken as a model for military and political leadership. This model was further developed by a series of Islamic political philosophers, including Al-Farabi (870–950), Avicenna (930–1037), Ibn Bajja (d. 1138), and Ibn Tufayl (d. 1185). Eldest among Russia's Muslim regions, Dagestan has contributed to Islamic thought through the work of Sufi writers such as Magomed Abu Bakr ad-Derbendi (early eleventh century), Abu Khamid al-Ghazali (1059–1111), and Magomed Yaragsky (d. 1839).

Venturing beyond more restrictive conceptions of theological doctrine, the Sunni faith draws upon the divinely mandated law, the *sharia*, which prescribes social and political relations as spiritual mandates comparable to the individual's ritual obligations to God. Sharia offers a comprehensive, and often codified, body of social laws that it derives from Koran and the hadiths (anthologies based upon Mohammad's statements and deeds). At the core of sharia is the recognition that its laws depend upon enforcement from *dawla*, or the state. Political philosophy and jurisprudence are integral elements in the study of classical Islam.

Confrontation and Compromise Among Competing Forms of Social Organization

In recent periods, two expansive social organizations have competed for control of the North Caucasus: Russian and Islamist. Because each has encountered opposition from traditional local structures, it is useful to consider three alternative forms of social organization as having joined in competition for preeminence in the North Caucasus. First, there have been the local systems of parochialism, egalitarianism, and self-determination that are traditional to North Caucasian societies. While these vary dramatically among themselves,[22] they have proved, in varying degrees, resistant to the hierarchical forms of organization that a long series of empires have attempted to impose upon them. Second, there has been the hierarchical system of dominance and subordination that is more or less traditional to Russian society.[23] Third, there have been systems of expansionist absolutism advocated by Islamist extremists. Variations of these three systems— traditional-local, Russian, and expansionist Islamist—have competed on and off in the North Caucasus for the past 200 years.

During these years there have been periods in which each of these principles was in ascendance, and periods in which each was in decline. There
were periods in which each system was advanced by its proponents in stark
opposition to the others, and periods of relative compromise. This spirit of
compromise was illustrated perhaps most stunningly when the Dagestani
highlanders forced the Mongols to pay them tribute. But a more important
instance occurred in the latter half of the nineteenth century when the Russian
imperial administration in Dagestan accepted traditional village law (*adat*)
and political organization, along with village-based Islamic functionaries, and
played their parochialism against efforts by some Islamic leaders to organize
another wave of expansive popular resistance.

By contrast, the Soviet Union offered North Caucasians different forms
of compromise. On the one hand, the Soviet Union persecuted Islam, and
imposed a stark system of hierarchy and domination in keeping with Russian
traditions. Yet at the same time, Soviet collectivism was roughly concordant
with traditional highland village life. Moreover, Stalin's ethnic policies
paid lip service to local traditions of kinship and parochialism by carving
the region into a series of titular republics, wherein linguistic and cultural
distinctions were subsequently reified. In the post-Stalin period, the Soviet
Union offered North Caucasians tangible benefits in terms of security and
economic development.

Political stability in the North Caucasus has been strengthened by such
periods of relative compromise. On the other hand, periods of stark opposition
among any of these three social systems have tended to undermine regional
stability. Have these oppositions been heightened by Moscow's efforts to recentralize political control through the assertion of a hierarchically organized
political system in place of parochial democratic structures? In the absence
of tangible improvements in local security and economic development, are
these efforts more likely to precipitate or to prevent the further destabilization of the region?

In the face of globalizing pressures of the twenty-first century, most local
residents realize that North Caucasian parochialism is not sustainable. Hence,
the questions are, which of the two competing approaches to a more expansive
mode of social organization will eventually consolidate the region, and what
kind of terms will that system reach with the traditional cultural and economic
requirements of the region?

The Russian system has had advantages including: (1) political inertia
resulting from current Russian control; (2) the legacy of Soviet security and
economic benefits; (3) unattractive features of proximate states in the South
Caucasus; (4) the Yeltsin administration's willingness to compromise with
local sociopolitical structures. For example, from 1994 to 2003,[24] the Russian

Federation accommodated Dagestan's uniquely democratic political system, despite the fact that the latter boasted a distinctive ethnic electoral system and the federation's only executive that was either collegial in its nature[25] or indirectly elected.[26] Each of these singularities was inspired by the requirements of Dagestan's ethnic heterogeneity and the traditional sociopolitical structures to which it has given rise.[27] Similarly, both the Yeltsin and Putin administrations proved willing to compromise and cooperate with leaders of the region's traditional Sufi Islam in their struggles with a strain of expansionist, Islamist extremism known locally as "Wahhabism." Examples of compromise are the certification of the Islamic Party of Russia,[28] and Putin's application for Russian membership in the Organization of the Islamic Conference. Examples of cooperation are Putin's June 2000 appointment of Mufti Akhmad-Khadji Kadyrov to administrative leadership of Chechnya,[29] and political authorizations extended to the Spiritual Directorate of the Muslims of Dagestan.[30]

These are precisely the sorts of compromises from which the region's Wahhabis have been prevented by their absolutist ideology. Wahhabism is an expansive mode of social organization whose adherents seek to establish an Islamic state in the North Caucasus. Hence it can achieve its ideological objectives only insofar as it overcomes both the Russian mode of social organization and the traditionally parochial societies of the region. Thus far Wahhabism has proved unprepared to compromise with either of these. Moreover, since Wahhabis seek to establish an expansive Islamic state in the North Caucasus, they would require the region to divorce itself from existing nation states in a manner that is unlikely to provide economic or security benefits to local residents. Finally, the austere tenets of Wahhabism are incompatible with the moderate practices of the region's traditional Sufi Islam,[31] and have been fiercely rejected by overwhelming majorities of local residents.[32] For all of these reasons, Wahhabism has been regarded as an unattractive alternative by most North Caucasians, and the Russian system therefore should not have had great difficulty in consolidating its control over the region by means of moderate compromises with the traditional requirements of local communities.

Hence, it seems surprising that Moscow adopted a much less compromising political strategy after Putin rose to power. Since the spring of 2000, Moscow's program of administrative recentralization has been gradually shifting the political balance of the region in a manner that seems to be ultimately less conducive to Russian management. This is because it has undermined previous political compromises without offering widespread economic benefits or tangible security improvements. On the contrary, there is a general sense in the region that security has deteriorated. Indeed, the strategy of Wahhabi leaders has seemed, at times, to advertise this point by way of periodic terrorist atrocities as well as by targeting government and law enforcement officials for assassination.

Meanwhile wealth has become more concentrated as genuine opportunities for legitimate economic advancement have diminished. To be sure, Moscow has been heavily subsidizing the republics of this region. Dagestan, for example, has regularly received more than 80 percent of its budget from the federal center, while Ingushetia has received in excess of 85 percent. Yet federal mandates have required that some of this money be allocated for material purchases from Moscow suppliers, and too much of the remainder has lined the pockets of a diminishing number of political elites in the south. Overall, corruption and economic disparity have increased in the North Caucasus, while political access and local accountability have narrowed. Gradually, the region has seen the development of hierarchies of power and subordination that resemble those of Russian colonial domination in the early nineteenth century, although with local elites occupying rungs that were previously held by Russian administrators.

During the period of conquest, early Russian colonialism ignored the region's traditional egalitarianism in order to empower local potentates as administrative vassals. The result was increasing economic disparities, corruption, and political repression. Those conditions inspired the murid movement in Dagestan, which later spread to Chechnya. The murid movement drew upon the structure of local tariqah Islam with its groups of students (murids) and their Islamic teachers (sheikhs). Muridism was a political ideology devised in opposition to the Russian colonial hierarchy, and drawing upon Islamic teachings such as: "A true Muslim can neither subordinate, nor be subordinated to, another man."

In other words, when the hierarchical and expansionist features of Russian colonialism became incompatible with local traditions, the Dagestanis turned to a political interpretation of Islam that they devised as a counterweight, culminating in twenty-eight years of brutal warfare from 1831 to 1859. In order to sustain their struggle against the Russian empire, murid leaders such as Imam Shamil had to wage a simultaneous war against the parochialism of the local villages and their traditional codes of law, known as *adat*. Shamil sought to unite all of the villages of the northeast Caucasus in one expansive imamate under the rule of Islamic sharia.

Thus in the early nineteenth century, the traditional Russian system of hierarchy and domination drove many Dagestanis and Chechens toward an Islamist response. However, the murid ideology that they devised was also expansionist and therefore also at odds with the traditional parochialism of the region. This contributed to its defeat in 1859, after which a series of tsarist, Soviet, and democratic administrations found various means of compensating, or compromising with, local sociopolitical needs.

The period that began with the Dubrovka Theater hostage crisis in Moscow in October 2002 and culminated in the Beslan school hostage crisis in North Ossetia in September 2004 may be viewed as a watershed in the North Caucasus. The intervening months saw a series of democratic setbacks in the region, including the manipulation of Chechnya's constitutional referendum, the manipulation of the Chechen presidential election, the imposition of a new constitution upon Dagestan, the assassination of Chechnya's president, and the manipulation of a second Chechen presidential election. Meanwhile Ingushetia was gradually destabilized after the Kremlin instigated the withdrawal of its popular president, Ruslan Aushev, and his replacement by Murat Zyazikov, a former officer of the Russian Federal Security Service, who sought to compensate for his political weakness by means of brutal repression.

Did the destabilization of Ingushetia foreshadow events in neighboring republics following the centralized appointment of local governors? Ironically, Moscow's program of recentralization seems to have contributed to precisely those problems in the North Caucasus that it was advertised as preventing.

If Moscow had stimulated local economies while playing the neutral arbiter among the region's relentless political rivalries it might have earned the enduring loyalty of the local peoples. If, instead of umpire, it prefers to play empire, then it may reap their resentment. Might Moscow have been wiser to support economic development together with democratic procedures in the North Caucasus? In order to answer these questions it will be helpful to take a closer look at the complex history of confrontation and compromise among the three systems of social organization that have competed for this region over the past two centuries.

2

Murids and Tsars
Islamic Ideology as an Antidote to Russian Colonialism

In the mid-sixteenth century, Tsar Ivan the Terrible established alliances in Dagestan and Kabarda with local chieftains who sought to balance Ottoman and Persian influences in the region. At the end of that century, the first Russian fort was raised where Dagestan's Sulak River meets the Caspian Sea.[1] In 1722 Peter I's Caspian campaign became Russia's first direct military intervention in Dagestan, though it eventually furthered the interests of Persia. In his manifesto dated June 15 of that year, Peter declared that the "Russian Army joined our friend, the Iranian Shah Hussein, against the Dagestanis, Hadji-Daud and Surkhai-Khan, that rose against their sovereign" and raided Russian merchants. A large Russian army marched down the west Caspian corridor, seizing Derbent and its environs. At about the same time, Peter furthered Russian incursions into northern Dagestan by founding the Russian city of Kizliar.[2] Yet difficulties in other regions of Peter's far-flung empire forced the withdrawal of Russian troops, and by 1732 Russia had ceded Dagestan to Persia.

By the latter half of the eighteenth century, Russia was consolidating its control of the Stavropol region, and initiating military incursions southward toward the mountains. Beginning in the 1760s, Russia expanded its presence in the region with a chain of fortresses that eventually stretched across the plains of the North Caucasus and that served as the origin for several contemporary cities and towns.[3] This Russian presence was anchored with the construction of a military outpost at Mozdok (now in North Ossetia) in 1763, followed in 1790, by the fortress of Vladikavkaz.[4] As early as the 1780s, Catherine the Great initiated expansionist warfare against North Caucasian clans.[5] In 1806, Russia annexed Kabarda and Derbent, and Ossetian leaders recognized Russian control. In 1818, Russian fortifications were established in Grozny and Nalchik, and by 1844 a fortress had been erected at Petrovsk, now known as Makhachkala. This chain of Russian forts, running east and west along the base of the mountains, precipitated a century of conflict with the highlanders of the region.

In addition to this military challenge, Russian expansionism posed a yet more serious demographic threat, as the flow of settlers southward disrupted the local economy and drove the local population further upward into less arable highland territories.[6] As early as the seventeenth century, Christian Cossacks had begun to settle along the Terek River, and congregated in the town of Kizliar in northern Dagestan.[7] Skillfully playing the Cossacks against the Muslim natives, St. Petersburg's policies for undermining Islam and converting its subjects to Russian Orthodox Christianity "added a cultural and spiritual dimension to the threat."[8]

These new incursions mobilized the diverse societies of the North Caucasus in a variety of ways. In the northwestern Caucasus, the Circassian tribes sought closer alliances with one another, while also striving to play the Ottomans against the Russians.[9] Resistance was largely passive in Kabarda and northern Dagestan, but the northeastern highland clans of Chechnya and Dagestan began to organize a fierce Islamic resistance. In 1783, the same year Russia annexed the Crimea, a Chechen religious leader known as Sheikh Mansur Ushurma emerged. Proclaiming the unity of the highland clans, Mansur called upon them to participate in a jihad against the Russians. He relied on religious as well as political leaders from throughout the region, and evidently tapped into Sufi networks, in order to gather a sufficiently large force to wage devastating guerilla attacks that inflicted several defeats upon the Russians. While there are various claims regarding the extent of Mansur's Sufi connections, and though he was without widespread support in Dagestan,[10] there is no question that Mansur's organizational, as well as his tactical, innovations were an important legacy to subsequent Islamic resistance in the region. In the end, Mansur was captured by the Russians, and died a prisoner in the Shlisselburg fortress in 1791.[11]

In 1796, Russian forces occupied Derbent, and by 1803, the Avarian Khanate voluntarily submitted to Russian rule. Yet it was another decade before Russia formally acquired Dagestan through its Gulistan Treaty with Persia in 1813. During the next fifty years, it devoted much of its military resources to its efforts to establish control of the region. By 1818 there was a widespread revolt against the ruthless tactics of the Russian Commander in the Caucasus, General Aleksey Petrovich Yermolov. Against entire populations, Yermolov waged a form of total warfare with tactics that included mass deportations, scorched earth, and mass starvation. For episodes that might be characterized as "genocidal" today, he was criticized by his contemporaries, and even cautioned by the tsars Alexander I and Nicholas I. Yet he notoriously responded to this criticism with the claim that "Gentleness in the eyes of Asiatics is a sign of weakness, and out of pure humanity I am inexorably severe."[12]

Though their severity was barely diminished, the efficacy of Yermolov's destructive tactics was partially mitigated by structural peculiarities that he encountered in the North Caucasus at the micro, as well as the macro, level. At the micro level, Yermolov's tactic of razing highland villages to the ground was rendered somewhat less devastating by the Chechen propensity for wooden dwellings, which facilitated the reconstruction of their villages. The Dagestani preference for stone construction was a relative liability.[13] More important, at the regional level, the decentralized nature of highland life substantially undermined the efficacy of Yermolov's methods. Because of the traditionally parochial nature of highland life, the region was fragmented into a mosaic of village-states, which had to be conquered one at a time. As was the case in their resistance to all preceding empires, the decentralized nature of North Caucasian life, itself a product of the mountains, helped the local peoples to resist imperial conquest.

The difficulties that Yermolov faced as a result of the region's traditional sociopolitical fragmentation were especially significant in the case of the Chechens, who lacked any overarching political structure. Chechen society was organized according to a seven-tiered kinship structure, centering on clans (*teips*) that in turn composed larger federations (*tuhums*).[14] The only unifying body that the Chechens recognized was the Mekh Kel, an egalitarian assembly of clan leaders, which exercised limited authority in cases where unanimity was lacking.[15] In Chechnya, Islamic zealotry went hand in hand with an egalitarianism that recognized neither class distinctions nor aristocratic privilege. As Reynolds puts it:

> Every Chechen male was an *uzden*, or "freeman." It is only a slight exaggeration to say that every Chechen was in effect free to act as he saw fit within the bounds of the Chechen code of behavior, which admired courage and resistance as much as it disdained weakness and submission. Yermolov's strategy of intimidation was far less effective against such a decentralized and resilient society.[16]

Yet if the traditional fragmentation of Chechen society was an obstacle to Russian expansion, elsewhere in the region the opposite was the case. In their effort to establish their power, Russian administrators exploited the ethnic diversity of the region through a strategy of "divide and rule." Relatively unified groups, such as the Circassians, were subdivided among a number of artificial ethnicities that stressed previously subsidiary ethnolinguistic distinctions. Other Russian policies favored Christians in Armenia, Georgia, and Ossetia over the region's Islamic population, and settled Cossacks in the territories of numerous ethnic groups. The Transcaucasus fell under Russian control long before the Eastern Caucasus had been subdued.

Library of Congress Cataloging-in-Publication Data

Ware, Robert Bruce.
  Dagestan : Russian hegemony and Islamic resistance in the North Caucasus / by Robert
Bruce Ware and Enver Kisriev.
  p. cm.
  Includes index.
  ISBN 978-0-7656-2028-6 (cloth : alk. paper)
  1. Dagestan (Russia)—Ethnic relations—Political aspects. 2. Dagestan (Russia)—
Relations—Russia. 3. Caucasus, Northern (Russia)—Relations—Russia.
4. Russia—Relations—Russia (Federation)—Dagestan. 5. Russia—Relations—Russia
(Federation)—Caucasus, Northern. 6. Dagestan (Russia)—History. 7. Caucasus, Northern
(Russia)—History. 8. Islam—Russia (Federation)—Dagestan. 9. Islam—Russia (Federation)—
Caucasus, Northern. 10. Muslims—Russia (Federation)—Dagestan.
I. Kisriev, E. F. II. Title.

DK511.D2W37 2009
947.5'2—dc22   2008047517

Printed in the United States of America

The paper used in this publication meets the minimum requirements of
American National Standard for Information Sciences
Permanence of Paper for Printed Library Materials,
ANSI Z 39.48-1984.

CW (c)   10   9   8   7   6   5   4   3   2   1

Russia's nineteenth century struggle to control the North Caucasus took the form of a military administration that combined autocracy with the traditional local influences of Islam and adat, that is, local customary law. It produced a form of government that was at once bureaucratic in its form and arbitrary in its policies. Bureaucratic appointees, who often were imported from Christian areas of the Caucasus, especially Georgia and Armenia, arrived at relations of patronage with members of the local "aristocracy."

In Dagestan, there were efforts to establish the traditionally hierarchical power structures that had enabled centuries of Russian expansion. Hence the tsarist administrations relied upon the local "aristocracy," though the social status of this group differed substantially from its Russian counterpart. The confiscation of lands for the imperial treasury was followed by distributions of those same lands to local elites who agreed to cooperate with the new rulers. This imposition of the Russian model of sociopolitical organization led, on the one hand, to the elevation of a pseudo-aristocracy of loyal local elites, and, on the other hand, to the enslavement of the formerly free *djamaat*, or village, populations, who were reduced to the misery of forced labor.

These practices undermined traditional systems of sociopolitical relations among the local population. The result looked less like the construction of a new social system than the demoralization of the old. Formerly democratic highland societies degenerated into little tyrannies, in which arbitrary power was propped up by the strength of the Russian military. Ordinary citizens had to choose between submission to these petty tyrannies and armed resistance. This resistance drew upon a potent combination of Islamic and clan-based solidarity, together with the self-reliant individualism and egalitarianism that traditionally characterized "free societies" in the area. In the Northeast Caucasus it was neither national groups nor village chiefs that organized the fight against Russian expansion. Rather it was tribal federations fighting under a novel variant of Islamic organization known as muridism, a religious ideology of political resistance based upon Sufi traditions.

Thus the pressures of colonialism led to the formulation of a new Sufi ideology of liberation and self-determination. The murid movement depended upon the traditional organization of mystical Sufi brotherhoods, or *tariqahs*, that consisted of *murids*, or students, around an Islamic teacher, or *sheikh*. Muridism initially emerged within the Naqshbandi Sufi brotherhood, where it appeared as a spiritual response of Dagestan's formerly free djamaat population to the critical changes in the sociocultural conditions of life, inspired by the divisive politics and the harsh administration of the tsar's occupation officials. This movement had the goal of spiritual purification of Muslims from the imposition of a foreign religion, the perceived impurities of the new society, and the inequities of the new aristocratic order.[17]

These political goals were expressed in the concept of *gazavat*, or war of liberation. This doctrine was propounded by Mullah Magomed from the Yaragi djamaat of southern Dagestan after he became the highest Sheikh-Murshid of the Naqshbandi brotherhood. Magomed Yaragsky's early statements were exclusively moral admonitions and appeals. The erosion of traditional Dagestani norms and values led him to preach a strong spiritual response. Gradually, the sheikh developed a doctrine that evoked the spiritual aspirations and social demands of the djamaat population.

At the basis of his teaching was the concept of the freedom of a Muslim from subordination to anyone. His main idea was that "A Muslim cannot be a slave, or anybody's subject; he should not pay taxes; and there should be equality among Muslims."[18] The conclusion that followed was that Dagestanis who called themselves Muslims were not in fact such, since they had been subordinated by local rulers and oppressed by foreigners. It made no difference that the former subjugation was to Muslims and the latter was to Christians. Yaragsky's admonition simply implied that the true Muslim was free from oppression in all forms, and that the unfaithful were those who either oppressed or suffered oppression. Conversely, a Christian who lived freely and did not oppress another man was not to be considered an enemy of the Muslims.

This approach demanded a revision of one of the Pillars of Islam, namely *zakat*, or mandatory charity. The word literally means "purification," since it was believed that a tithe given for those in need purifies and legitimizes material prosperity. Zakat contributions are based upon income from different kinds of profit and property. Yet in the Dagestani practice of those years, zakat had become a mandatory tax that not only was used for its intended purpose but also was misappropriated by those who regulated its collection and distribution, including mullahs, kadis or judges, and other clerics.

Based on his conviction that "a Muslim is a free man and should not pay taxes to anyone," Magomed Yaragsky rejected customary practices for the distribution of zakat. He cited passages from the Koran such as the following: "If you give charity openly, this is good, but if you secretly help the poor it is better for you, and it covers all of your bad deeds."[19] According to Magomed Yaragsky, passages such as this implied that zakat should not be a mandatory tax that one man pays to another, but rather the duty of a free man to his God, serving exclusively to support the poor, and others in need. Following from this view, the sheikh decided to refuse the portion of the zakat that his djamaat customarily dedicated for his personal allowance. He declined his traditional remuneration by way of a penance before the people of his village that also affirmed his new ideology:

I am very sinful before Allah and the Prophet. Until now I understood neither Allah's will, nor the Prophet's predictions. Only by the mercy of the Most High have my eyes now been opened . . . I used the fruit of your fields, and was enriching myself at your expense, but a sheik should not take even a tenth of your property, and a judge should take only what Allah promised him for his service. I did not observe these Commandments, and now my conscience accuses me. I wish to redeem my guilt, and beg for forgiveness from Allah and you, and return everything that I previously took from you. Come here: all my possessions should become yours! Take them and divide them among yourselves.[20]

The sacrifices and insights of the Sheikh of Yaragi showed the way (*tariqah*) for those who sought to become true Muslims, the way that was known as *gazavat*. On the one hand, gazavat indicated a war of liberation from oppression. Yet, as used at Yaragi at the time, gazavat was neither a war that intended to bring the faith to pagans nor an attack on infidels; it was not *jihad*, or holy war. Rather gazavat was the zeal of a Muslim on his way to Allah.[21] As proclaimed by Magomed of Yaragi, gazavat was rebellion against oppression, whether the source of oppression was the local customs, or the local "aristocracy," or the soldiers and bureaucrats that served the tsar.[22]

This interpretation of Islam was criticized, at that time, by some well-known Dagestani *ulema*, including Barka-kadi of Akushi and Said of Arakani Mirza-Ali.[23] Yet whether or not the teachings of Magomed of Yaragi were consistent with tariqah traditions, the organization of his adherents was in accord with the Sufi model of the tariqah brotherhood (*taifa*), consisting of a union of murids (students, apprentices, disciples) around their *murshid* (teacher, sheikh). In the end, it was not the scholarly esoterica, but rather the political significance of the new ideological approach that defined its social response. In his notes "On the Beginning and Development of *Muridism* or Spiritual Muslim War in Dagestan in 1823–1834," K.I. Prushanovsky, the captain of the General Staff of the Russian Army, described the effect of Magomed Yaragsky's penance upon the surrounding populations:

Since then the doors of the Mosques were rarely closed; men and women, even children, crowded in the Temples of the Prophet, prayed to God, cried, and promised not to commit sins. The word about Mullah Magomed was spread across the whole of Dagestan, and Dagestanis started flocking to the village of Yaragi from every corner; they were looking for his blessing, sworn to follow his teaching, admit him as their Murshid, and declare themselves as his Murids.[24]

In the Kurinskii khanate, where the village of Yaragi was located, there soon began ritual, mystical initiations of children involving symbolic wooden swords marked with admonitions, such as "Muslims! Gazavat! Gazavat!" In other parts of Dagestan, especially Avaria, the followers of Yaragsky's teachings brandished real weapons.

In 1824, Kazi-Magomed of Gimri, with the approval of his sheikh, Magomed Yaragsky, was elected *imam* (that is, military and political leader of Muslims) and declared gazavat. His success in the struggle against local khans, or aristocrats, and Russian garrisons laid a strong foundation for the new supra-djamaat, or imamate, a united, political organization of mountaineers. After Kazi-Magomed's death in battle against the Russian army in 1832, Gamzat-bek was declared imam. He was followed, in 1834, by Shamil, whose twenty-five-year war with the Russian empire attracted international attention.[25]

The movement of muridism was emerging as a moral response to the degradation of the sociopolitical basis of djamaat society under external pressure from the empire to the north. Yet its organized opposition to those external pressures soon culminated in expansionist efforts to unite Muslims throughout Dagestan with those of Chechnya. In turn, the efforts to achieve this unification implied an internal struggle against not only the presumptions of the local aristocrats but also the particularism of the djamaats, which fractured Dagestan into hundreds of little states.

The struggle of the murids to overcome the djamaats soon became a struggle against the customary law, or adat, upon which each djamaat was based. Ironically, before the rise of muridism, the civil laws of the djamaats were not regarded as adat, which is to say that they were not regarded as being opposed to sharia. Rather they were considered to be consistent with sharia.[26] Sharia jurisprudence permits the approval of laws that correspond to the demands of conditions and circumstances where they are made.[27]

The redefinition of djamaat laws as adat, or as something opposed to sharia, is an ideological innovation dating only from the beginning of the nineteenth century, when it was the view adopted by the emerging political-religious movement, muridism. It was tantamount to a redefinition of the djamaat as being contrary to Islam. In the course of organizing a North Caucasian resistance to Russian conquest, murid leaders also declared war against the independent mountain "republics" and "principalities" in order to unite all Muslims under the banner of purified Islam. Essentially, the war against adat on behalf of sharia meant a rejection of the constitutions of the djamaats with a view toward the unification of the imamate.[28]

No sooner had the Russians begun to contain traditional forms of Caucasian resistance than their hierarchical administrative methods gave rise to the murids. But, while the murid movement arose in opposition to the external pressures of Russian colonialism, it quickly embarked upon an effort to transform the internal structure of North Caucasian society. This was because the murids could mount an effective opposition to the Russian empire only by uniting the Muslims of Dagestan and Chechnya. Thus, in their efforts to resist the Russians, the murids were compelled to wage war against traditional North Caucasian social structures, for there was no other way for them to expand and strengthen their mode of Islamic organization. Yet this required a transcendence of the particularism inherent in Dagestan's traditional djamaats, or village states, as well as in the traditional Chechen kinship structures. Hence, in order to wage their twenty-eight-year war against Russia, the murids also waged war upon the local djamaats, seeking to replace their customary law, or adat, with a more restricted understanding of Islamic sharia law.

Through its own revealing dialectic, the murid resistance to Russian domination that was initiated in the name of traditional North Caucasian values of equality and self-determination soon became a struggle against traditional North Caucasian parochialism. The same political fragmentation that had long underpinned Caucasian resistance to imperial domination was a problem for the murid approach to social organization no less than it was for the Russians. For millennia, traditional North Caucasian social structures had resisted imperial expansion. Yet with the rise of muridism in the nineteenth century, the North Caucasus saw a struggle between three competing models of social organization: traditional, Islamist, and Russian. By the middle of that century, the traditionally particularistic social structures of the Northeast Caucasus were under assault from both Russian and Islamic modes of expansionism.

The Repression of the Islamic Leadership Under Military Rule

Further ironies followed the surrender of Shamil in 1859. Shamil's political campaign against the djamaats was brought to a close when the tsarist administration created the "Dagestani Oblast of the Russian Empire." Yet, at the same time, his religious campaign was defeated when, as a counterweight to muridism, Russian administrators founded the new province on the traditions of the djamaats with an emphasis upon adat. Sharia was to be strictly limited, while the Sufi brotherhoods were subsequently persecuted. This system of government was presented as a "military-people's administration." Because the administration was "military," Russian civil laws did not apply in Dagestan. A limited form of adat was preserved within the internal life of the djamaats, and sharia was still used to determine relations between husband and wife, parents and children, and cases involving stealing or cheating that did not exceed fifty rubles.

The regime in the djamaats remained much as it had been prior to Shamil, except that the councils of "village elders" and "village judges" were appointed by the military administration. Clerics were removed from power but kadis became members of the courts. They served as consultants on issues of Islamic justice, maintained records, and managed the exclusively religious affairs of the djamaats. Village assemblies were also allowed, but they were deprived of any real power or significance. The authors of a text dated April 26, 1868, and titled "The State of Agricultural Management in Dagestan," explained these concessions as an "unwillingness to create opposition" to Russian administrative power among the religious leadership of the djamaats. They wrote:

> Thus, adats, and the djamaat administrations that are based upon them, serve us as a firm foundation in the approaching lengthy and covert fight with the Islamic clerics for influence over these people. The clerics will not remain indifferent to the fact that their influence is weakening, mainly due to the loss of their right to judge and prosecute.[29]

Russia's conquest of the North Caucasus had cost the lives of 20,000 of its soldiers. More than 60,000 had been wounded and 6,000 had become captives. After the war, Russia's presence in the region could be sustained only at the cost of a quarter of its imperial budget. The burden of these costs deterred the Russian military administration from any further attempt at interference with existing, economic, social, and legal systems. Dagestan saw no further attempt at "grand agrarian colonization."[30]

Unlike Russia's initial attempt, in the early 1800s, at a more strictly hierarchical colonial organization that ignored local traditions, Russia's late nineteenth-century military-colonial organization sought to compromise with traditional village structures, including lower level Islamic officials, in an attempt to build local alliances against the resurgence of an Islamic expansionist ideology, such as muridism had supplied.

Yet despite these concessions, rebellion continued in the second half of the nineteenth century. Revolts broke out in various parts of Dagestan in 1861, in 1862, and in 1866. A widespread revolt began in 1871, when Gadzhi-Magomed, from the Avar village of Sogratle, was elected Dagestan's fourth imam. The revolt was ruthlessly suppressed. Gallows were erected in Derbent and Gunib, where about 300 leaders of the resistance, including Dagestan's foremost religious leaders, were hung in front of thousands of people who had been specially chosen to represent their djamaats as witnesses. About 5,000 people, including children and the elderly, were exiled to remote regions of Russia. During the Russo-Turkish War, 1877–78, Dagestanis and Chechens nevertheless joined forces once again against Imperial Russia.

On the eve of World War I, Dagestan saw a powerful protest movement known as the "opposition to the introduction of Cyrillic characters into the written language." All village records had previously been kept by kadis in Arabic. Inevitably, this proved unacceptable to the tsar's administration. Numerous programs were introduced to replace the Arabic language with Russian. Finally, in 1913 a formal edict was signed. Record books in Arabic were confiscated from the kadis, who were released from their duties. New Russian-speaking clerks were appointed, whose salaries were to be paid by the djamaats. Tensions brewed over a period of several months. By the autumn of that year, deputations from various parts of Dagestan were arriving at the provincial administration in Derbent, all of whom requested a reversal of the edict. The envoys were arrested and the organizers of the protest were repressed. In February and March 1914, mass resistance had begun in some regions of Dagestan, and by that summer the entire province was enveloped in protest. The officials backed down, agreeing to postpone the reform. It was canceled after the beginning of the war.

The "military-people's" administration in Dagestan was intended to be a temporary and transitional measure when it was introduced in 1861. However, every time that the question of a civil government was raised, the corrupt Caucasian administration found a reason to extend its "temporary order." Colonial in its essence, the local regime was nevertheless preserved until the fall of tsarism.

Revolutions and the Resurgence of Islamic Organization

The reforms of the February revolution of 1917 did not reach Dagestan immediately. Up to April 1917, the administration of the military governor continued to function. Since the life of the majority of the population remained traditionally parochial and interior to the djamaats, and since only a thin layer of well-to-do, European-educated Dagestanis participated in political affairs, the regime change was of little interest to most of the locals.

Having been liberated from feudal and bureaucratic controls, life in the djamaats gradually began to return to traditional forms of self-governance. The process was not without serious intra-djamaat conflicts, though these remained localized. The role of the Islamic clergy was definitive in these processes. During the years in which the tsarist regime had sought to limit their influence, the kadis, mullahs, sheikhs, and ulema had managed to preserve their authority among the people of their djamaats. Indeed the discourse of the local political class was saturated with Islamic values.

During the course of growing democratic and revolutionary agitation in tsarist Russia, the importance of Islam in Dagestan was enhanced. According to the census of 1897, there were 571,154 people in Dagestan. Of these, 52,826 were literate, and over 75 percent of these, nearly 40,000 people, could read Arabic. By 1904, Dagestan had 685 Islamic schools[31] with a total of 5,118 students. Ten years later in 1914, there were 743 *maktabs* (mosque schools for younger pupils) and *madrassas* with over 7,000 students.[32] The Mavraev publishing house, which opened in 1903 in Temir-Khan Shura,[33] published large editions of the Koran, as well as more than 100 other religious titles, authored by Dagestani ulema in the Arabic language. More Islamic spiritual literature was published by Mikhailov publishing house in Port Petrovsk (now Makhachkala), as well as in Baku, Bakhchisarai, Simferopol, and other cities.[34]

In 1917, on the eve of the revolution, Dagestan had only 183 secular schools with 13,000 students. Yet there were 2,311 maktabs and 400 more madrassas, where 45,000 students studied under about 2,500 teachers. There were more than 1,700 mosques.[35] In May 1917, Dagestanis were well-represented at the First Convention of Muslims of Russia.

In the preceding month, Islamic societies had been organized in Temir-Khan Shura, Port Petrovsk, and Derbent. On April 15, an all-Caucasian convention of Muslims convened in Baku. From out of this convention emerged two Islamic political organizations, one for the South Caucasus and one for the North Caucasus.

The Union of Allied Mountaineers of the North Caucasus (*Soiuz ob"edinennykh gortsev severnogo kavkaza*), or UAM, was an inclusive movement embracing highlanders from across the region. The movement held its first congress on May 1, 1917, in Vladikavkaz. It was intended to provide spiritual guidance for the Muslims throughout the mountains, and soon vowed to institute sharia at the foundation of the judicial system. Among the leaders of the organization was Nazhmuddin Gozinskii, an ethnic Avar, who later assumed the title of Mufti of Dagestan and the North Caucasus. Its leadership was drawn primarily from the pool of North Caucasians with advanced Russian educations or with Russian bureaucratic experience. Yet when the organization held conferences at Vladikavkaz, Andi,[36] and other locations, it also demonstrated substantial popular support.[37]

This was because the UAM attempted to transcend the divisions of ethnicity, religion, and language by focusing upon the highland culture that encompassed all of the indigenous peoples of the North Caucasus. The organization attempted to cooperate with Orthodox Christian Cossacks alongside peoples against whom the Cossacks had fought for centuries. The UAM's leadership recognized the demographic challenge that inward migration presented to all of the small Caucasian groups, and attempted to forge a common strategy for their survival.[38]

This UAM envisioned the successful integration of the North Caucasus into a democratic Russian society. While the UAM rejected the autocratic abuses of the tsarist administration, and while it honored Imam Shamil, it also sought to locate itself within a rapidly changing Russia by drawing a sharp distinction between the monarchy and the Russian people, and looking toward cooperation with the latter. According to Reynolds:

> The UAM leadership saw Russia not merely as a source of oppression, but also as a window to the advanced societies of Europe and the wider world. They were products of Russian education, and though fierce patriots and partisans of the Caucasus, they understood the benefits their people stood to gain through inclusion in a single state with Russia. Integration with Russia offered access to education, technology, and other aspects of modernity that the mountaineers needed if they were to develop into a prosperous society.... Russia's colonial adventure had not been a total failure, and had even produced a class of mountaineer patriots that identified the best interests of their people with remaining part of Russia.[39]

Thus, in 1917, the revolutionary uprising in Petrograd undermined Russia's colonial organization in the south. The temporary decline of the Russian Empire created opportunities for the resurgence of local and indigenous, as well as Islamic, structures. In response to this resurgence of traditional North Caucasian social fragmentation, the UAM was a regional organization that recognized the need to transcend traditional ethnic and religious structures, in order to reach a compromise between the latter and a rapidly transforming Russian society. As a regional organization, it sought to mediate the vertical organization of the late Russian Empire in order to provide a sphere of regional autonomy conducive to economic preservation and local social practices.

3

Soviet Rule in the North Caucasus

Betrayal of Islam and Construction of Ethnicity

Like the earlier collapse of the tsarist regime, the October revolution had no immediate consequences in the North Caucasus. Yet by the summer of 1918, Dagestan had become the scene of interventions from the south as well as from the north. Life in Dagestan's cities had grown significantly more complicated. The economy declined and livestock, in particular, were depleted due to incessant military operations in those Dagestani lowlands that traditionally provided winter pastures. Famine and extreme poverty contributed to a social degeneration with which traditional political institutions were no longer able to cope.

In August 1919, General Anton Denikin led his anti-Bolshevik forces into Dagestan, where he was perceived by the local population as attempting to restore the power of the tsar. This inspired a spontaneous mass movement that quickly developed into a war of national liberation. The main goal of this movement was the independence of Dagestan. The movement was supported even by local Bolsheviks, but it was led by the Islamic clergy. At the forefront of the movement was Sheikh Ali Gadzhi (Akushinskii) from the ethnic Dargin Akusha djamaat. Other prominent leaders were Sheikh Uzun-Hadji of Salta, and Mufti Nazhmeidin Gozinsky. In the autumn of 1919, at the height of the united resistance to Denikin's army, Sheikh Uzun-Hadji proclaimed the "Northern Caucasian Emirate" with its capital in the Chechen village of Vedeno.[1] Mountain guerrilla warfare pushed Denikin out of Dagestan, though his forces lingered on the northern plains and in Port-Petrovsk. The arrival of the Red Army confirmed Dagestan's liberation from the White forces, and Bolshevik control over the North Caucasus was soon consolidated.

Though the Bolsheviks initially were opposed to federalism, it nonetheless provided a framework for managing and incorporating the nationalist movements that appeared on the periphery of the Russian Empire as it approached its collapse. The traditional "divide and conquer" strategy, which had served for the expansion of that empire, was consequently reflected in the 1918

Constitution of the Russian Soviet Federated Socialist Republic (RSFSR). The constitution characterized the RSFSR as a "free union of free nations, a federation of the Soviet national republics."[2] As Pipes observed, Soviet Russia was "the first modern state to place the national principle at the base of its federal system."[3]

The Mountain Republic (Gorskaia Respublika), which lasted from 1918 to 1921, drew upon a common *gorskii* (mountaineer) identity in an effort to unite the North Caucasian peoples within a loose confederation. In January 1921, following the Bolshevik conquest of the region, it was established as the Autonomous Soviet Mountain Republic, including Chechen, Ingush, Osset, Kabard, Balkar, and Karachai districts. At the same time, the peoples of Dagestan were combined into a separate Dagestan Autonomous Republic. But whereas Dagestan endured as an aggregation of ethnic groups, the Mountain Republic was quickly dissolved into separate national units.

Beginning in 1922, it was partitioned among the Adygei, Chechen, Karachai-Cherkessian, and Kabardino-Balkarian autonomies. The dissolution of the Mountain Republic was completed in 1924, when its remaining territories were divided into the North Ossetian and Ingush Autonomous regions. As a consequence of this process of ethnic fragmentation, schools and infrastructure deteriorated in many areas.

These divisions were based upon the administrative, economic, and security concerns of the central authority, and not on concern for the locals. According to Abdurakhman Avtorkhanov,[4] the émigré Chechen historian, the fragmentation of the Mountain Republic into ethno-linguistic units was initiated by Moscow, motivated by a policy of dividing a rebellious population, and decidedly opposed by North Caucasian leaders. By fragmenting the Mountain Republic, and by subsequently stressing cultural, linguistic, and religious distinctions among its peoples, Moscow sought to diminish the threat of a North Caucasian alliance against Soviet power. The same policies later permitted Soviet ethnographers to insist that the North Caucasian nations were separated into several autonomous regions because their diversity rendered them incapable of peaceful coexistence.[5] Yet according to Soviet scholars N.G. Volkova and L.I. Lavsov,[6] the identity of North Caucasian inhabitants in the decades after the civil war was characterized not by nationalist aspirations, but by localized clan and village consciousness, which was complemented by an awareness of the encompassing North Caucasian gorski society.

Ethnic policy during this period owed much to Joseph Stalin, whose position as the first People's Commissary General made him effectively Minister of Nationalities. In his 1913 article on "Marxism and the National Question," Stalin had combined ethnicity, territory, and political administration within a conception of the national state. This was translated into actuality in 1922 when the establishment of the Soviet Union provided an elaborate, if often arbitrary, administrative hierarchy of ethno-territorial units.[7] In the North Caucasus, these administrative boundaries were repeatedly redefined throughout three subsequent decades. These adjustments occurred in response to insurrections among many of the national groups, insurrections that were themselves the result of the fragmentation process and its effect upon ethnic land holdings.[8] In this way, Soviet ethnic policy contributed to a vicious cycle of horizontal conflicts among various ethnic groups, resulting in no small part from the territorial fragmentation imposed by a vertically hierarchical system of Russian domination, and justified as a response to these same horizontal conflicts. This cycle has sporadically consumed the region to the present day.

The irony is that it was the alpine verticality of the local geography that had initially established the horizontal fragmentation of the local peoples. This same horizontal fragmentation had long helped to preserve these peoples from subsumption within the vertically hierarchical organizations of the empires that arrived, over the centuries, at the base of the mountains. Yet having now been incorporated by Soviet expansion, it was the vertical weight of the Soviet system that contributed to further horizontal fragmentations among these peoples.

The Betrayal of Islam in Dagestan

It was only at the eastern end of the Soviet's North Caucasian ethnic mosaic that a genuine multiplicity of ethnic groups came to be included in the same republic. By 1920, Red Army officers and local Bolsheviks had united with local guerrilla leaders to establish a new political order in Dagestan. Initially, however, this order resembled the old "military-people's administration." Power was maintained by military force, and apportioned through revolutionary committees appointed by Bolshevik leaders in Moscow. The similarities in the bureaucratic features of the new and the old orders led to widespread disappointment that soon issued in mass revolts. In September 1920, a large uprising took place under the banner of Islam that was led by Imam Nazhmudin Gozinskii, who was elected in the highlands of Avaria. Gozinskii demanded that the Bolsheviks reconsider their approach to the governance of Dagestan.

In response, the Bolsheviks offered compromise with traditional village structures as well as with Islam. They created local organs of power that were popularly elected. Revolutionary committees were replaced by "village soviets" (councils). Indeed, the Bolshevik slogan of "Power to the Soviets," in its initial presentation during the revolution and civil war, corresponded to the goals of the Dagestani highlanders, since it came close to approximating their traditional djamaat-based organization of political life.

Moreover, Moscow recognized the necessity of granting Dagestan political sovereignty. The Dagestan Autonomous Soviet Socialist Republic was declared in Temir-Khan Shura (now the town of Buinaksk) at the Emergency Convention of the Peoples of Dagestan, on November 13, 1920, in the midst of the warfare between the Bolsheviks and the recalcitrant highlanders.

Finally, the most important compromise made by the Bolsheviks was to give Dagestan "the right to govern based upon their laws and customs." Since adat had by that time been turned into a tool of colonial administration, and since sharia and the authority of the Islamic ulema (including mullahs, kadis, and sheikhs) had been systematically undermined, the slogan of "Islam and Sharia" was widely voiced after the fall of tsarism in Dagestan. On the basis of their political calculations, the Bolsheviks openly accepted sharia as a "legitimate right" of the Dagestani people. Attending the Emergency Convention of the Peoples of Dagestan in 1920, Joseph Stalin provided an assurance of this compromise:

> We have been informed that sharia has a very serious meaning among the peoples of Dagestan. We have also learned that the enemies of Soviet power are spreading the rumor that the Soviets will ban sharia. I am here to assure you, on the authority of the Russian Soviet Federative Socialist Republic, that these rumors are false. The government of Russia allows every nation to govern based upon the local laws and tradition. The Soviet government recognizes sharia as a legitimate, customary law, practiced among other nations of Russia. If the Dagestani peoples wish to preserve their law and tradition, then they should be sustained.[9]

The establishment of their republic on the basis of sharia law was initially perceived by the Dagestanis as the achievement of their independence. The Bolsheviks seemed to have sanctioned what the mountaineers sought for themselves: sharia and a return to the traditional power of djamaat councils, now called "soviets."

Yet shortly thereafter they witnessed the emergence of new structures of vertical power and control. In 1921, a District Sharia Legislative Department was created. In 1922, it became the Sharia Department of the *Narkomat*[10] of Justice of the Dagestan Autonomous Soviet Socialist Republic. In 1923, eleven district sharia courts were established as intermediaries between the judicial structures of the djamaats and the republic. The most authoritative and well-known religious leaders were appointed as heads of these district sharia courts. In 1924, the republic Communist Party Committee decided to establish official Islamic holidays, such as *Kurban-Bairam* and *Uraza-Bairam*.[11]

In 1925, there were 11,631 students in maktabs and madrassas in Dagestan.[12] In the same period, there were approximately 40,000 members of the Islamic clergy, including sheikhs, imams of mosques, mullahs, kadis, and ulema. This figure was equal to 4 percent of the total population of Dagestan, whereas for Russia as a whole, the proportion of the clergy was less than one-tenth of 1 percent of the total population.[13] If before the revolution, there were about 1,700 mosques in Dagestan,[14] in 1928, there were about 2,000.[15] That was just before Soviet authorities began the open persecution of Islam.

The establishment of state structures of administration required the gradual elimination of sharia structures. The process of restricting the prerogatives of sharia was under way long before their direct cancellation. By 1922, district investigative committees were created to control djamaat and district sharia courts. Simultaneously, cases involving land ownership were removed from sharia jurisdiction, and were assigned to separate, specialized courts known as district land committees. However, the latter applied the same norms of traditional law, based upon adat and sharia. In 1923, cases involving homicide and blood feud were also removed from sharia jurisdiction. In 1924, the sharia courts were deprived of public financial maintenance, including salaries.[16] In 1925, "village oral courts" were created in parallel with the sharia courts. The former were staffed by an official known as the "village bailiff" whose duties were similar to those of the traditional *chaush*, and who became the prototype for the village policeman.

On April 18, 1927, the Central Executive Committee and the Soviet of People's Commissars of Dagestan issued a decree that abolished the djamaat and district sharia courts, and criminalized the practice of sharia. Beginning in 1928, mosque schools and madrassas were shut down, and clergy were repressed. That same year, more than 800 of the most respected elders in Dagestan were sent into exile in Archangelsk, near the Arctic Circle.[17] This came at the same time as the enactment of the Tenth Article of the Criminal Law titled "On Crimes Related to the Antiquated Way of Life."

Throughout the remainder of the Soviet period Islam was repressed in Dagestan. Especially during the 1930s, Islamic leaders were persecuted and the tariqah orders were driven underground. Most active Muslims were arrested, many were executed, and some were exiled into the remote northern regions of the country. From the early 1930s mosques were closed on administrative order. By 1940 there were no openly active religious organizations in Dagestan. Nevertheless, underground Sufi orders survived in Dagestan's rural communities, and particularly in its highland villages. Still, without opportunities for formal study and communication with broader communities of Muslims, the Islamic education and practices of these groups suffered a gradual deterioration.

Thus in response to an early period of resistance, the Soviets offered compromises with local and Islamic structures. Dagestanis initially embraced these compromises within emergent and encompassing structures that fit more neatly within Russian traditions of hierarchical social organization. Yet within ten years after the proposal of these compromises, local and Islamic structures were abolished and their practitioners were persecuted.

Nevertheless, the Soviet Union offered North Caucasians other forms of compromise. On the one hand, the Soviet Union imposed a stark system of hierarchy and domination in keeping with Russian traditions. Yet at the same time, Soviet collectivism was consistent with traditional highland village life. Moreover, Stalin's ethnic policies paid lip service to local traditions of kinship and parochialism by carving the region into a series of titular republics, wherein linguistic and cultural distinctions were subsequently reified. Most important, the Soviet Union offered North Caucasians tangible benefits in terms of security and economic development. Over the ensuing decades the Soviet Union brought them pavement, plumbing, electricity, health care, education, and relative gender equality. Today many Dagestanis are nostalgic for the system that combined unparalleled security with unprecedented opportunity and international pride of place.

Soviet Ethnic Construction and Subsequent Disintegration

In the 1920s and 1930s the Soviets launched a number of programs designed to develop ethnic identities in the Caucasus through national language schools, newspapers, theaters, and so forth.[18] By the mid-1920s languages were standardized and alphabets were newly formulated in Latin script. The relative insignificance of ethnic identities at the outset of this period was indicated by the initial indifference of mountain residents, whether peasants or intelligentsia, to the development of exclusive national cultures. At the time, and as the Union of Allied Mountaineers had previously demonstrated, the North Caucasian peoples shared a cultural heritage that transcended their fragmentation along the lines of administrative, ethnic, linguistic, tribal, and clan divisions. According to Ormrod, the inhabitants of this society "exhibited little consciousness of themselves as members of their officially recognized national groups."[19]

Yet while radical nationalism was suppressed, ethnic identity was reinforced through cultural development programs, through ethno-territorial organizations, and through a system of internal passports (introduced in 1932), which documented the ethnic origin of every citizen. Zaslavsky explains that the

> Institutionalization of ethnicity created the prerequisites necessary for pursuing an ethnic policy, which combined divisive measures and integrative

techniques to prevent the organization of alliances between neighboring ethnic groups, to undermine the capacity of any existing ethnic group to act as a unified entity, and to co-opt the crucial sectors within each ethnic population into the Soviet regime.[20]

These policies were consolidated in the Soviet Constitution of 1936. In the North Caucasus region, the constitution recognized five autonomous republics (Abkhazia, Checheno-Ingushetia, Dagestan, Kabardino-Balkaria, and North Ossetia) and three autonomous districts (South Ossetia, Karachai-Cherkessia, and Adygea).

From 1942 to 1944 entire communities of Balkars, Chechens, Ingush, and Karachai were deported under appalling conditions to Soviet Central Asia on loosely supported allegations of collaboration with Nazi invaders. Their territories were allocated to other North Caucasian administrative units. Members of the other groups were sometimes forcibly resettled in their homes. Though the republics of Checheno-Ingushetia, Kabardino-Balkaria, and the District of Karachai-Cherkessia were reestablished in 1957, and though many deportees returned, this bitter period raised extremely contentious issues that have yet to be resolved.

In the period following Stalin's death, and in subsequent periods of Soviet liberalization, there were waves of ethnic radicalization in regions such as the North Caucasus that can be traced to the Soviet strategy of managing a multinational state. In other words, these recurrent waves of ethnic mobilization may be seen as illustrating the horizontal social fragmentation that was caused by the pressures of the vertical hierarchy of control that was constructed during the Soviet period. According to Lapidus and Walker,

> [t]he design of the Soviet state as a federation of ethno-territorial "union republics" that were, symbolically if not in fact, national states, both reified nationality as a central aspect of individual identity and created a setting in which liberalization would catalyze ethno-national mobilization.[21]

The national fault lines along which the Soviet state was structured revealed their fundamental instability during the period of accelerated liberalization that followed Mikhail Gorbachev's reforms. Both the political and the economic thrusts of these reforms played critical roles in the emergence of nationalism as a powerful political force in the perestroika period. On the one hand, glasnost and democratization tended to undermine the authority of Communist Party elites, while, on the other hand, the process of resource redistribution exacerbated tensions and produced widespread competition among existing groups. Resulting power struggles culminated in efforts to reestablish authority on a foundation of nationalist ideology. Liberalization encouraged provincial leaders to seek expanded economic autonomy and placed property rights, both individual and collective, at the forefront of dispute.

At the same time, the intellectual freedom that followed from glasnost issued in a reevaluation of Soviet policy and the assertion of diverse approaches to ethnic, economic, political, and social issues. With fewer restrictions on political expression, nationalist political movements emerged as vehicles of reform. Yet efforts to reformulate Soviet federalism also served as a vehicle for the nationalist agendas and personal ambitions of local elites. Chief among these was the challenge of the Russian Federation under Boris Yeltsin. Soviet authority was diminished by Gorbachev's ineffectual response to rapidly growing centrifugal forces.

Against this background a new union treaty was proposed with the intent of preserving the Soviet state through certain concessions to its administrative components. Critics, however, were concerned that the new treaty would undermine the authority of the central government. Efforts to uphold the latter by preventing the former culminated in the coup of August 1991. The dramatic failure of the coup contributed over the next four months to the disintegration of the Soviet Union, and to the subsequent rise of fifteen sovereign states, with Russia strongest among them.

Thereafter the same fissiparous forces that led to the demise of the Soviet Union were reproduced within the union republics from Tajikistan to Georgia. Economic chaos and political collapse drained the Union into a whirlpool of state formation by ever smaller ethnic and regional groups. The history of the Soviet Union culminated in an ironic and extraordinary dialectic: because of the extreme power concentrated vertically at the federal center and party control of all aspects of economic and political life, the sudden disintegration of the Communist Party led to a rapid and unrestrained, horizontal fragmentation of power, and to the effective independence of local elites. At the same time, and because of the enforced ubiquity of Marxist ideology, the de facto withering of the state left an enveloping moral vacuum that could be filled by motives no less potent than those of nationalism and Islam.

Competitions between the central institutions and the republics were exacerbated by Boris Yeltsin's personal competition with Gorbachev. According to Lapidus and Walker, Yeltsin's efforts to secure Russian sovereignty, which were inseparable from his political ambitions, led to a "horizontal" strategy that undermined central power by promoting ties among the republics.[22] The result was a catastrophic struggle between two compelling visions of Russia's future: Russia, on the one hand, as a sovereign national entity emancipated from far-flung and sometimes debilitating entanglements, and on the other hand, Russia as an imperial power.

Yet while Russian reformers initially welcomed national movements they began to fear that the drive toward self-determination might be directed not only against the Soviet Union but also against Russia itself. In early 1991, Aleksandr Tsipko observed that if Russia is only one of the Union republics then it does not differ from Tatarstan or Dagestan, and warned that the election of a president of the RSFSR could produce a "domino effect." His fears were soon realized as every one of the autonomous republics followed Russia's declaration of sovereignty.

Toward the end of the year, Yeltsin appealed for support from the autonomies in his growing battle with Gorbachev. Yet his position shifted when RSFSR autonomies began to seek greater recognition, as illustrated, for example, by Tatarstan's desire to become a signatory of the Union Treaty. At the same time, Gorbachev and conservative forces in the central authority began to support peripheral challenges to the Russian government. Thus, as Gorbachev appeared increasingly unable to preserve the Union, officials in the autonomies began to conclude that obstacles to local independence were not the work of Gorbachev and the collapsing Soviet center, but of Yeltsin and reformers in the Russian government. Their concerns were aggravated that autumn when Yeltsin reacted to Dzhokhar Dudaev's ascendance to the presidency of Checheno-Ingushetia by declaring a state of emergency and dispatching troops to enforce the Russian constitution in the rebellious republic.

Thus, the struggle for Russian sovereignty not only accelerated the disintegration of the Soviet Union, but risked the internal fragmentation of Russia itself. On the eve of its independence, in 1991, Russia's central authority faced a host of regional challenges. Yet the threat of political dissolution was, in some respects, an overt reflection of a deeper crisis of cultural self-identity. Many intellectuals despaired that the legacy of imperial expansion, the decline of the Orthodox creed, and the collapse of communist ideology left Russia in a cultural void without a coherent national ethos.

Russia was confronted by some of the same centrifugal forces that had fragmented the Soviet Union as some republics clamored for greater independence while others sank into border disputes that threatened their disintegration. At the same time, broad coalitions in the Urals, the Far East, the Western borders, and the Caucasus began to challenge Moscow's authority.

Mounting disagreement over Russia's "federation structure" interfered with the completion of a new constitution for the country. Along with the division of powers between Moscow and the republics, there were the disputes over the administrative jurisdiction and territorial boundaries. Inevitably, there was a debate about whether the components of the federation should conform to existing borders or should constitute new territorial units. At the time, Russian reformers joined with some ethnologists, such as Valery

Tishkov, to support a nonethnic federal framework patterned on the United States. They argued that an expansive and culturally heterogeneous country could preserve neither union nor democracy if administrative boundaries reinforced ethnic barriers.

Yet political realities precluded redistricting across ethnic lines. Soviet propaganda had long disparaged "bourgeois" territorial federalism that ignored ethnic identities, in favor of a recognition of the collective rights of communities that was afforded by the "socialist" form of federalism. Minorities privileged with their own administrative territories resisted change, and even nontitular residents of the autonomies saw economic advantage in the existing political units. Moreover, redistricting would have threatened the power of local elites. Consequently, after 1991 there was less interest in restructuring Russia's internal administrative divisions.

In the autumn of 1992, attention was drawn to ethnic unrest in the North Caucasus by incidents in North Ossetia, Kabardino-Balkaria, and in Karachai-Cherkessia, where nationalists were calling for distinct Karachai, Cherkess, and Cossack republics. Pressures mounted meanwhile for the separation of the Kabardin and Balkar territories. The same year saw a brief but bloody conflict between Ossetians and Ingush that resulted from territorial disputes simmering since the latter group was deported in 1944. Conflict continued across the border in Georgia, where volunteers from the Confederation of Peoples of the Caucasus and Cossack irregulars joined Abkhaz separatists, and where southern Ossetians cherished hopes of joining their cousins to the north in the Russian Federation.

Fires in the Caucasus were also fueled in 1992 by the legislative/executive conflict in Moscow, which led Yeltsin and his opponents into frenzied competition for the support of local officials. Russian nationalists in the Supreme Soviet, who might have been expected to resist local autonomy, instead formed an anti-liberal alliance with conservative deputies from the republics. Meanwhile Yeltsin not only made economic concessions in an effort to win the favor of local authorities but also extended considerable independence to the republics and regions with the conviction that economic decentralization would prevent conservatives from reversing privatization were they to return to power. This result was dramatically avoided, and Yeltsin's hand was temporarily improved by the misfortune of the military assault on the Russian Parliament in 1993.

With the resolution of the political crisis in Moscow, Yeltsin served notice that the central government would no longer tolerate interminable bilateral debates with each of the eighty-nine administrative units. And while the draft constitution that was approved by referendum in December 1993 made numerous provisions for Russia's ethnic minorities, many of its decrees were vague or contradictory, leaving much to future legislation, adjudication, and negotiation. Significantly, it did not describe the republics as "sovereign," an omission that undermined constitutional rights for national self-determination and led to widespread protests in the North Caucasus. At the same time, ethnic tensions in many areas were increased by the constitution's restriction of each republic to a single representative in the Upper Chamber of the new Russian legislature.

Ethnic Construction and Accommodation in Dagestan

Soviet efforts to concentrate vertical power issued in a deluge of horizontal disintegration that was foreshadowed by early Soviet ethnic policies. As these events swept across the broad Soviet stage, their Dagestani resonances acquired distinctively ethnic and religious tones. The period of "socialist construction" was marked by the rapid growth of ethnic self-consciousness and the development of national languages and cultures for all Dagestani groups. As a consequence of this ethnocultural heterogeneity, on the one hand, and the social and political indivisibility of Dagestan, on the other hand, it became necessary to establish means of ensuring proportionate ethnic representation at the highest levels of authority in the republic.

During the postrevolutionary years, and in the period of prewar economic development, the key positions in Dagestan were occupied by the prominent representatives of the local ethnicities. Only during the period of the prewar political purges (1937–38) did the ethnic composition of the organs of power become a secondary consideration.

After the war, ethnic considerations were once again crucial. In 1948, the first secretary of the Dagestani regional committee of the Communist Party, an Azeri named Aziz Aliev, who was appointed during the war by the Central Committee, was returned to Azerbaijan, and the position was filled by a local Avar named Abdurahman Daniyalov, who worked during the war as a chairman of the Cabinet of Ministers of the Dagestan Autonomous Soviet Socialist Republic. In turn, a Lezgin filled Daniyalov's previous position, and a Kumyk headed the Supreme Soviet. The traditional rotation of ethnicities occupying these three high positions in Dagestan endured to the end of the communist era.

Kremlin representatives also participated in the distribution of power in Dagestan. Ethnic Russians could be classified into two categories: (1) those whom Moscow assigned to political positions in Dagestan, known as "visitors," and (2) local ethnic Russians, known as "natives." The first category of Russians invariably occupied two important positions: the second secretary of the Communist Party of the republic, and the chairman of the Committee for State Security (KGB). Local Russians usually managed the Makhachkala committee of the Party and served in positions such as deputy prime minister, vice-chairman of the presidium of the Supreme Soviet, ministers and deputy ministers of various ministries, and party leadership positions in outlying areas with predominantly Russian populations. The latter included Kizliarsk and Tarumovsk regions, and the city of Kizliar.

In 1967, Abdurahman Daniyalov was replaced as first secretary of the Dagestani regional committee of the Communist Party by a Dargin named Magomed-Salam Umakhanov. A Kumyk became chairman of the Cabinet of Ministers (Sovmin), and an Avar headed the Supreme Soviet. In 1983, there were further changes among the highest officials: an Avar named Magomed Yusupov replaced the Dargin Umakhanov and became first secretary of the Party, in which post he remained up to 1990. His position in the Sovmin was occupied by a Dargin, and a Kumyk became chairman of the Supreme Soviet (Verkhovny Soviet). In the course of each of these replacements, the ethnicity of the highest official was changed, and that of the other two highest appointees was altered accordingly. All appointments conformed to the principle that the three highest positions should be occupied by the representatives of three different Dagestani ethnicities. From 1948, the following "troikas" were formed and subsequently replaced: (1) Avar–Lezgin–Kumyk, (2) Avar–Dargin–Kumyk, (3) Dargin–Kumyk–Avar, (4) Dargin–Avar–Kumyk, and (5) Avar–Kumyk–Dargin.

By the beginning of perestroika, the "troika" of Dagestan's highest positions was occupied as follows: an Avar named Mukhu Aliev served as first secretary of the Communist Party, a Kumyk named Abdurazak Mirzabekov was chairman of the Sovmin, and Magomedali Magomedov, a Dargin, was chairman of the Presidium of the Supreme Soviet. The unwritten prerequisite of a "triumvirate" shared among representatives of different Dagestani ethnicities helped to preserve Dagestan's political stability through the strains of this period. All of the new political structures and social movements that struggled for power in those days found themselves tightly restricted by ethnic communities in the augmentation of their authority as well as in their proliferation among groups of people. Indeed, Dagestan's multiple ethnic mobilization movements also served to counterbalance anything that might have advanced the hegemony of any particular ethnic group. In this way, the unrelenting pluralism of Dagestan's ethnic diversity limited extremist developments during these chaotic years.

The first genuine crisis in the Dagestani system of power occurred in August 1991, after the putsch of the GKChP (the State Emergency Committee), when the activity of the Communist Party was banned. In Dagestan, this led to a breach of the principle of ethnic parity in the highest positions. Mukhu Aliev, the Avar leader of the Communist Party, was thereby prevented from power sharing, and the government lurched closer than ever to a loss of control. Instead of a traditional triumvirate of the highest leaders, there emerged an unstable diarchy, in which the two highest remaining positions were occupied by a Dargin and a Kumyk.

The principal result of the complicated developments that took place between September 1991 and July 1994 was that none of the political groups managed to achieve unilateral control over the republic.[23] The consequent pluralism was incorporated with care and considerable difficulty into the development of Dagestan's constitution, which was ratified on July 26, 1994. Yet it was the institutionalization of ethnic pluralism, with all of its counterbalancing forces, that prevented Dagestan from following Chechnya that year, into separatist extremism and conflict.

4

Democratic Dagestan

Ethnic Accommodation in the Constitutional Djamaat

As a consequence of Soviet national policies, the citizens of Russian emerged from the Soviet period with a heightened sense of ethnic identity. This was true nowhere more than in Dagestan, where the Soviets had formally recognized fourteen different ethnic groups, but where there are in fact many more. For example, Dagestan's largest ethnic group, the Avars, were an amalgamation of fifteen ethnolinguistically distinct nationalities. The Dargins, Dagestan's second largest ethnic group, were a composite of three ethnolinguistic groups. Thus, there were, more accurately, at least thirty ethnolinguistic groups in Dagestan. Depending upon the criteria that one employed in distinguishing a language from a dialect, the count could be considerably greater with many of Dagestan's djamaats displaying their own ethnolinguistic peculiarities. Most of these languages and dialects lived on in village conversation, while Dagestan's fourteen officially recognized languages flourished in their own newspapers, magazines, theaters, and radio and television programs.

Dagestan's largest national group included the Akhvakhs, Andis, Archins, Avars, Bagulals, Bezhtins, Botlikhs, Chamalals, Didoi, Ginukhs, Godoberins, Gunibs, Karatins, Khvarshins, and Tindins All of these groups were aggregately identified as Avars, which are consequently Dagestan's largest ethnic group. In the 2002 census, Avars totaled 758,438, or 29.4 percent of Dagestan's population.

The second largest group was the Dargins, including Kubachins and Kaitags, who comprised 16.5 percent of the population, with 425,526 people. Living nearby the Dargins, in the central regions of the Dagestani highlands, were approximately 139,732 Laks, constituting 5.4 percent of the total population.

The Lezgins occupied the southernmost tip of Dagestan, traditionally inhabiting an area that extends from the Caucasian highlands to the shores of the Caspian Sea and into neighboring Azerbaijan. Unlike the Avars, members of this group were registered officially as separate nationalities. These were proper Lezgins, with 336,698 people or 13.1 percent; Tabasarans, with 110,152 or 4.3 percent of the population; Rutuls comprising 24,298 or 0.9 percent; 16,000 Aguls with 0.9 percent; and 8,168 Tsakhurs or 0.3 percent of the total population.

On the Caspian lowland to the north of Derbent, back to the foothills and north on the Tersko-Sulak plain lived an Altaic people known as the Kumyks, whose language belonged to the Turkic branch. Kumyks number 365,804 people, or 14.2 percent. In the same region, and predominantly in the Khasaviurt district, lived Chechen-Akkins, or Aukov Chechens, a Vainakh people: 87,867 Dagestanis, or 3.4 percent, were of Chechen ethnicity.

North of these groups, along the Terek River, in the Kizliar and Tarumovsk districts, and including the town of Kizliar were concentrated 120,875 Russian nationals comprising 4.7 percent of Dagestan's population. In the semiarid region further to the north lived 38,168 members of another Turkic group. These Nogais made up only 1.5 percent of Dagestan's population, but another 37,000 Nogais were nearby in Chechnya and the Stavropol region of Russia.

Though Sunni Muslims predominated, Dagestan also contained 111,656 Shiite Azeris constituting 4.3 percent of the population, and significant populations of Christians and Jews. In the southern part of the Caspian lowland, in the town of Derbent and in the nearby foothills, lived 825 Mountain Jews, also known as Tats, whose language belonged to the Iranian group. They constituted 0.03 percent of the population. These figures are summarized in Table 4.1.

According to Russia's Census in October 2002, the population of Dagestan was 2.57 million people.[1] Dagestan's rural population totaled 1,474,000, or 53 percent of the total. City dwellers totaled 1,102,000 Dagestanis, or 43 percent of the total population. The population of Makhachkala was 545,000, accounting for more than 21 percent of the republic's population.

While Dagestan's cities have long been multiethnic, the countryside traditionally has been a mosaic of ethnic territories. There the scarcity of land and the paucity of economic development have not deterred the most expansive birthrate in the Russian Federation—1.8 children for each Dagestani woman, versus 1.3 for Russia as a whole. At the same time, life expectancy for Dagestani males was sixty-eight years, versus an average fifty-eight years throughout Russia.[2] During the last three decades of the twentieth century, Dagestan's population doubled, as it bumped along at or near the bottom of the list of Russian republics for a wide range of socioeconomic indicators. Against a background of impending demographic disaster, the disintegration of the Soviet Union only accelerated the pace of Dagestan's ethnic mobilization. How did the Dagestanis keep the lid on their ethnic pressure cooker as the dynamics of nationalization and democratization were increasingly energized?

Table 4.1

Population of Dagestan's Ethnicities According to the 2002 Russian Census

Ethnicity	Population	%	Ethnicity	Population	%
Whole population including:	2,576,531	100	21. **Dargins** including:	425,526	16.5
1. **Avars** including:	758,438	29.40	22. *Kaitags*	4	0.00
			23. *Kubachins*	57	0.00
2. *Andis*	21,270	0.80	24. Jews	1,478	0.06
3. *Archins*	7	0.00	25. **Mountain Jews***	1,066	0.04
4. *Akhvakhs*	6,362	0.25	26. Kazakhs	619	0.02
5. *Bagulals*	18	0.00	27. **Kumyks**	365,804	14.20
6. *Bezhtins*	6,184	0.24	28. **Laks**	139,732	0.40
7. *Botlikhs*	—	—	29. **Lezgins**	336,698	13.10
8. *Ginukhs*	525	0.02	30. **Nogais**	38,168	1.50
9. *Godoberins*	2	0.00	31. Ossetins	897	0.03
10. *Gunibs*	972	0.04	32. Persians	719	0.00
11. *Didoi*	15,176	0.59	33. **Russians**	120,875	4.70
12. *Karatins*	6,019	0.23	34. **Rutuls**	24298	0.90
13. *Tindals*	33	0.00	35. **Tabasarans**	110,152	4.30
14. *Khvarshins*	107	0.00	36. Tatars	4,659	0.20
15. *Chamalals*	3	0.00	37. **Tats***	825	0.03
16. **Aguls**	23,314	0.90	38. Ukrainians	2,869	0.10
17. **Azeris**	111,656	4.30	39. **Tsakhurs**	8,168	0.30
18. Armenians	5,702	0.20	40. **Chechens** including:	87,867	3.40
19. Belorussians	547	0.02			
20. Georgians	876	0.03	41. *Chechen-Akkins*	116	0.00

Notes: Dagestan's titular ethnicities are in bold font. Ethnic groups that have been administratively classified as components of larger ethnicities are in italic font. Other ethnicities (e.g., Ukrainians) are included only if their population exceeded 500 people. Peoples included in the table comprise 97.8 percent of the total population of Dagestan.

*In Dagestan, Mountain Jew and Tat are often considered one ethnic group.

The numbers in this table derive directly from the official Russian census of 2002. However, the numbers for some groups are too low to be credible. For example, the town of Botlikh is the administrative and cultural center of the Avar sub-group known as the Andis. The table lists a count of 21,270 Andis. Yet there are 0 Botlikhs registered in Dagestan, and only 4 Botlikhs registered in all of Russia. Similarly, only 7 Archins, 2 Godoberins, 3 Chamalals, 33 Tindins, and 107 Khvarshins were counted in Dagestan. These low numbers appear because the census questionnaire allowed respondents to choose only one ethnic categorization. Avars were concerned that the fragmentation of their ethnic group among its fifteen subgroups would undermine the status that they enjoy as Dagestan's largest ethnic group, and might have affected the number of legislative seats that they held. Hence, they launched a campaign to persuade members of subgroups to register themselves as Avars and not as members of subgroups. Had respondents been permitted to select multiple self-categorizations then the count of these Avar sub-groups would have been more meaningful.

There were similar problems with the Dargin and Chechen subgroups. All but 4 Kaitags and 57 Kubachins described themselves as Dargins. All but 116 Chechen-Akkins described themselves as Chechens.

(continued)

Table 4.1 *(continued)*

As a result of this oversight in the census questionnaire there is no accurate official count for these sub-groups. At best, there are expert estimates for these populations as follows:

Andis	40,000
Archins	2,000
Akhvakhs	6,000
Bagulals	5,000
Bezhtins	7,000
Botlikhs	4,500
Ginukhs	500
Godoberins	3,500
Gunibs	3,000 (including 350 residing in Georgia)
Didois	8,000
Karatins	7,500
Tindals	12,000
Khvarshins	1,000
Chamalals	8,000

The Collapse of Central Authority and the Rise of Ethnic Politics

Evidently Karl Jaspers was wrong in his insistence that authoritarian regimes cannot be eliminated from within.[3] He may have been correct in his assertion that a totalitarian system cannot be changed from below, but he overlooked the possibility that the regime, and indeed the entire political system, could be changed from above when elites transform the system in order to achieve their private objectives. The demise of the Soviet Union and the rise of Russia's bare-knuckled capitalism could be described as revolution from above.

Party and government elites, along with factory managers and other industrial leaders, who were closest to the distribution of financial and material resources prior to perestroika, the policy of "restructuring" initiated by Mikhail Gorbachev in the 1980s, were best positioned to exploit social and political changes to their own advantage. Many of these were able to amass huge resources during the social transformation. At the same time, new, and generally younger, elites emerged informally from among those with the energy and daring to profit from social upheaval. Preoccupied by their competition with one another, the older elite failed to prevent the rise of these new bosses, in no small part because the former required the support of the latter.

The transformation of the Russian elite was reproduced in Dagestan with peculiarities resulting from its social structure and cultural diversity. First, the abolition of the old hierarchy resulted in markedly less reticent, more assertive elite behavior. The destruction of this reticence resulted from, and led to, the introduction of new principles for the selection of elites.

Generally, these changes resulted not so much from the replacement of old apparatchiks with new leaders, but from the political rise of an entrepreneurial and financial elite unknown in the Soviet Union. Whereas it might have been supposed that the collapse of the cumbersome Soviet regime would result in the simplification and rationalization of government institutions, the opposite occurred. Throughout the 1990s the number of state officials increased by 50 percent in the Russian Federation, and by 100 percent in Dagestan. This "swelling" of state agencies, together with relations between old and new elites largely determined the character of both Russian and Dagestani politics during that decade.

Shortly after the collapse of the communist regime, Dagestan saw few changes in the highest echelon of power. Yet it was not long before altered structures of political power began to yield changes in political personnel. Throughout the remainder of the 1990s, there were two principal types of influence in Dagestan, corresponding to a Weberian distinction between authority and power: (1) formal-legal authority primarily exercised by the highest officials of all three branches of government; and (2) informal, extralegal power that depended upon (a) financial capacity, (b) charismatic appeal, and (c) force, including violent acts and threats thereof from well-armed ethnic and religious organizations. Elites who enjoyed a combination of formal and informal influence saw their influence expand most dramatically. This intersection could be approached by either formal or informal routes: (1) some high officials enriched themselves, attracting acolytes and establishing extrainstitutional support networks; (2) some popular leaders of ethnic organizations or other mass movements, and wealthy individuals acquired official positions through appointment or popular election. Meanwhile, those elites whose power remained primarily formal or primarily informal tended to become marginalized, and in many cases, radicalized.

Old and new elites could be distinguished by the political tactics that they employed. The old regime relied upon extraeconomical levers of influence, including moral and ideological inducements as well as formal-legal mechanisms of control and political repression. By contrast, the new elite was largely indifferent to ideological considerations. Its power was measured by the material benefits that it bestowed and was supplemented by extralegal suppression and threats thereof.

Increasingly, Dagestan saw the emergence of a new class of political "bosses," the primary motivation of whom was the corporate interest of a tightly connected group of people. While the term "boss" evokes connotations of corruption and even criminality that are often appropriate in this context, it is also intended to connote an informal, highly personal, and sometimes charismatic, capacity for the acquisition, amalgamation, and retention of power. It was often the case that informal operations led to an increase in material prosperity, followed by the "bosses" entrance into formal power structures. Elections provided newer elites with legitimacy and sometimes contributed to their reconciliation with their elder peers.

Nevertheless this transition was not smooth. For example, in 1996–97, there were thirty-two reported cases of criminal pressure on state officials. Fourteen officials were assassinated, including seven members of the assembly. The fact that not one of these assassinations was solved does not mean that the murders went unpunished. According to a spokesperson for the then-minister of internal affairs Magomed Abdurazakov, suspects in assassinations were often found murdered themselves.[4] Since many of these attacks involved explosions in public places, it might have been observed that Dagestan's elite was responsible for a significant portion of its terrorist activity, a fact as ominous as it was remarkable.

If these developments led to increasing insecurity among Dagestan's political-economic elites, they also contributed to increasing tensions between these elites and the general population. By the end of the 1990s, the richest 10 percent of Dagestan's population was thirteen times wealthier than the poorest 10 percent, ranking among the greatest discrepancies of wealth anywhere in Russia. Average income in Dagestan was one-third the average for Russia as a whole. This placed Dagestan's average salary below the living wage in the rest of the federation and eight times lower than the average in Russia's wealthier regions. Moscow's average income, for example, was five times higher than Russia's living wage. Moreover, debts owed in salaries to Dagestan's 2 million people (a figure that includes underage, retired, and other nonworkers) was in excess of 131 billion rubles. Dagestan was also among the six Russian regions with the highest backlogs in the payment of child allowance.

During these years, Dagestan's wealthy elite formed an increasingly tight circle. By the end of the decade there were about 200 clans in Dagestan that had managed to acquire huge resources and that consequently defined the system of political relations. Money that Moscow provided for the republic was being siphoned by these individuals who openly flaunted the law, leading lavish and ostentatious lifestyles in mansions and palatial, often fortified, compounds. The nucleus of this financial elite consisted of approximately 1,000 families with 6,500 members (or 0.3 percent of the population). This highest elite was supported by another 5–7 percent of the population who had significantly improved their financial situation. Another 20–25 percent managed, often by means of extraordinary effort, to raise their income two to five times above the living wage. Approximately, 70 percent of the population lived in deep, and deepening, poverty. Apart from electrification, rural life was often characterized by nineteenth-century living conditions. Even in the capitol, the overwhelming majority lived in crumbling apartment blocks where electricity and running water were at best unreliable, and where water, when it ran, had to be treated before it could be consumed.

These tensions reverberated along the ethnic and clan divisions that had been established among Dagestan elites. Whereas the communist regime initially declared proletarian internationalism, it later underwent a political erosion, first affecting its creative elite and then its political and scientific elites. The last two decades of the Soviet Union were remarkable for the increasing attention devoted to ethnic factors. Whether in Moscow or the republics, declining confidence in the established social structure led to an ascendance of personal loyalties, which developed naturally along ethnic lines. Latent nationalism sank deep roots the decaying Soviet society.

Communist cosmopolitanism had never been more than a thin veneer on Dagestan's historically multinational social structure, and it was initially among Dagestan's elites that this structure began to regain political significance. By the time of perestroika, ethnic political structures were completely reestablished. With the collapse of the communist regime, Dagestan's governing elite lost the support of previously existing bureaucratic structures, but recovered support through informal networks of friends, relatives, and community members of common ethnic heritage. Yet when grassroots ethnic organizations began to arise, they were often resistant to consolidation by governing elites who now sought to strengthen their vertical, intraethnic connections. The ensuing political process focused upon competition between formal elites, who sought to acquire influence over newly emergent national movements, and informal leaders of national movements, who sought to acquire institutional authority.

This transformation of Dagestan's multiethnic political balance was the prevailing political factor in the early 1990s. Those ethnic communities, which were previously without political power, and which acquired political significance only insofar as they were objects of ethnic policies determined by a distant, authoritarian regime, suddenly attained political prominence. Political mobilization in the republic was based neither upon ideological nor partisan divisions, but upon ethnic consolidation.

By the end of 1991, Dagestan's political scene was characterized by increasingly complex ethnic alliances and shameless demagoguery on the part of older, Soviet-style leaders who were attempting to carve out niches for themselves in the rapidly evolving environment of nationalist politics. Suddenly deprived of support from the Soviet bureaucracy, Dagestan's political elites were casting about desperately for new bases for their authority. In the administrative vacuum of autumn 1991, it was clear that subsequent support would have to be popular in nature. Since power had stopped flowing from the top down, there was an urgent need to open new channels through which it could flow from a populist base.

At the same time, the ominous implosion of the Soviet government opened a new era of immanent social chaos. In this new power vacuum, Dagestanis turned reflexively toward their traditional modes of social organization. Thus they spontaneously embarked upon a revival of village-centered political organizations. Yet because most Dagestani villages are monoethnic, this revival of Dagestan's traditional, subethnic political units was initially expressed, throughout the early 1990s, in the Sovietized categories of national groups. In the tumultuous economic and political realignments of those years, national movements sprang up to defend traditional ethnic prerogatives against the encroachments of rival groups and shifting power structures.

For example, under the banner of Sadval (or Unity), the Lezgin national movement was primarily concerned with the separation of Lezgin people along the newly internationalized border between Russia and Azerbaijan. The border cut the Lezgin population approximately in half, although given the assimilationist policies of the Azeri authorities, the Lezgin population of that state is undoubtedly greater than it appears. A circle of Lezgin intelligentsia in Dagestan and Azerbaijan initially conceived of the combination of all Lezgin territory into a Republic of Lezgistan. The proposal became increasingly popular as the border between Dagestan and Azerbaijan acquired international status, severing families, friends, and economic ties. Yet the Lezgin movement lacked unity, for whereas Sadval was headed by Olympic wrestling champion Ruslan Ashuraliev, the Lezgin National Council was under the guidance of racketeer-turned-financier, Marat Ramazanov.

The name of the Nogai national movement, Birlik (or Unification), proclaimed its goal of combining Nogais of Dagestan, Chechnya, and Stavropol. Under the leadership of B. Kildasov, Birlik also addressed the population displacements that threatened traditional Nogai villages and pastures. This included the migration of Kwarel Avars who were being driven out of the high mountains of northwestern Georgia onto Nogai lands.

The Lak People's Movement was headed by a famous former sportsman-karatist and businessman[5] named Magomed Khachilaev. The Dargin national movement, called Tsadesh (or Unity), garnered less support than its counterparts because Dargins were relatively successful at solving their problems at the village level. An exception to this was the tense relationship that existed, in these years, along the border of the Dargin and Kumyk territories. This was particularly the case in the Kaiakentskii raion in the south and the Khasaviurt raion in the north, where there were problems in the villages of New and Old Kostecks, inhabited respectively by Dargins and Kumyks.

The migration of mountain people to the plains also raised problems for the ethnic Russian population, mostly Cossacks residing along the Lower Terek River. This was especially true in the districts of Kizliarsk and Tarumovsk, where Russians became a minority in lands that once were almost exclusively Slavonic. Cossack interests in this area were defended by a Kizliar-based group of Terek-Cossack troops, whose leader was Ataman Alexander Elson, and by the Slavic Movement of Russia, under Sergei Sinitsin. Moreover, a group called the "Russian Community" formed in Makhachkala in 1994 with the aim of unifying the Russian population against criminal elements. Because the urban Russian population lacked the extended familial networks that supported other groups (indigenous Dagestani clans are commonly retributive), they were especially vulnerable to crime.

Each of Dagestan's ethnic segments sought to spread its influence not only in politics but also in economic and financial concerns, education, the media, health care, public works, and even cemetery administration. Yet while these segments of the society contended for horizontal influence, the vertical connections within each segment were subject to proliferation and reinforcement as they were cultivated by those ethnic elites who depended upon them for support. The culmination of this horizontal and vertical expansion was a circle of friends and relatives that presided over the political, economic, social, cultural, religious, and health care organizations in each community, further entrenching the elitist elements of Dagestani democracy. Dagestan's new political organization was soon expressed in informal social structures, later dubbed "ethnoparties."[6] The primary characteristic of all ethnoparties was that they tended to be clan-based and local, each anchored in the life of a djamaat. Since nearly all Dagestani djamaats are monoethnic, and since all ethnic groups encompass numerous djamaats, the ethnoparties were essentially the vehicles through which the djamaats competed within the politics of the republic.

New Roles for the Traditional Djamaat

Prior to both the tsarist and Soviet regimes, Dagestani life was dominated by a system of djamaats, or traditionally localized communities, organized politically, and defined along territorial and historical lines. Typically, a djamaat was, and is, a village or a group of villages with a historical connection. Each djamaat consisted of a few, and sometimes as many as ten, different tribal or ancestral structures, known as tuhums. Each tuhum was a broadly extended and closely connected family. Governments of the djamaats traditionally consisted of councils of elders drawn from each of the constituent tuhums. That is, a traditional djamaat might be considered as a plural association consisting of segmented kinship structures, and governed cooperatively by elites drawn from each of these segments. The independent djamaats were governed by the adat, which structured a complex of economic, political, and sociocultural norms that collectively distinguished Dagestan as a coherent cultural entity.

For more than 500 years, Dagestan had been a separate country, set apart from Shiites in the south, Christians in the west, and Chechens to the north. From the end of the fifteenth century, Dagestani life was defined not by tribal relations, but by the civil and political structures of the djamaats, which operated in a manner analogous to the ancient *poleis*. From this period forward, the civil and judicial structures of the djamaat successfully transcended ethnotribal connections, which thereafter gradually diminished in their significance. The adat restricted the intratribal solidarity among members of the djamaat and demanded the subordination of kinship concerns to the political integrity of the community.

Despite the independence and sovereignty of the djamaats, a unified Dagestan emerged through common faith in Islam and an integrated intelligentsia consisting of educated ulemas.[7] Hence, Dagestan's ethnolinguistic diversity did not play a decisive role in its early political development. Citizens of most djamaats spoke the same language, but this was not the reason for their connection. On occasion, indeed, ethnic homogeneity of some djamaats tended to provoke resorts to artificial extraethnic distinctions. In short, ethnic identification was not a factor in the sociopolitical discourse of traditional Dagestan. Rather it has been traced to Soviet ethnic policies, and to the national movements that sprang up in the late 1980s and early 1990s as loci of grassroots agitation and elite legitimation.[8]

Though the national movements remained a factor, their significance faded as the social transformation progressed, and especially as Dagestan's 1994 Constitution provided new sources for authority. Gradually, the national movements gave way to traditional structures of social solidarity that offered an informal foundation for the formal political system under construction by Dagestani elites. Thus, the djamaats began to reemerge through the course of the transformation and the consequent struggle for control of the economic and political legacies of socialism. Despite the superficial appearance of national movements and Western-style political parties, Dagestani political life settled increasingly into its traditional village patterns.

The resulting political organizations have been described as "ethnoparties" because they displayed many attributes of Western-style political parties: aspirations toward the expansion of their power by political means; ideological like-mindedness; organization; authoritative leadership and a broad circle of activists; financial support; and support of the masses. However, ethnoparties were peculiar in that the bulk of their membership and the base of support derived from a single djamaat. An ethnoparty might include some activists from another ethnic group, but all key positions of leadership and support were filled by djamaat members. Every ethnic group received representation through its ethnoparties, yet because ethnoparties typically were concerned primarily with local interests they did not represent an entire ethnic group. Larger ethnic groups such as Avars, Dargins, Kumyks, and Lezgins had several such ethnoparties. Yet even the smallest of Dagestan's ethnic groups fielded multiple ethnoparties. The leaders of ethnoparties might unite with leaders of the same ethnicity, but they might also form alliances against other leaders of their ethnic group by uniting with other ethnic groups.

As a result, Dagestan saw the emergence of djamaat-based elites. The elites devoted all of their efforts to maintaining and strengthening their control over their supporters by proportionate measures of pressure and concession. In this way, the traditions of the Dagestani djamaat, transcending kinship and ethnic structures, provided a basis for the stabilization of a political system, which however fragile, nevertheless endured in the face of extraordinary crises, while providing for Dagestan's peaceful integration into Russia's federal system.

Small-scale political organization was ideally suited to Dagestan's rugged terrain, where groups clustered in alpine valleys, and the people on the other side of the mountain spoke a different language. But after the revolution, when the Soviets combined a multiplicity of small ethnolinguistic groups to form the Republic of Dagestan, the traditions of the djamaat became the basis for a political organization that transcended not only blood, but also ethnolinguistic barriers. Unlike many Chechens, who never fully accepted Russian rule, the Dagestani's developed a transethnic, Dagestani identity and settled fairly comfortably within the Soviet federal system, which was, for them, in some respects, the djamaat writ large. Just as the djamaat was a political structure that transcended the kinship cleavages of its constituent tuhums, so the Republic of Dagestan, and indeed the entire Soviet Union, were political structures that transcended the kinship structures of their constituent ethnic groups.

In the tumultuous, post-Soviet period, these traditional structures reemerged with traditional responsibilities for local governance. Yet the djamaats also reemerged with new responsibilities in their role as the territorial bases for the ethnoparties that acted on behalf of the interests of local populations in the competitive politics of the republic. While these ethnoparties were distinct from the national movements that emerged during perestroika to advocate the interests of the principal ethnic groups, they were nevertheless related to the national movements in a number of different ways. For example, the Lak national movement, Kazi-Kumuch became the nucleus of an ethnoparty, and its leader, Magomed Khachilaev, became the genuine political leader of the Laks, prior to his arrest in 1999 and his death at the hands of his bodyguard the following year. On the other hand, the Dargin national movement Zadesh had little to do with the Dargin ethnoparties. For the most part, national movements were phenomena of the early 1990s that were soon subordinated to ethnoparties or reduced to fronts for the latter.

Constant maneuvering among these ethnoparties was a major source of political instability in Dagestan; yet paradoxically it also did much to sustain the fragile balance among Dagestan's ethnic groups. Ethnoparties tended to diminish the significance of Dagestan's other political, economic, and ideological polarities. At the same time, they formed a system of counterbalances that maintained an intricate equilibrium of ethnic power through a multiplicity of limited and countervailing oppositions. This dynamic balance, which followed from the extremity of Dagestan's ethnic heterogeneity was responsible for the unique character of Dagestani politics. Though Dagestan's numerous local conflicts sometimes became acute, they were limited by the djamaat structure of Dagestani politics, and therefore rarely spread beyond the local level.

At the same time, the existence of ethnoparties tended to fragment the political elite and thereby inhibited the articulation and realization of common social objectives. This appeared in contrast to neighboring Russian republics with titular nationalities. During these same years, perhaps for the same reason, Dagestan did not produce the charismatic leadership that flourished in other regions of the Caucasus. Moreover, because Dagestani politics was based upon the perpetual struggle of ethnic elites it was nearly impossible for the government to focus upon external issues affecting the republic as a whole. Regardless of their importance, external issues were at best a secondary concern, and all the more so when a tough solution was required. If it is relatively easy, and often advantageous, for a united political elite to focus upon external threats and problems, an effort by Dagestani elites to resolve such difficulties could only weaken their domestic position. Any decisive solution would have resulted in new cleavages around which the population would have polarized, dividing one's supporters and enlivening new opponents. Similar considerations often inhibited decisive resolution of domestic problems. Thus the incessant efforts of elites to counterbalance one another and the efforts of the government to maintain stability also tended to inhibit the decisive resolution of fundamental problems. As a consequence, Makhachkala's external relations (with Baku, Tbilisi, Grozny, and Moscow) were chronically problematic. Yet it was this same counterbalancing among elites that gave rise to Dagestan's distinctive democratic system. It was a process that began near the start of perestroika.

Renewed Nationalism and Recycled Elites

In 1983, a wave of changes swept Dagestan. Magomed-Salam Umakha-nov, a Dargin, retired from his position as Communist Party secretary and was replaced by an Avar named Magomed Yusupov. This ethnic rotation at the highest level mandated corresponding rotations in order to maintain the delicate ethnic balance. Hence, the fifty-three-year-old Dargin, deputy prime minister, Magomedali Magomedov, was promoted to the vacant position of prime minister.[9] Magomedov had been promoted to the post of deputy prime minister in 1979, having served as secretary of agriculture in the party apparatus since 1975. As a result of these changes, control of the two top positions was switched between Avars and Dargins, Dagestan's two largest ethnic groups.

Soon thereafter, Yusupov elevated a forty-three-year-old Avar named Mukhu Aliev in the party apparatus by appointing him secretary of the Personnel and Organization Department. Aliev had previously served as first secretary of the Communist Party of the Sovetskii raion of Makhachkala.[10] Though leadership of the Personnel and Organization Department was not a high-profile position, the appointment placed Aliev in a key gatekeeping role. In a sense, the post was the local equivalent of the party role through which Stalin had propelled himself to power. While Aliev did not exploit the responsibilities of this position, his influence grew enormously. This was, in part, because Yusupov's policies concentrated upon economic development, leading to organizational shifts and high-stakes personnel appointments that Aliev controlled.

Meanwhile Magomedali Magomedov's lackluster performance as prime minister came to an end in 1987, when he was replaced prior to the official age of retirement. To fill the vacant position of prime minister, Yusupov appointed "his man," a well-qualified economist and an ethnic Kumyk named Abdurazak Mirzabekov. This required another ethnic rotation in which Alipasha Umalatov, a Kumyk, was retired from his position as chairman of Dagestan's Supreme Soviet, and the position was given to Magomedali Magomedov.

By all indications this meant that Magomedov's career was finished. From here he would never become first secretary of the Communist Party, and in three years he would reach the age for retirement. Indeed, Dagestanis referred sardonically to the chair of the Supreme Soviet as the "pre-retirement position." Thus, at the age of fifty-seven, Magomedov was preparing to step aside. As he was then the eldest and most obscure of Dagestan's leaders, nothing foreshadowed his further ascent.

At the same time, the forty-seven-year-old Aliev also seemed to reach the ceiling of his career. Since the current first secretary was Yusupov, an Avar, the traditions of Dagestan's ethnic balancing required that his successor not be an Avar. Thus, because he was an Avar, Aliev could not become the next first secretary. On the other hand, the position of prime minister usually did not go to a party bureaucrat, such as Aliev, but to a recognized economist and manager. These factors suggested that the next first secretary of the Communist Party of Dagestan would be the Kumyk prime minister, Abdurazak Mirzabekov. History, however, took a different turn.

In 1990, when the Communist Party of the Soviet Union became "a vestige of the past," Yusupov left his position, and moved to Moscow to take a diplomatic position. On his recommendation, Mukhu Aliev was elected to replace him as first secretary. At the same time it had become clear that Gorbachev aimed to shift power from the party bureaucracy to local legislatures, as part of a reform package that promised openness and flirted with democratization. Gorbachev himself set the pace for this transition at the federal level when he combined the positions of party leader with the chairmanship of the Supreme Soviet of the USSR, and thereafter concentrated his attentions primarily upon the latter. Across the Soviet Union there were spontaneous efforts to mimic this development at the regional level. For example, in the Chechen-Ingush Republic, Doku Zavgaev, the recently appointed first secretary of the Communist Party was readily elected chairman of the Supreme Soviet. Yet this trend took an unexpected turn in Dagestan as a consequence of its multiethnicity; and it was precisely at this point that a new, and uniquely Dagestani political process emerged.

It all began when both the party leader, Mukhu Aliev, and the prime minister, Abdurazak Mirzabekov, demanded the resignation of Magomedali Magomedov from his post as chair of Dagestan's Supreme Soviet. Seeing Magomedov as a weak leader on the verge of retirement, each of them sought to clear his path of Magomedov so that he might move into Magomedov's position as speaker of the legislature.

Faced with an ultimatum from Aliev and Mirzabekov, Magomedov unexpectedly refused to step down, responding with what seemed at that time to be unthinkable impertinence. It was rumored that Magomedov stormed out of their meeting with the words, "It's no longer for you to decide!" Magomedov, it seems, had realized that the shift of power to the legislatures had unexpectedly placed him in a stronger position than those of Aliev and Mirzabekov.

It is also possible, that Mirzabekov was secretly gratified by Magomedov's stand because Mirzabekov was attempting to prevent greater power from falling to his chief rival, Aliev, and was relatively unconcerned about Magomedov, whom he regarded as a political cipher. Since Mirzabekov was concentrating upon his efforts to prevent Aliev from mimicking Gorbachev by combining his leadership of the party with leadership of the legislature, he may have welcomed Magomedov's unexpected obstinacy, assuming that he could dispose of Magomedov once he had overcome Aliev. At the time, this might have seemed a likely outcome to Mirzabekov since power was also shifting from the party to the government executive. In Makhachkala, the tight rows of limousines (personal Volgas) had already moved from the Obkom (party headquarters) to the Sovmin (the building that housed the Cabinet of Ministers).

On April 24, 1990, the first Convention of the People's Representatives of Dagestan elected Magomedov as chairman of the Supreme Soviet. According to rumor, Magomedov had promised Aliev and Mirzabekov that he would "retire soon." Meanwhile Mirzabekov continued as prime minister, and Aliev remained leader of the increasingly irrelevant Communist Party, having just sustained the loss of the fifth amendment of the Soviet Constitution, which had once proclaimed the Communist Party as "the ruling and directing power."

Uniquely in Dagestan, however, the Communist Party clung to power not because of its inherent authority, but because it had become one of the traditional, and therefore indispensable "branches" for the ethnic distribution of power. In Dagestan, a representative from each of the three largest ethnic groups—the Avars, the Dargins, and the Kumyks—had traditionally occupied the three highest positions in the republic. In 1990, the Kumyk, Mirzabekov, was Dagestan's prime minister, and the Dargin, Magomedov chaired the Supreme Soviet. The Communist Party retained power because it was headed by an Avar, Mukhu Aliev, and the realities of Dagestan's ethnic politics were such that the Avars could not be excluded from power regardless of the vicissitudes of the Communist Party.

Yet shortly thereafter, in August 1991, when Boris Yeltsin came to power, the Communist Party was banned, and Mukhu Aliev was left not only without power but also without a job. His office, along with the rest of Makhachkala's Communist Party headquarters, was sealed shut. Aliev retained power only as an ordinary representative of the assembly of Dagestan, which was headed by Magomedov.

Throughout the preceding year, actual political power had been gradually shifting from the offices of the Committee of the Communist Party to executive officials, and especially to the cabinet headed by Mirzabekov. However, Dagestan's slow drift toward political crisis produced additional adjustments in the balance of power. Increasingly, the threat of mass protests, the potential for ethnic clashes, and threats of destabilization placed the focus on representative bodies. Under these conditions there gradually emerged a new spirit of discussion, negotiation, and open compromise, all of which tended to enhance the authority of the Supreme Soviet.

Magomedov's position at the head of the Supreme Soviet provided increased influence with which he artfully maneuvered himself toward the center of events. A year later, when the Communist Party was abolished, Magomedov's position was strengthened once again. Mukhu Aliev, who was then the Communist Party leader in Dagestan, managed to obtain a position as Magomedov's first deputy. He accomplished this transfer with great difficulty, and in defiance of Magomedov's wishes. Thus, at the time of the regime transition, ethnic parity had prevailed and power was again distributed among the triumvirate of Magomedov, Aliev, and Mirzabekov. Yet this had occurred to the unexpected advantage of Magomedov.

Thus the transition away from Communist power, which proceeded relatively smoothly in much of the rest of the Soviet Union, became a uniquely tense and trying process in Dagestan. The real de facto power was concentrated in the hands of a Kumyk, Mirzabekov; de jure power, such as it was, was in the hands of a Dargin, Magomedov; while the largest ethnic group in Dagestan, the Avars, lost their representation in the highest echelons of power. Mirzabekov demonstratively refused to be pulled into the political struggle, single-handedly managing all the economic problems of the republic, some of which seemed to offer prospects for genuine economic development.

This left Magomedov managing the tumultuous political process, wherein he suddenly revealed himself to be a subtle and sensitive politician who could yield when necessary, and yet still press his issues as required. All at once, and completely unexpectedly, he emerged as a brilliant political operator. One might speculate that the planned and predictable certainties of the Soviet system had a stifling effect upon Magomedov's inherent political talents, which therefore blossomed only in the vortex of bureaucratic demise. One might say almost exactly the opposite of Aliev, who was now eclipsed by Magomedov.

The loss of "the Avar position" of power only served to intensify Dagestan's political tumult. Political stability required some move toward the restoration of ethnic balance. The highest-ranking Avar at that moment was Magomed Abdurazakov, who served as interior minister. Under the circumstances, the power of this position stood to be dramatically increased.

Ethnic Protests and Emerging Elites

Yet only a month after the fall of the Communist Party, in October 1991, the Kumyk national movement, known as Tenglik (Justice), launched a series of massive protests demanding Abdurazakov's resignation as head of the Interior Ministry. These protests featured widespread involvement and support from Kumyks hailing from many of Dagestan's raions. All of this was indicative of a sharp increase in tensions between Kumyks and Avars. These tensions resulted from the economic uncertainties of that year, and from the consequent spike in the migration of Avars from their hardscrabble, highland villages to the lowland cities and pasture lands that had traditionally belonged to the Kumyks. As a consequence of these displacements, Kumyks became a minority in their traditional ethnic territory. Many Kumyks were also resentful of traditional Avar political power, and looked to Mirzabekov's ascendance and Aliev's demise as a watershed that could potentially restructure local political power to the advantage of the Kumyks. For both of these reasons, they welcomed the sudden turn of events as an opportunity to limit, and possibly to undermine, Avar power. Under the leadership of Salav Aliev, Tenglik called for an end to resettlement and called for an autonomous Kumykstan, perhaps within a federated Dagestan.

In response, the Avar national movement emerged and grew rapidly. On October 12, 1991, an "All-Avar National Convention" was convened with 810 participants from all raions of Avaria. The convention was dominated by elites and intellectuals of the old school, who were relatively moderate in their outlook. Eschewing radical declarations, the convention dedicated itself to the preservation of peace in Dagestan, together with the preservation of Avar power, and the prevention of efforts to remove Avar officeholders.

On October 22, without prior announcement or discussion, the fourteenth session of the Supreme Soviet of Dagestan proposed to appoint an Avar as a deputy of the chairman of the Supreme Soviet. That same day the Kumyk national movement, Tenglik, blocked the Baku-Rostov highway near the village of Aksai in the Khasaviurt raion. Tenglik also organized a blockade of the Makhachkala Airport, and a massive rally on Makhachkala's central square in front of the main government buildings. The stated aims of this protest were "against the personnel policies of the Supreme Soviet, and for the resignation of the Supreme Soviet and the Cabinet of Ministers of the republic." The subtexts of these demands were the prevention of the appointment of an Avar as deputy to the chair of the Supreme Soviet, and the removal of Abdurazakov as head of the Interior Ministry.

While the representatives of the Supreme Soviet wanted to discuss the situation "on the streets," Magomedali Magomedov ignored these events and concentrated exclusively on the election of his Avar deputy.[11] His goal was to choose, as one of his deputies, an Avar who would be personally loyal to him. Possibly this appointment could have made it easier to remove the Avar interior minister. There are no reasons to suppose that Mirzabekov, a Kumyk, was conspiring with Magomedov, but it is possible that Mirzabekov would also have been interested in Abdurazakov's departure from the Interior Ministry.

Old-fashioned "party ethics" would have required Magomedov to nominate Aliev as his Avar deputy. However, focusing upon the criterion of personal loyalty, Magomedov chose an obscure individual who had formerly served as a party secretary in one of the rural districts. Recognizing this as a power play on Magomedov's part, the Avars persuaded Magomedov's Avar nominee to withdraw his candidacy in favor of Mukhu Aliev. The exchanges between supporters of Magomedov and Avar representatives were openly hostile. As a response to Aliev's candidacy, Magomedov's faction nominated Takibat Mahmudova, a female Agul representative from Kaspiysk who was connected through her marriage to one of the most powerful Dargin clans, the Omarovs.

This was an astute move on Magomedov's part. As one of Dagestan's smallest ethnic groups, the Aguls have the sympathy of other smaller groups, who sometimes resent the power of the larger groups. Moreover, the Aguls have cultural and historical affiliations with the Lezgins, the fourth largest ethnic group that, arguably, has been excluded from its fair share of influence. Takibat's nomination was consequently assured of support. Yet Takibat's affiliation with a powerful Dargin clan meant that she would also be accessible to Magomedov's influence. The Supreme Soviet debated the nominations until late at night, and the election was postponed until the next morning. On the following day, October 23, there were 113 votes for Aliev, and 75 votes for Takibat Mahmudova. This left Aliev five votes short of victory. The problem was unresolved, and was set aside for the future.

Following this unsuccessful election, the Supreme Soviet moved on to discuss the Kumyk protests and their transportation blockades. During this discussion, the head of the Dagestan branch of the KGB, Viktor Moshkov, informed the session that Chechens from the Chechen national movement, Vainakh, had joined with the Kumyks in their highway blockade near the village of Aksai. The Chechens were joining with the Kumyks because they were involved in similar territorial disputes with the Avars in Dagestan's Novolakskii raion, from which the Chechens had been forcibly deported in February 1944.

Meanwhile, outside of the assembly hall, Makhachkala's central square, which had been abandoned by the Kumyks at the close of the preceding day, was now rapidly filling with buses, trucks, and cars from the Avar regions. They responded to a call by the National Front of Imam Shamil. Prior to this moment, the activities of this group had been largely confined to the Kazbekovskii and Khasaviurtovskii raions. There it had worked to thwart Chechen efforts to reclaim lands that they had lost in the deportation of 1944, and which had subsequently been occupied by Avars.[12] The Imam Shamil Front was energetically led by Gadzhi Makhachev, a youthful newcomer from Khasaviurt with a record of two prior convictions for thuggery. Makhachev had nothing to do with the old-guard, Avar elite, who had been preaching moderation.

At his impromptu Avar convention in the central square, Makhachev declared that all actions of Tenglik were "serving the old Kumyk nomenclature and are anti-Avar." Then, leading a group of his supporters, Makhachev broke into the meeting of the Supreme Soviet, and declared that "if the highways are not cleared by the government within the next three hours, the people from the square will do it for them." In no uncertain terms, Makhachev was publicly threatening violent conflict between the Avars in the square and the Kumyks and Chechens who were blocking the highways. In his unscheduled address to the assembly, Makhachev accused high-ranking Kumyk officials and representatives in the Supreme Soviet of covert involvement in Tenglik's activities, including the illegal protests. These Kumyk officials included Abduragim Beksultanov (chairman of the Khasaviurt Raion Council); and representatives Arsen Atabiev, Tazhitdin Batyrbiyev, and Arsen Ataev (who were involved in the administration of the Supreme Soviet); Bagautdin Gadjiev (the trade minister); and Toturbii Toturbiev (the head of Dagestan Hydro-Construction).[13]

After his speech, Makhachev led the column of cars and buses to Aksai, where Tenglik blocked the highway. It appeared that a major ethnic conflict would ensue, pitting the Avars, on one side, against Kumyks and Chechens on the other. Had there been an actual clash, the history of Dagestan and the North Caucasus would have taken a dramatically different turn. The Ossetian-Ingush conflict that took place a year later, and the Chechen war that started soon after would have looked like episodes of a single expansive and bloody war, occurring on all sides of the traditional Vaynakh (that is, Chechen and Ingush) territories, which was sparked by those Aksai events.

It took enormous efforts of both Avar and Kumyk leaders and persistent mediation of the government officials to prevent the clash of Avars against the Kumyks and Chechens. The highway was opened, but the tent camp near Aksai (called "Tenglik-kala") remained in place for a long period of time, persevering in the protests, but no longer threatening Dagestan's main highway.

Magomedov's Political Art

It was in this new, intensely nationalized, political framework that Magomedali Magomedov began to reveal his previously dormant political skills. At the following session of the Supreme Soviet, he suggested the election of not one, but two deputy chairs to include both competing candidates: Mukhu Aliev and Takibat Mahmudova. This plan easily carried the Supreme Soviet. At the same time, he pushed to establish positions for three additional deputies to the prime minister on the ground that this would create greater opportunities for ethnic balancing. Mirzabekov protested this move, and offered his resignation, which was not accepted. The three new positions of deputy prime minister were filled by Said Amirov (Dargin), Narbek Aidzhigaitkanov (Nogai), and Zeidullah Yuzbekov (Tabasaran).

Another echo of the struggle for ethnic balance in the highest echelons of power was the forcible takeover of the Spiritual Directorate of the Muslims of Dagestan (known locally as the DUMD) by a group of Avar Islamic leaders in February 1992. Dagestan's Kumyk mufti, Bagautdin Isaev, was overthrown by direct armed actions, and an Avar named Said-Akhmed Darbishgadjiev was installed in his place. Magomedov and Mirzabekov took a quietly passive approach to this overthrow because it was the most harmless possible compensation for the power positions that the Avars had lost. After that they could claim that "the Avar branch of power" was represented in the form of "the spiritual leadership" of Dagestan.

These events marked the first time that Magomedov achieved his personal objectives by means of an astute indirection that ultimately contributed to Dagestan's emergent political pluralism. His achievement was the recognition that he would never secure a complete victory in these matters and that a full frontal attack upon his political adversaries would therefore prove counterproductive. Instead he sought to achieve his objectives of marginalizing Aliev and Mirzabekov, and neutralizing their respective power bases in the Avar and Kumyk communities, by personally presiding over an effort to achieve more complex forms of ethnic balancing, all in the name of avoiding ethnic civil warfare. However inadvertently, this was the beginning of Dagestan's development of its own unique form of consociational democracy (see below), involving a dynamic political interplay of ethnic social segments.[14] Operating under enormous pressure, Magomedov successfully subordinated Mukhu Aliev, an otherwise strong politician, as a member of his own team of deputies, where Aliev's influence was balanced by that of Magomedov's supporters including Takibat Mahmudova. At the same time, he weakened one of his main competitors, Prime Minister Mirzabekov, by encumbering him with new deputies of diverse ethnicity, and defanging Tenglik's forceful protests.

Magomedov's management of Mirzabekov was particularly astute. Claiming to expand multiethnicity and support ethnic balancing, Magomedov planted "his man" at the highest level of Mirzabekov's government. This was the young and inexperienced Said Amirov, who had developed wide contacts through his management of a Soviet retail butchery operation, that is, through the culinary favors that he had bestowed upon his friends, and through the predaceous fears that he had inspired in his enemies. Though Amirov was developing a reputation for ruthlessness, he had demonstrated his complete loyalty to Magomedov.

As a contrast to Magomedov's artful ascent, Mukhu Aliev had barely managed to cling to power. His influence was now diluted by the bureaucratic structure of the Presidium of the Supreme Soviet, and by three other deputies who were loyal to Magomedov: Akhmadov (the Lezgin first deputy), Hizri Shikhsaidov (a Kumyk), and Takibat Mahmudova (who "talked like an Agul, but walked like a Dargin"). Among other things, this meant that Magomedov was able to solve all of his administrative problems by a vote of four to one.

Mirzabekov's wings had also been clipped. His operation of the government had been encumbered, against his will, by three new deputies, two of whom served primarily to legitimize the installation of Said Amirov. Amirov's primary purpose was to limit the independence of Mirzabekov's financial dispensations, which had previously been extravagant. A couple of days after these personnel innovations had been completed in Dagestan, in early 1992, Russia embarked upon "liberal economic reforms" under Yegor Gaidar. The "socialist economy" collapsed as natural resources, public assets, and private savings accounts were openly looted.

Three months after his appointment as deputy prime minister, Said Amirov survived an assassination attempt. An assailant fired upon his car; a bullet was lodged in his spine, and he became a paraplegic. He underwent treatments for a year, during which he was absent from Dagestan's political scene.

Thus the pluralistic system of multiethnic balancing that soon developed in Dagestan, owed much to Magomedov's self-serving maneuvers in his struggle with Aliev and Mirzabekov. From this clash there emerged a system in which neither political power, nor material wealth, nor even the resolution of key problems could be monopolized by any single individual, faction, or ethnicity.

Moreover, it became impossible to rule by agreements among three top officials of the republic. During the late Soviet period, Dagestan was ruled by a triumvirate comprised by the top Avar, Dargin, and Kumyk leaders. Now, however, Magomedov required broader support in order to maintain his position in power. Not only the politicians of the second and third echelons but also local leaders participated in the political process, and even leaders of the larger ethnicities could not hope to govern without support from some of the smaller ethnicities. None of the numerous ethnoparties could achieve dominance in power, but any of them could, if there were a will, provoke serious social destabilization. There were plenty of resources and manpower for these sorts of intensive, and potentially destabilizing, political activities.

Yet if it was extremely pluralistic and participatory, the political system that emerged was also remarkably stable in its system of balancing claims to power. Even more remarkably, open and (relatively) fair elections and referenda settled political struggles in a peaceful and democratic manner. At the same time the media became truly pluralistic and independent. None of the political leaders could avoid journalistic exposure of his financial machina-

Table 4.2

Results of Three Referenda on the Establishment of an Office of the Presidency of Dagestan (%)

Date of referendum	For	Against
June 28, 1992	10.6	87.9
December 12, 1993	30.8	68.1
March 7, 1999	21.6	74.8

tions because there were always some political forces who were interested in throwing light upon them, informing the media, and thereafter supporting media freedoms.

However, the following events indicated that Magomedov had not entirely abandoned his hopes for unlimited power. On May 21, 1992, during the seventeenth session of the Supreme Soviet, he introduced a discussion "on the improvement of the system of executive power in Dagestan." It soon became clear that Magomedov wished to introduce a system of presidential power in the republic. The representatives were taken by surprise when they were asked to make a decision about establishing a Dagestani presidency. Clearly Magomedov hoped to win a general election.

When the Supreme Soviet voted on the issue, 106 were for it, and 112 were against.[15] The measure was supported by Magomedov and all his deputies with the sole exception of Aliev. With this defeat in the Supreme Soviet, Magomedov proposed to put the question to a referendum. Almost all of the deputies voted in favor of this proposal. On the referendum ballot the initiative appeared as follows: "Do you think it necessary to establish the position of the president of Dagestan elected in a general election?" Yet only 10.6 percent of the electorate favored this proposal, while 87.9 percent were opposed. Those opposed included some who were already growing suspicious of Magomedov, but many Dagestanis voted against the measure because they feared a concentration of power in the hands of any single ethnic group. Two similar referenda also failed in later years for similar reasons. The results are shown in Table 4.2.

When the work on the new Constitution of Dagestan began, it was unclear how to establish the branches of government without a president. The committee that worked on the Constitution held regular meetings, argued bitterly, and adjourned without any solution.

In October 1993, a serious crisis occurred in Moscow, pitting the Supreme Soviet of the Russian Federation against Russian President Boris Yeltsin. The Dagestani leadership avoided the demonstration of any preference in this struggle. Yeltsin's victory over the Supreme Soviet gave him the power to embark on rapid economic reforms, and to hastily complete a new Russian Constitution. In December 1993, a referendum on the Constitution of the Russian Federation occurred simultaneously with elections for two federal legislative chambers, the new Russian parliament or State Duma, and the Federal Assembly of the Russian Federation. Magomedov was elected to represent the fifth Dagestani electoral district in the Federation Assembly along with an Avar named Ramazan Abdulatipov. Meanwhile Mukhu Aliev remained a representative in Dagestan's Supreme Soviet, and Magomedov's deputy.

The Constitutional Djamaat

Thereafter, the ratification of the new Constitution of Dagestan became a necessity that could no longer be postponed. When it was finally proposed, it was clear that the Constitution had been molded by the practice of permanent struggle in the highest echelons of power combined with the complex parity among pluralistic political forces. As it happened, the Constitution was crafted neither by elder statesmen nor by political scientists, but by the three rival politicians—Magomedov, Aliev, and Mirzabekov—seasoned in the political struggle among themselves. Based upon their experience of this internecine struggle, they devised an original approach to the institutions power. The result was a collegial executive known as the State Council (Gossovet [SC]), which consisted of one representative from each of Dagestan's major ethnic groups. This innovation was complemented by electoral laws that effectively secured proportional ethnic representation in Dagestan's National (or People's) Assembly (*Narodnoe sobranie*).[16]

The Constitution required that the chairman of the SC be selected from a field of more than a single candidate, by secret ballot in Dagestan's Constitutional Assembly.[17] The first deputy of the chairman of the SC was included in the SC automatically as the prime minister. When the Constitution was drafted, it was assumed that Magomedov would become chair of the SC, that Mirzabekov would occupy the position of prime minister, and that Aliev would lead the new legislature. The regular term for the chair of the SC was established as four years, but the initial term was regarded as transitional with a two-year limit. By all appearances, these three leaders agreed among themselves that Magomedov would get the position of the chairman of the SC for two years on a strictly transitional basis, after which he would retire at the age of sixty-six. To guarantee his departure, the Constitution established (in Article 93) that "the chairman of a particular ethnic group cannot remain in power for two terms."

On July 26, 1994, Dagestan's new Constitution was ratified at a convention of the Constitutional Assembly. The same Constitutional Assembly also selected the new SC headed by Magomedov. In this election Magomedov ran not against Mukhu Aliev, but against an Avar named Magomed Tolboev, a well-known test pilot who had participated in the Soviet space program. Mukhu Aliev later took Magomedov's position as chairman of the legislature, now to be known as the National Assembly. In early 1995, more specifically, Aliev was elected to the assembly from his native Khunzah djamaat, and was thereafter elected as chairman of the assembly.

With the ratification of its new Constitution, Dagestan emerged from a dangerous period of transitional uncertainty. Following the demise of the Soviet Union, the Dagestanis reflexively remained within the Russian Federation, adopted a new constitution, and set about the development of a unique political system. The republic saved itself when the collapse of authoritarian state structures led to the revival of traditional, and often compensatory, values, institutions, and social organizations.

The overarching framework for this revival was provided by the tensions of the post-Soviet era that forced the Yeltsin administration into a series of political compromises. These compromises relaxed the vertical power of the central bureaucracy, and offered local elites unexpected latitude for horizontal political development. In Dagestan, the peculiar means for the reemergence of traditional institutions had much to do with competition among Soviet-era elites, such as Magomedov, Mirzabekov, and Aliev. Its medium was the ethnic constructs that had come to dominate Dagestani life in the Soviet period. Yet at its core were social structures anchored far more deeply in the history of Dagestan's village life. The traditions of the djamaat at the informal foundation of Dagestan's political system had much to do with this period of fragile success, but so did the quasi-consociational expression that those traditions received in Dagestan's democratic constitution. The 1994 Constitution echoed the traditions of the djamaat insofar as it provided a codified framework for transcending kinship structures through the cooperative interactions of elites. Dagestan's ethnic diversity became the defining feature of its political system, which conformed inadvertently with consociational models at a number of different points.

The Consociational Djamaat

Arend Lijphart defines consociational democracy "in terms of both the segmental cleavages typical of a plural society and the political cooperation of the segmental elites."[18] He explains that in a consociational democracy "the centrifugal tendencies inherent in a plural society are counteracted by the cooperative attitudes and behavior of the leaders of the different segments of the population," and he emphasizes that pragmatic accommodation among elites is the principal feature distinguishing the consociational model. In particular, Lijphart's account has lent currency to concepts of a "grand coalition of the political leaders of all significant segments of the plural society" and the "mutual veto or "concurrent majority" rule, which serves as an additional protection of vital minority interests.

Many consociational models[19] have involved a macrostructural emphasis upon proportionality among ethnic groups and the expression of ethnic autonomy through federal arrangements. To one extent or another, all of these investigations have underscored the importance of approximate long-term parity, proportionality, reciprocity, and autonomy in achieving accommodation among ethnic groups. However, none of these studies has considered a case that compares with the ethnic heterogeneity of Dagestan.

The key to the Dagestani system was the approximate parity among its four largest ethnic groups: Avars, Dargins, Kumyks, and Lezgins. Since no group was large enough to govern on its own, Dagestani politics was characterized by a process of shifting balances and counterbalances among these four groups. Elites from Dagestan's other thirty ethnic groups could be compared to wandering electrons that ceaselessly transferred themselves from one ethnic nucleus to another in order to maintain a dynamic parity of political forces. This feature became all the more important in that the larger groups were effectively complex combinations of ethnoparties, which sometimes detached from their own ethnic group to unite with others. These features were evidently unprecedented in the consociational literature, and when taken together with the approximate parity of the four main groups (which these features also helped to sustain), they were among the great secrets of Dagestan's political stability. It is significant that these uniquely transient groups of elites actually strengthened the political system in so far as they facilitated a highly flexible political structure that could shift to respond to a crisis or to correct the overall balance against the ascendance of any particular group. This occurred through an elaborate, sometimes ingenious, set of institutions and practices set forth in Dagestan's 1994 Constitution.

Article 88 of the Constitution required that "there cannot be more than one representative of each of fourteen major ethnic groups" on the republic's chief executive body, the State Council; and a representative of the same ethnic group cannot "be elected chairman of the State Council for two consecutive terms" (Article 93). Indeed, the collegial nature of this executive had a consociational basis. Among the reasons that Dagestanis thrice rejected referenda that would have created an individual presidency was their fear that this would give too much power to a single ethnic group. Hence the chair of the SC was elected by its members for a fixed term, a restriction intended to provide for the rotation of the chair among the Council's members. This system of rotation was devised as a compromise among ethnic elites who feared, first, a violent and precipitous ethnic struggle for this powerful position, and second, the loss of ethnic balance through the influence of an individual executive. The chair of the SC appointed two deputy chairs.

The 1994 Constitution distinguished the Cabinet of Ministers (*Sovet ministerov*) from the SC, while subordinating the former to the executive power of the latter. However, the ministers were responsible to the chair of the SC and not to that body as a whole. As a consequence of this detail, the chair of the SC became the most powerful position in the land, wielding quasi-presidential powers on a de facto basis, while remaining formally a member of the collegial executive. The head of the cabinet, or prime minister, was, at the same time, one of the two deputy chairmen of the SC.

The Constitution also established the National Assembly, to which representatives were first elected in March 1995, with subsequent sessions elected in March 1999 and March 2003.[20] While the first election was highly contentious, involving violent incidents and several fatalities, the subsequent elections proceeded more smoothly. The assembly consisted of 121 members, of whom the chairman, two deputy chairmen, the heads of five standing committees, and one or two members of each committee (about twenty-five people), served on a continuous basis.[21] The function of the assembly was largely restricted to legislation and budgetary allocations.

The National Assembly also comprised half of the Constitutional Assembly. The latter was formed from the entire National Assembly plus an equal number of delegates (i.e., 121 + 121 = 242 total delegates) elected from the municipalities and raions particularly for the occasion of any given convention of the Constitutional Assembly in the same ethnic proportions (see below) as the delegates to the People's Assembly. The Constitutional Assembly considered constitutional amendments and elected members of the SC.

Each member of the Constitutional Assembly could nominate one candidate for the SC, and the three individuals from each ethnic group with the greatest number of nominations were then placed on a ballot for the SC. Any member of the Constitutional Assembly could vote for any SC candidates regardless of nationality. This system of selection promoted political integration and stability since it favored individuals with cross-national support. Due to the extent of Dagestan's ethnic diversity, candidates with support from several nationalities were likely to receive more nominations than those whose support was concentrated within a single group. Single-group candidates were even less likely to triumph in the assembly's final vote. It is significant that no leader of a national (monoethnic) movement was ever elected to the SC. Those who were elected were regarded as the most influential members of their ethnic groups, but they did not attain their positions through ethnic chauvinism. This process was intended to ensure that the government was made up of individuals and interests that favored stability and sought moderation and conciliatory solutions to conflicts occurring between segments of the population.

Yet the power of the National Assembly was progressively overshadowed by the expanding executive power of the SC. Through the incessant political maneuvers of Magomedali Magomedov, the chairman of the SC came to be significantly more powerful than the chairman of the assembly. Thus from the early years of its democratic system, Dagestan was gradually edging from its de jure collegial executive toward a de facto presidential system despite the fact that a formal shift to a presidential system was rejected in three referenda. Moreover, as the first (and only) chairman of the SC, Magomedov declined to yield his position at the end of his two-year term, precipitating a constitutional crisis (see below). Ironically, the system was internally undermined by the same self-serving maneuvers among political elites that had helped to bring the system into existence.

Dagestan's Electoral System

Article 72 of the Dagestani Constitution guaranteed the "representation of all the peoples of Dagestan." Dagestan's first democratic electoral system was designed to avoid the marginalization of any group and to ensure the representation of all nationalities in proportion to their numbers. These objectives could not be ensured unless the authorities had complete control of the nomination process, which would clearly be at odds with democratic purposes. The Dagestani government consequently depended upon informal agreements among ethnic groups. Where this was insufficient the Electoral Commission had the authority to allocate seats to members of a given ethnic group.

The first challenge came in the results of city council elections held in 1994, shortly after Dagestan adopted its democratic constitution. For example, in Makhachkala's council election Avars, who constitute 20 percent of the population, took 50 percent of the seats; Dargins with 10 percent of the population won 30 percent of the seats; Kumyks and Lezgins won only two seats each despite the fact that they respectively constitute 14 percent and 10 percent of the city's inhabitants. With 10 percent of the population, Laks held only a single seat, and though 20 percent of the city was Russian they held no seats at all. In the same year, the coastal city of Kaspiysk elected no Lezgin, Russian, or Kumyk representatives though Kumyks counted for 10 percent of the municipal population, Russians for 22 percent, and Lezgins were the largest national group. Though Kiziliurt was 15 percent Kumyk, no Kumyks were elected. While accepting that individuals should be elected on their merits, and while encouraging cross-national voting, the government was nonetheless concerned that such results could leave some groups feeling marginalized.

The weeks that followed these elections saw the emergence of a popular consensus, which included the elected council candidates, in support of the conclusion that such assemblies were neither representative nor legitimate. Such were the ethnic pressures, and such was the history of Dagestan's ethnic accommodation, that it was not regarded as respectable to serve on such an unrepresentative assembly.

In order to save the situation, and in classic Dagestani style, the republic's leadership quickly increased the number of seats and formed new electoral districts, where elections were soon held to choose more representatives. In Makhachkala, for example, ten new seats were created, and a new election was held in which Dargins and Avars were barred from candidacy.

Elsewhere, similar restrictions were applied regarding the ethnicity of the candidates. Whereas residents of all ethnic groups were qualified voters, only candidates of specific ethnicities were permitted to stand for office. The result was a remarkably proportionate representation of some of Dagestan's smaller ethnic groups. Moreover, the designation of ethnic electoral districts produced a marked alteration in the election campaigns. Issues of ethnicity were dropped altogether since all of the candidates were of the same group. Hence, ethnicity became a nonissue as personal qualities and political views came to the fore. Many public debates among candidates served to establish and test rules of the campaign. Both the campaign and the election of the additional representatives were conducted without serious disturbance. Clearly, Dagestani society was prepared for this innovation, which was quickly given a legislative foundation, and was further applied, with great success, during the election of the first People's Assembly in March 1995.

A law "On Elections to the People's Assembly of Dagestan" laid down a procedure guaranteeing the representation of all the constituent nationalities in proportion to their share of the republic's population. Of the 121 single-mandate electoral districts for elections to the assembly, sixty-six districts with multinational populations were designated by the Electoral Commission as "national electoral districts" (e.g., an Avar district, a Lezgin district, etc.). Within these districts only candidates of a single predetermined nationality could run for election, though voters of all national groups could select from among these candidates. This was done to avoid interethnic confrontations during elections and to achieve the necessary proportions of ethnic representation. Of the sixty-six nationally defined electoral districts, twelve were Avar districts, twelve Kumyk, ten Russian, seven Dargin, five Tabasaran, five Azeri, four Lezgin, four Chechen, three Lak, two Tat, one Nogai, and one Tsakhur.

Most of the remaining fifty-five electoral districts were in mountainous regions, whose populations were largely monoethnic. The exception was the Rutul region, where two electoral districts were established: one for the Rutuls and one for the Tsakhurs, the least numerous of the republic's peoples. Table 4.3 shows that as a result of these careful arrangements, each of Dagestan's fourteen principle ethnic groups achieved, in 1995 as well as in 1999, a representation in the assembly that was almost precisely proportionate to its representation in the total population. However, the proportion of Chechen representatives was somewhat lower, and that of Dargin representatives was slightly higher, than their respective population proportions. Notably, for an Islamic society, the Tats, or Mountain Jews, benefited, in both Assemblies, from slight overrepresentation.

Some ethnic groups (such as Kumyks, Azeris, Russians, Chechens, and Tats) live entirely in multiethnic rural regions or in Dagestan's multiethnic cities. Other ethnic groups (including Avars, Dargins, Laks, and Lezgins) inhabit primarily monoethnic territories. Thus, for example, the twenty-one Avar representatives who were not from designated Avar districts were from districts in which the population was overwhelmingly Avar.

This system of designated ethnic electoral districts was widely criticized by Dagestan's democratic intelligentsia, who regarded it as a violation of civic equality and the individual's right to stand for election in a district of choice. Prior to the election, in February 1999, this system was scrutinized, at the insistence of certain democratic organizations, by the Constitutional Court (*Konstitutsionnyi sud*) of the Republic of Dagestan. The court concluded that designated electoral districts did not violate Dagestan's Constitution, and that they were consistent with guarantees that are made to minorities by Articles 1, 2, 4, 5, and 72.[22]

In addition to designated ethnic districts, Dagestani electoral laws initially provided for seven women's districts and several "professional" (or "full-time") districts. Whereas ninety-six representatives served on a part-time basis, while retaining their principal means of employment, the remaining twenty-five representatives served full-time as administrative officers of the assembly or members of standing committees. In principle, only individuals who were able to leave their jobs for full-time parliamentary positions were permitted to run from districts that were designated for full-time representatives.

The "professional" districts were justified on the expectation that winning candidates would include many thugs who lacked education sufficient to ensure the routine operation of the body. Thus, twenty-five districts were reserved for candidates with higher education, particularly in law and economics, who were prepared to work full-time in the assembly as a sort of standing commit-

Table 4.3

Distribution of Ethnic Electoral Districts and Ethnic Representation in Dagestan's First and Second Assemblies Compared with Representation in Population

Ethnic group	No. ethnic electoral districts, 1995	No. ethnic electoral districts, 1999	No. representatives, 1995	No. representatives, 1999	% Assembly, 1995	% Assembly, 1999	% Population 1995–1999*
Avars	12	12	33	33	27.3	27.3	27.90
Dargins	5	7	21	21	17.3	17.3	16.00
Kumyks	12	12	16	15	13.2	12.4	12.50
Lezgins	4	4	14	14	11.6	11.6	12.50
Russians	10	10	10	10	8.6	8.6	7.00**
Laks	3	3	6	6	5.0	5.0	5.00
Tabasarans	5	5	5	6	4.1	4.9	4.50
Azeris	5	5	5	5	4.1	4.1	4.20
Chechens	4	4	4	4	3.3	3.3	4.50***
Nogais	0	1	2	2	1.6	1.6	1.60
Tats (and other Jews)	2	2	2	2	1.6	1.6	0.80
Rutuls	0	0	1	1	0.8	0.8	0.80
Aguls	0	0	1	1	0.8	0.8	0.75
Tsakhurs	1	1	1	1	0.8	0.8	0.30

Notes:

*Approximate.

**Whereas explosive birthrates in Dagestan, and anti-Caucasian sentiments elsewhere in the Federation, have contributed to increases in other ethnic populations since 1996, Russians are emigrating out of Dagestan.

***While this number excludes refugees, Chechen immigration to Dagestan has been high as a consequence of instability in Chechnya; and while Dagestani law prevents the sale of apartments to Chechens, some Chechens disguise their ethnic identity through falsified documents. Many others reside in Dagestan illegally. Hence, this figure is problematic.

tee. Other representatives were permitted to retain current employment, and to attend assembly meetings as necessary. Candidates in the "professional" districts signed releases at the time of their registration guaranteeing that in the event of electoral victory they would resign their current posts to work full-time in the assembly.

Due to fears that women would not receive proportionate representation, seven districts were designated where there would exclusively be female representatives—only women could be elected in these seven districts. But women were also eligible for election in any other district. This would have been a remarkable initiative in any society; in an Islamic environment, it was stunning. One of these seven districts received ethnic, female, and professional designations, which meant that only women of determinate ethnicity and education were allowed to stand.

Electoral districts were also defined nationally for regional and town assemblies so as to ensure ethnically proportional representation in local government. For example, in the Khasaviurt raion the administration determined the ethnic allocation of the thirty-nine seats of the local council: Avars (fourteen), Kumyks (thirteen), Chechens (nine), Dargins (two), and Lezgins (one). Since most of the raion's villages were monoethnic their seats were assigned to their respective nationalities. Where villages were mixed, the seat was assigned to the largest nationality. In urban areas electoral districts were reserved for specific nationalities when their members constituted the bulk of the inhabitants. Leaders of different nationalities were able to arrive at an agreement concerning the allocation of more ambiguous districts. The Electoral Commission refused to recognize the validity of candidates from groups other than those to which a district had been assigned. Neither Kumyks nor Chechens in Khasaviurt have been entirely satisfied with their allotments.

While remarkably successful in some respects, this system also encountered difficulties. From the beginning some of the individuals elected to "professional" seats refused to resign from their existing positions. Promises not withstanding, these people generally enjoyed good careers that they declined to interrupt for a temporary political post. Dagestani courts proved ineffectual at enforcing their obligations.

Following formal protests, the Constitutional Court abolished "women's" districts on the grounds that they violated the Constitution, Articles 19, 21 (Parts 1 and 2), and 32 (Parts 1 and 2). The court decided that such districts undermined individual equality and discriminated against men.[23] However, when several men immediately declared their candidacy in these districts, public opinion was aroused against them. Perhaps in part for this reason, women held six seats in the Second Assembly.

Consociational Inadvertency

Thus the inevitability of federal compromises, a history of social pluralism, and the internal dynamics of elite rivalries together culminated in consociational innovations that enabled the Dagestanis to pluck a fledgling democracy from the tumult of the 1990s. Because it combined the extremes of ethnic heterogeneity and economic deprivation, Dagestan might have seemed the most likely candidate for intercultural warfare. Yet alone among all of their neighboring territories, the Dagestanis were able not only to avoid protracted ethnic conflict but also to sustain political stability, and, at least for a period of years, to achieve a political transcendence of the ethnic and religious cleavages that might otherwise have fragmented their society. This achievement, remarkable by regional standards, had much to do with the patently consociational features of Dagestan's 1994 Constitution. The Dagestanis improvised a unique system of consociational democracy that accommodated the relentless pluralism of their society and maintained a dynamic balance among competing interests.

Yet clearly there was no intent to base the Dagestani political system upon consociational models. Rather the consociational features that characterized Dagestani politics from July 26, 1994, to July 26, 2003, may be attributed to the general demands of any highly segmented society, as filtered through ancient social traditions that were, themselves, influenced by such demands. It is significant that Dagestan's traditional political system was also based upon political structures that specifically transcend the bonds of kinship through governments based upon written law and the consensual administration of elites. This was, in fact, the function of the traditional Dagestani djamaats, based upon the application of adat by councils of elders drawn from the constituent tuhums. In other words, the djamaats historically have displayed protoconsociational features that have served to influence the political culture within which Dagestan's constitution was framed.

There is little difficulty in identifying consociational elements of Dagestan's 1994 Constitution. For example, it is difficult to imagine a better illustration of Lijphart's grand coalition than Dagestan's State Council, with its fourteen representatives of Dagestan's principal ethnic groups. The original constitutional mandate for the rotation of the chair of the SC after four-year terms, was a particularly interesting arrangement from a consociational standpoint since it seemed to guarantee that no elite from any single group could retain power for long enough to establish an ethnic dynasty in the various branches of power. However, constitutional amendments to this institution edged Dagestan toward a de facto presidential system, and eventually concentrated disproportionate power in a single segment of the population. This concern was all the more significant following the February 15, 1998, election of Said Amirov to a highly influential position as mayor of Makhachkala. Like the chair of the State Council, Amirov was a powerful Dargin, who, in fact, was previously appointed by Magomedov to the post of vice-prime minister. Nevertheless, rivalries between Magomedov and Amirov inevitably developed over time.

Yet while these events brought Dagestan closer to a de facto presidential system, the fundamental structure of the SC remained both consensual and consociational. It should also be emphasized that the successful elections of SC and assembly members, though not without some irregularities and disturbances, were evidence of the success of this coalition in representing the components of Dagestani society.

A second important feature of consociational models is the mutual veto, which once again, appeared prominently in Dagestan's political system. Any of the 121 representatives to the National Assembly could block the passage of any legislation that significantly affected the member's ethnic group, particularly if the legislation involved ethnic boundaries or territories. As described in Article 81 of the Constitution, an override required a two-thirds majority: "During the review of questions concerning changes to the current administrative-territorial arrangements, and likewise to the demographic linguistic, socioeconomic, and cultural environment of the peoples of Dagestan, in the case of disagreement with the projected draft law of a deputy or group of deputies from the said territory, a decision is reached by a vote in which not less than two-thirds of the total number of deputies of the People's Assembly agree."

Dagestan's 1994 Constitution contained numerous arrangements to provide for proportionality, the third feature of the consociational model. Representatives to the assembly were elected from districts that were identified with particular ethnic groups in order to guarantee remarkably precise proportionality. Elections to local government bodies often involved similar arrangements, and proportionality was also an objective that guided government appointments at all levels.

Further illustration of proportionality in Dagestani politics was provided by a remarkably consociational innovation that the authors called "packet replacement."[24] In view of Dagestan's complex ethnic balance, personnel replacements were a difficult issue at any level of government, and this was especially the case in the higher echelons. The replacement of any high-ranking official resulted in a dramatic swing of the ethnopolitical pendulum. Suppose, for instance, that the Ministry of Health were headed by an Avar minister who was approaching retirement. If another Avar were appointed in his place, then the Avars would achieve a dynastic control of health services, which would alarm all of those other groups that would not benefit from sustained Avar patronage throughout the lower echelons of health care. On the other hand, if a member of any other nationality were appointed, then Avar representation would be reduced and members of that group would consequently be disturbed. Of course, an Avar could be appointed to another position, but this approach tended toward a dangerous game of administrative musical chairs. For example, if a Dargin replaced the Avar in the Health Ministry, then another Avar would have to receive a compensatory post. If this resulted in the displacement of a Kumyk, then the latter had to be given another position even if it displaced a Lezgin or a Lak, and so on. Once the process of replacement began, it could be difficult to stop.

Packet replacement was the solution to this problem that was innovated informally by the Dagestani government. This approach involved the simultaneous replacement of several ministers together with high-level staff members. Selections were made by considering the size and significance of potential resistance to any candidate. Since this process had a propensity to snowball, even highly placed officials were unable to control it, and there was ultimately no recourse save consensual pragmatism and mutual accommodation.

In 1996, for example, the government managed to replace six ministers by this method. The shift required the abolition of one post and the establishment of another highly authoritative position, and efforts were made to appoint compliant, instead of charismatic, individuals. Opponents of the adjustment were "neutralized" by the sheer mass of interested participants and observers. The details of the procedure provide a number of helpful illustrations.

In April 1996 the appointment of a Dargin named Gamid Gamidov as minister of finance substantially disrupted the existing ethnic balance. Efforts to restore a condition of parity were undertaken by the SC, and by Chairman Magomedov in particular. These efforts were successful because of their introduction of an extensive packet replacement program, which resulted in changes to nearly a third of the cabinet ministers and their staffs.

Table 4.4 shows the ethnic distribution of seven cabinet posts before and after the introduction of packet replacement. Line 1 refers to the secretary of the Security Council, a post that did not exist prior to the shift. An influential Avar cosmonaut, military officer, and politician named Magomed Tolboev, who formerly represented Dagestan in the Duma and who competed with Magomedov for the chair of the SC in 1994, was appointed to the post. The second line describes the retirement of the Dargin minister of conservation and natural resources, and his replacement by a young and talented Dargin representative to the assembly. The latter vacated his post in the assembly, which was filled by another Dargin. Line three shows the retirement of the Dargin minister of social security and his replacement by an Avar of impec-

Table 4.4

Ethnic Distribution of Ministerial Posts Before and After Replacement

No.	Before	After
1.	None	Avar
2.	Dargin	Dargin
3.	Dargin	Avar
4.	Avar	Lezgin
5.	Avar	Avar
6.	Lezgin	Russian
7.	Avar	None

cable reputation. The fourth line refers to the difficult and controversial retirement of the Avar education minister and his replacement by an authoritative and widely respected Lezgin. The retirement of the Avar minister of health, indicated by line five, led to the appointment of a distinguished member of the same ethnic group. The sixth line follows the replacement of the somewhat underqualified Lezgin minister of zoning and land use by his hardworking Russian deputy. Line seven refers to the elimination of the post of the Information Ministry, and the consequent elimination of an Avar minister whose adamant Communist approach had earned her a reputation for obstinacy. The Ministry of Information was replaced by the State Committee of Information and the Press, which was headed by the Lak deputy of the former information minister.

The new appointments were carefully selected for their contribution to competent administration and ethnic parity. The success of packet replacement in this instance was due in part to the large number of people who carefully followed the process, who had interests in its outcome, and who were able to overcome others who opposed these changes. Additionally, the retiring ministers avoided stigma and disgrace through their very numbers. This exchange took place on August 2, 1996.

A further consociational feature of Dagestan's 1994 political system was the high degree of autonomy that it permitted to each segment with regard to its internal affairs. Most of Dagestan's thirty-nine raions are monoethnic, and were allowed to exercise complete control over their internal cultural and agricultural affairs. Both during and after the Soviet period, the Dagestani government supported ethnic groups and protected national cultures.

Indicative of this concern was the establishment of a Ministry of Nationalities with responsibility for external relations in keeping with the external ramifications of Dagestan's ethnic issues. The Ministry funded six national theaters (sharing three buildings) as well as locally administered, mixed cultural centers in Makhachkala and in various raions. It supported radio broadcasts in eleven languages and television broadcasts in nine. It financed eleven newspapers in the major indigenous languages and multiple language editions of a women's magazine. Though these newspapers claimed independence they were generally supportive of the government. In addition, there were numerous unsubsidized ethnic publications.

Many of the national movements (especially the Kumyk Berlik and the Lezgin Sadval) agitated for a confederated political system incorporating ethnic regions with a greater degree of autonomy. Yet after reaching their zenith in the early 1990s, these national movements were of declining significance. Their leaders either rose to institutional positions, or descended into criminality. A few groups experimented with ethnic assemblies, but these were without political power.

While Dagestan's approach to ethnic autonomy thus fell short of the full-blown federalism that Lijphart invoked,[25] it was not inconsistent with Nordlinger's concern that segmental autonomy encourages secession.[26] In Dagestan, these darker possibilities were ever-present concerns, which served not only as a restriction on structural arrangements but also as a force for the moderation and speedy resolution of conflicts. Yet while Dagestan's political system responded quickly to characteristically local crises, it was often prevented by this same political fragmentation from responding effectively or with anything approaching long-term strategy to internal political problems. It was also deeply vulnerable to external pressures. Subsequent chapters will examine these problems externally in terms of the rise of Islamist extremism, and pressures from Chechnya and from Moscow. The remainder of this chapter, will examine these problems as they appeared internally, almost from the beginning, in terms of corruption at the highest levels of Dagestan's political system.

The Corruption of Dagestan's Executive

The primary thesis of modernization theories is that assimilation and integration are promoted by the social mobilization that comes with modernization. Modernization introduces universal interests and homogenizing influences that may serve to transcend long-standing social divisions, while at the same time, stimulating new cleavages, including class and intergenerational divisions, that cut across the traditional segmentation of a plural society. Improvements, for example, in agricultural and industrial technology, transportation, and mass communication have profoundly affected traditional patterns of social interaction.

In Austria, Belgium, and the Netherlands this process has involved the weakening of vertical cleavages between ethnic and religious segments of these societies, accompanied by the emergence of new horizontal stratifications, along economic, educational, and generational lines, for example. Yet this is possible precisely because the consociational system has already furnished the foundation for the resolution of religious and ethnic conflicts.[27] Thus modernization and consociational democracy have often been viewed as making mutually reinforcing contributions to the development of plural societies.[28] Within this development, consociational democracy appears as an "historical phase," the very success of which "permits its replacement rapidly or slowly by a more competitive (democratic) model."[29]

However, modernization theories also concede that integration and assimilation may be impeded when modernizing forces increase contacts between members of different groups more rapidly than these can be accommodated by integrative institutions. The slow process of assimilation can be reversed in modernizing societies when the increasing pace of transactions between members of different groups renders their differences more conspicuous.[30] In such cases, segmental identification and competition may be increased by modernization.

At the same time, segmental identification may be increased by democratization, which encourages the establishment of organizations for the pursuit of pluralistic interests, the formulation of factional agendas, and the expression of segmental demands. In much of the consociational literature, social pluralism is taken as an independent variable and democracy is treated as the dependent variable, such that the question is whether a segmented society can sustain a democratic regime. Yet this causal relationship involves an inherent reciprocity. Thus democracy also appears as the independent variable and pluralism becomes the dependent variable, such that democratization may be linked to an intensification of segmental cleavages.

In the case of Dagestan, wide-scale economic modernization and development did not accompany democratization, and there was consequently no basis for the establishment of new, horizontally cross-cutting, economic and educational cleavages, such as those that eventually developed in Austria, Belgium, and the Netherlands. Yet democratization did encourage new forms of factionalism as elites and their ethnoparty supporters competed intensively for existing economic and political spoils.

Whereas Dagestan's unique system of consociational democracy had once seemed to hold great promise, it appeared that the process of democratization vastly outpaced that of economic development. And whereas the former might have been supported and eventually advanced by the latter, the lack of economic development accentuated the darker features of Dagestan's democracy. As elites competed for limited and, in some ways, shrinking resources, Dagestan's democracy gradually descended into a maelstrom of factionalism, clannishness, cronyism, corruption, and self-seeking until it was a democracy only in name. And if Russia's democratic revolution had begun at the top, then the corruption of Dagestan's democracy begin with the constitutional manipulation of the chief executive position on behalf of a small circle of elites.

Dagestan's Constitution stipulated that the SC should be elected at four-year intervals, but the first SC (according to the transitional chapters of the Constitution) was elected only for two years. By February 1996, it became clear that Magomedov would not surrender power in June at the end of this two-year term, but intended to continue for another two years. Mukhu Aliev insisted on Magomedov's departure on the ground that Magomedov had no constitutional right to extend his term. By this time, however, Magomedov had significantly strengthened his political position. Moreover, there were the other thirteen members of the SC who had similar interests in extending their two-year transitional term for an additional two years, to make their tenure in office a regular four-year term. Those same members were, of course, the most influential representatives of their ethnic groups.

Near the end of the two-year, "transitional" term, Magomedov's supporters as well as supporters of the other members of the SC organized a campaign for collection of signatures for the amendment of the constitutional article that restricted the term of the SC (the transitional Article 10, which stated that the first SC would serve only half a term). Try as he might to prevent this, Mukhu Aliev was doomed to lose this fight. There was no hope of his alliance with Mirzabekov, the Kumyk prime minister, who simply ignored the political struggle. The non-Avar assembly representatives were offered incentives by the executive branch. Even the Avar ethnoparties most staunchly opposed to Magomedov were reluctant to unite behind Aliev because he had held himself aloof from the fractious confrontations and alliances among various groups. In those days, Aliev was the exception that proved the rule. He was neither interested in becoming a *silovik* (a Russian official drawn from the security or military services) nor concerned to join in those negotiations and compromises that would oblige him to pay others with favors for their services.

Almost single-handedly, Aliev resisted Magomedov to the end. During the session of the assembly that finally canceled the transitional article of the constitution, there was an open confrontation between the two men so heated that the famous Avar poetess, Fazu Alieva, had to remove her headscarf and throw it between them in order to prevent a fist fight.[31]

Aliev and other Avars appealed to the Constitutional Court, which nevertheless voted on March 19 to uphold the cancellation of the transitional article. The article was canceled by the assembly on March 21, 1996. The following day that cancellation was ratified at a meeting of the Constitutional Assembly convened expressly for this purpose. The term of the SC was formally extended by two years until the summer of 1998.

That same day, the leaders of numerous Avar ethnoparties (Magomed Sheikhov, Esenbulat Magomedov, Ahmed Gamzatov, Zagalav Abdulbekov, and others) delivered a televised statement calling for restraint and urging their supporters not to protest on the central square. Magomedov's victory was complete. On the next day, March 22, 1996, the Constitutional Assembly formally extended his powers for an additional two years.

Just over a year later, Magomedov managed to remove Mirzabekov from his position. This time it was Mukhu Aliev who withheld his support from Mirzabekov. In August 1997, by a vote of eight to six, the SC voted to relieve Mirzabekov as prime minister, and nominated Magomedov's loyal Kumyk deputy, Hizri Shikhsaidov, to replace him. The National Assembly promptly approved the nomination.

In 1998, Magomedov once again reached the end of his term. This time it seemed that his retirement was constitutionally inevitable. Yet Magomedov maneuvered to strengthen his position by balancing among various, often competing, ethnoparty leaders. It might have been more difficult for Mago-medov to manage this had Aliev employed similar political tactics, but the latter refused to enter the political fray. He did not form his own ethnoparty; he did not surround himself with a group of supporters; he did not build alliances with other leaders; and he did not promise anything for loyalty and support. Moreover, this time Aliev withdrew from the attempts to prevent Magomedov's reelection.

On Monday, March 9, 1998, Aliev went to Moscow, and was sent from there to Strasbourg. No sooner had he departed when Magomedov's supporters once again began collecting signatures for the cancellation of Article 93 of the Constitution, requiring that the chair of the SC could not be held by a representative of the same ethnicity for more than one term. Magomedov's supporters proposed to amend the article to read: "The same person should not be elected to this position for more than two terms in the row." It took little time to collect signatures from the majority of the representatives of the National Assembly (different sources reported from 86 to 112 signatures of support from a total of 121 members of the assembly). According to the Constitution of Dagestan, an amendment to the Constitution requires the support of two-thirds of the members, or eighty-one representatives. On March 18, 1998, the National Assembly enacted the amendment without any serious resistance by a vote of 86 to 14.

Ensuing political protests were insignificant. An Avar named Saigid-pasha Umakhanov[32] tried to organize a Committee for the Defense of the Constitution. The group held a few meetings on the central square of

Makhachkala, but they were not well publicized and were attended by less than 2,000 people.

Yet if grassroots support was marginal, these meetings attracted some significant elites. From among Dagestan's leadership, the meetings were attended by Kurban Mahmudgadjiev (the Avar chairman of the Makhachkala City Council), Nadirshah Khachilaev (the Lak State Duma deputy, and the head of the Union of the Muslims of Russia), and Adallo Aliev (a well-known Avar poet, who was at that time the deputy of Movladi Udugov in the Dagestani-Chechen political movement Islamic Nation).

On June 25, 1998, the selection of the new SC took place during a session of the Constitutional Assembly. This time, Magomedov was not even challenged by an Avar, but rather by a Dargin named Sharapudin Musaev. Musaev served as chairman of the republic's Pension Foundation prior to his removal in 1999 on charges of corruption. He and other officers of the foundation made their fortunes by regularly delaying pension payments and using the money to make millions of dollars for themselves. In a secret ballot, Musaev received 78 votes to Magomedov's 162. The assembly also approved Magomedov's nomination of Hizri Shikhsaidov for prime minister.

These events were followed by the nomination and election of the remaining twelve members of the State Council. Only three seats were unopposed: in contests for seats allotted respectively to Aguls, Russians, and Tats, one of two candidates withdrew in favor of the other. In the cases of the Aguls and Tats, the remaining candidate was a woman. This Agul woman was none other than Takibat Mahmudova, who had previously served as Magomedov's loyal deputy in the Supreme Soviet. Candidates for the nine remaining seats won by slim majorities. Nearly 50 percent of the SC were new members from the following nationalities: Avar, Lezgin, Lak, Rutul, Tabasaran, and Tsakhur. Representatives were reelected from the following groups: Agul, Azeri, Chechen, Dargin, Kumyk, Russian, and Tat.

By that time, the situation in Moscow had started to change, and the Kremlin was becoming more proactive in the affairs of the Russian regions. In September 1998, the Yeltsin administration intervened in Dagestan for the first time. The deputy of the interior minister of the Russian Federation,[33] Vladimir Kolesnikov, arrived in Dagestan, and, in an unprecedented manner, arrested a series of high-ranking Dagestani leaders. The carefully targeted arrests left no room for doubt about whom Moscow intended to support: Many of those arrested by Kolesnikov had opposed Magomedov's reelection Kolesnikov arrested the Dagestani minister of justice, a Kumyk named Tazhudin Bizhamov. He arrested Kurban Mahmudgadjiev (chairman of the Makhachkala City Assembly), and Magomed Khachilaev (leader of the Lak national movement). He issued an order for the arrest of Sharapudin Musaev (the manager of Dagestan's pension fund who had run against Magomedov in the election of 1998), but Musaev took refuge in his native village of Kuppa, where even the special services of the federal government could not reach him. However, one of Musaev's supporters, the Dargin mayor of Kaspiysk, Ruslan Gadjibekov, was arrested while he was still inside the government building. The Russian State Duma was scheduled to consider removing the legal immunity of the Dagestani deputy, Nadirshah Khachilaev, but Nadirshah decided not to wait for the vote and took refuge in Chechnya. An Avar named Esenbulat Magomedov was arrested on a street in Makhachkala. He was a member of the National Assembly, the head of Zapcasprybvod (Western Caspian Fishery).

On May 17, 2001, the Russian State Duma enacted legislation prohibiting republic heads from seeking third terms unless it was specifically permitted by local law. Since Magomedali Magomedov would reach the end of his second term in 2002 (or the end of his third term if the transitional term were counted separately), it seemed impossible for him to seek reelection. Nevertheless, the Council of the Russian Federation subsequently canceled the Duma's decision and permitted regional heads to be seated for a third term. While this removed federal restrictions from Magomedov, he still had to contend with Dagestan's Constitution.

Initially, it appeared that Article 93 would prevent Magomedov from reelection following the expiration of his second term in June 2002. Moreover, it appeared that it might be more difficult for Magomedov to obtain a favorable amendment of the Dagestani Constitution due to increased federal scrutiny of Dagestan's constitutional arrangements intended to bring the latter into alignment with that of the federation. Yet Magomedov, once again, found a way to evade the Dagestani Constitution.

On May 31, 2001, at the end of the session of the Dagestani People's Assembly, new legislation was hastily distributed and pressed to a vote. It stated: "The restriction established in Article 1 of the law of the Republic of Dagestan 'On the Changes of Article 93 of the Constitution of the Republic of Dagestan,' according to which the same person cannot be elected to the position of chairman of the State Council for more than two terms, does not apply retroactively, and applies only to events occurring after the introduction of the law."[34] According to this new legislation, the same person could not be elected to this position more than twice during or after 1998. Since Magomedov was elected to the position only once during this period, he was eligible for reelection. Magomedov had held the chair of the SC continuously for eight years from 1994 to 2002. Depending on how one reckoned his first term, which had initially been set as a two-year "transition," these eight years constituted either two or three terms. Yet the Constitutional Court ruled that only one of these terms was constitutionally relevant.

Throughout the following year Magomedov consolidated support, discouraged serious competition, and effectively ensured another victory. When it came in June 2002, his reelection was a foregone conclusion. Magomedov's new prime minister, a Kumyk named Atai Aliev, played the role of an electoral contender, though Magomedov did not make a single speech regarding his program. Of the 242 votes in the Constitutional Assembly, Magomedov received all but one. Perhaps Atai Aliev felt obligated to vote for himself.

Electoral Corruption in Dagestan

Dagestan's local elections were, for the most part, free and fair. The 1995 National Assembly election was marred by several acts of violence, and there were a few violent incidents in Dagestan's Buinakskii raion during the 2003 Duma election. Yet most local council elections, and the election of Dagestan's National Assembly in 1999 and 2003, were conducted without violence or substantial irregularity. When minor irregularities occurred, they were usually protested, investigated, and resolved. In such cases, the preferred form of protest was the blockade of federal roads by villagers who demanded investigations in particular districts. Some blockades lasted for a few days, forcing authorities to arrange detours.

Yet many of these elections were nevertheless characterized by frequent incidents of vote buying. Often candidates provided civic improvements for an entire village in advance of an election. In some rural areas, communities delivered clear, well-organized requests to candidates. Candidates were asked to repair roads, install water or gas lines, drill wells, and the like. If the tasks were completed prior to the election, the candidate received electoral support.[35] After the 1999 National Assembly election, commentary in one local newspaper observed:

> Democracy in Dagestan turned out to be plutocracy, with the smell of money everywhere. If before the election day the "gifts" for the voters were covered ("Here is a gift for the holiday." "Please take it; we just want to help you." "Do you need anything to be paved?"), desperate candidates became lavish on the day of the election, offering 100, 200, 500 rubles for a vote. Proclamations about "public interests" and "interests of ordinary people" were abandoned: they were simply tastelessly buying votes without sentimental comments. The record price paid to one voter was 2,300 rubles. A family in the same district "earned" 19,000 rubles.[36]

Electoral laws restricted a candidate's campaign spending to a sum equal to fifty minimum monthly salaries, which was given to each candidate. Expenditures of personal savings or other private funds was forbidden. Yet this restriction was generally ignored because the sum was far too small for even the simplest campaign. In practice there was little oversight of campaign spending.

Yet if vote buying and occasional violent incidents were problems in Dagestan's local elections, there was evidence that federal elections were marred by massive electoral fraud. In 1996, there were numerous, if largely uninvestigated, allegations of ballot stuffing in support of Boris Yeltsin's election to the Russian presidency. Whereas Dagestan voted 29.2 percent for Yeltsin in the first round of the election, Yeltsin received 51.7 percent in the second round amid widespread whispering, and credible anecdotal evidence, of fraud.

In the 1999 Russian State Duma election there was little effort to hide improprieties. While Magomedali Magomedov and the State Council were supporting the Unity Party, Said Amirov agitated for the Fatherland-All Russia (FAR) Party of Luzhkov and Primakov. A survey conducted by Kisriev[37] just before that election showed that 47 percent of Dagestanis favored the Communists, 21 percent supported Vladimir Putin's Unity party, and 20 percent were for FAR. However, the Dagestani government would not permit this study to be published in Dagestan.

Evidently, this was, in part, because the republic's government took an active role in attempting to influence the voters toward the achievement of maximum representation for the republic in the Duma, and toward the achievement of ethnic balance among the representatives. In addition to the republic's two single mandate districts, the government judged that it had a good chance to win seats for more Dagestanis through the party lists. Toward this end, leaders did their best to ensure that as many Dagestanis as possible appeared near the top of party lists. They appealed for the preference of Dagestani candidates on many grounds: the Dagestani victory in repelling insurgents from Chechnya a few months earlier, the fact that Dagestan is the largest republic in the North Caucasus, and their "special relationship with Putin" who once proclaimed his "love" for the people of Dagestan. They reckoned that if the Communists, Unity, and FAR each received no less than 25 percent of the Dagestani vote, then Dagestan would have three additional representatives in the Duma.

The following Dagestani candidates were well-placed in the party lists: on the Unity Party list was Gadzhimed Safaraliev (Lezgin, physicist, rector of Dagestan State University); on the FAR Party list was Magomed-Kadi Gasanov (Dargin, director of an enterprise called Adam-International, supporter of Amirov); on the Communist Party list were Hapisat Gamzatova (female Avar) and an ethnic Russian named Sergei Reshulsky. Since the Communists usually attracted substantial support in Dagestan, the government found it "necessary" to "readdress" their "excessive" ballots to Unity and FAR. Dagestani officials argued that similar techniques had been employed in other North Caucasian republics where the government is less pluralistic than in Dagestan. Like other North Caucasian republics, Dagestan was prepared to present itself monolithically in its dealings with the federal center. When it came to federal politics, ethnic, ideological, and political differences were increasingly pushed to the rear.

When the election took place on December 19, 1999, there was a 74 percent turnout. Since the first Duma election, in December 1993, Dagestan was divided into two single-mandate territorial districts with approximately 550,000 voters in each. These were the Buinaksk Electoral District, No. 10 (including the southern half of Dagestan, below the forty-third parallel), and the Makhachkala Electoral District, No. 11 (essentially north of the forty-third parallel), together giving Dagestan two seats in the lower chamber of the legislative organ.

In the Buinaksk District, the victor was Gadjimurad Omarov, a wealthy businessman who had lived for the preceding four years in Moscow. He won 27.6 percent of the vote, upsetting two well-known political figures. They were a Kumyk surgeon named Askerkhanov, who served in the Duma in 1995, and Magomed Tolboev, former secretary of the Security Council of Dagestan, and representative in the first Russian State Duma in 1993, whom Magomedali Magomedov had defeated in his first bid for the chair of the State Council in 1994.

Tolboev had been expected to win, but the government had pinned its hopes upon Askerkhanov because he was a Kumyk and they had no other Kumyks to promote. Omarov was accused of vote buying and there were published discussions of his controversial practices, which also included the performance of services on behalf of voters.

The single mandate Makhachkala District went overwhelmingly for Gadzhi Makhachev. Makhachev was the controversial leader of the Avar national movement, who had once filled Makhachkala's central square with his supporters, and who had by this time become the vice-prime minister of Dagestan, representative to the Dagestani People's Assembly, and head of the Dagneft oil company. There was little surprise in Makhachev's 62.4 percent victory.

With regard to the party lists, the government managed to exceed even its own expectations, securing six Duma representatives from the republic. The six Dagestani representatives elected to the Duma in 1999 were: Gadzhimurad Omarov (Avar, single-mandate district SMD), Gadzhi Makhachev (Avar, SMD), Sergei Reshulsky (Russian, Communist Party of the Russian Federation [KPRF]), Hapisat Gamzatova (Avar, KPRF), Gadzhimed Safaraliev (Lezgin, Unity), and Magomed-Kzadi Gasanov (Dargin, FAR). In addition, a

Dagestani Lak, residing in Moscow, was elected to the Duma from the Liberal Democratic Party of Russia (LDPR). This success may have served to encourage the further "reassignment" of votes in subsequent elections.

Officially, the Communists received 37.1 percent of the vote, Unity 29 percent, and FAR 28.6 percent. Amirov allowed himself to be persuaded that FAR should receive slightly less than Unity. The Communists protested that their votes were "readdressed" to Unity and FAR, but Magomedov asserted that the vote was fair. The chairman of the Election Committee announced that the committee had received numerous complaints concerning voters who were bribed, and that these had been forwarded to the office of the public prosecutor. Because Dagestanis historically have depended upon Moscow for economic support, they have taken a calculating approach toward the Kremlin. Dagestani leaders offer Dagestani support for Kremlin officials, while also playing upon Kremlin fears of instability. Dagestan's consistent manipulation of federal election results may be understood in this context.

In the case of the Russian presidential election of March 26, 2000, the *Moscow Times* discovered evidence of massive electoral fraud in Dagestan.[38] Based on anecdotal evidence and a survey of 16 percent of Dagestani precincts, the *Times* report claimed that 88,263 votes were stolen from the Communist presidential candidate, Gennady Zyuganov, and transferred to Vladimir Putin. The report then assumed that fraud occurred at the same level in all other precincts and extrapolated to the conclusion that 551,000 Dagestani votes were illegally allocated to Putin.

While agreeing that there was evidence of massive fraud, Ware pointed to methodological concerns in the *Times* study, and derived an alternative estimate of 275,000 to 375,000 fraudulent votes for Putin.[39] There were also questions concerning the *Times*'s assumption that electoral fraud in Dagestan was orchestrated from Moscow. It was possible that it might have occurred on the initiative of Makhachkala officials anxious to win the favor of the Putin regime. Since Dagestani officials blatantly transferred votes to both United Russia and the KPFR during the 2003 Duma election (see below), and since they transferred votes to each party in precisely those proportions necessary to maximize Dagestan's representation in the State Duma, there is reason to hypothesize that Dagestani officials manipulated federal electoral results in order to benefit the republic in its relations with the Russian Federation.

This hypothesis is consistent with observations that Dagestan's local elections were relatively free and fair. When Dagestanis were opposed to one another in a local election, then the victory of one over another was not clearly beneficial to the republic. However, there was considerable anecdotal evidence that Dagestanis tended to believe that when Dagestani candidates were opposed to non-Dagestani candidates in a federal election, then the republic was likely to benefit through the election of the Dagestani candidates. Dagestanis tend to identify themselves with Russia, but they identify themselves even more strongly with Dagestan. (See Table 6.1, page 130.) While they are generally loyal to Russia, Dagestanis also tend to view federal politics in terms of an us/them polarity.

Prior to the 2003 Duma election, Dagestani leaders persuaded the Central Electoral Commission to add one single-mandate district in Dagestan, making a total of three such districts. The addition was justified in terms of a significant increase in Dagestan's population in the interval since the 1989 census. Designated as Derbentsk District, No. 12, Dagestan's third electoral territory was established at the expense of other regions of Russia with declining populations.[40] These three single-mandate elections seated Asanbuba Nudurbegov (Lezgin) in the Derbentsk District; Magomed Gadzhiev (Avar) in the Buinaksk District; and reelected Gadzhi Makhachev (Avar) in the Makhachkala District.

In addition to the representatives from its three single-mandate districts, Dagestan gained an additional four representatives from the party list election. Three of the latter were from the United Russia list: Magomed Gasanov (Dargin), Gadzhimed Safaraliev (Lezgin), and Mamma Mamaev (Lak). The KPRF seated one representative from Dagestan, a Lezgin named Makhmud Makhmudov. Surprisingly, three of Dagestan's seven seats in the Russian State Duma were held by Lezgins.

In addition to these, four more Dagestanis were elected to the Duma from party lists in elections outside of Dagestan. Sergei Reshulsky, an ethnic Russian and KPRF activist from Dagestan who was previously elected in 1999, was elected in 2003 from the federal Communist list. Suleiman Kerimov, a Lezgin entrepreneur and billionaire, who resides in Moscow, was seated from the LDPR list. In other Russian regions, an Avar was seated from the United Russia list, and a Lak was elected by the LDPR.

While the Duma elections in Dagestan's three single-mandate districts were relatively fair and free of irregularities,[41] the results from the party list election were not credible, and appear to have been manipulated in two different ways. First, it appears that there was massive ballot stuffing in most, or all, districts, and, second, that there was widespread tampering with electoral protocols. Together these manipulations appear to have achieved three tactical and three strategic political objectives. From a tactical standpoint, it appears that the irregularity of the party list election: (a) artificially inflated Dagestan's total voter turnout; (b) massively skewed the result in favor of United Russia, the party of power; and (c) also somewhat skewed the result in favor of the KPRF. The achievement of these three tactical objectives seems to have secured the following three strategic goals: (1) The election successfully seated all Dagestanis who could possibly have won a place in the Duma; (2) The election evidently provided Kremlin officials with a demonstration of the loyalties and abilities of Dagestani officials; (3) It may have left officials in Moscow indebted to officials in Dagestan, thereby facilitating subsequent federal support, particularly in the form of budgetary subsidies.

If there was electoral fraud affecting party list contests during Dagestan's 2003 Duma election, how does it seem to have occurred? First, the official totals for Dagestan's electorate may be higher than the actual number of people who are qualified to vote.[42] Moreover, many voters are absent from the places of registration, especially in winter when the weather restricts opportunities for gainful employment in the mountains. There is also increasing indifference toward elections, with some voters boycotting the polls. Together, these factors suggest that in many districts there was a considerable margin between the number of votes that are officially allowed and the number that are actually cast. These circumstances create opportunities for stuffing ballot boxes with an additional 15–50 percent of the total ballots. Most of these fraudulent ballots would probably have supported United Russia, since it is the party of power, with which many Dagestani officials wish to cultivate closer relations, and toward which officials therefore sought to influence voters. It appears that ballot boxes were stuffed in virtually all polling places, though some of the remoter, mountain regions may have provided the greatest opportunities.

Second, it appears that after the ballots were counted and the percentages of the vote for each party were tabulated, the electoral protocols were routinely revised in order to inflate the total number of voters participating in the election without altering the relative percentages of the vote for each of the parties. It appears that members of Dagestani electoral commissions agreed to this maneuver because it was committed not to benefit one party at the expense of others, but rather to increase the official voter turnout. This is because the number of Dagestanis seated in a Duma election depends upon the total number of votes, and not upon the percentage of that vote for each party. For instance, a low result for the United Russia party in Dagestan could have resulted in a seat for only one candidate from the North Caucasus, who would not have been a Dagestani.[43] However, the second and third candidates on the United Russia party list were both Dagestanis, Gasanov and Safaraliev, and the sixth was Mamaev. The higher voter turnout, and the higher numbers of votes received by United Russia allowed for those three Dagestanis to be seated. There were also some indications that votes were also added for the Communists in order to seat Makhmudov, the Dagestani who was first on the KPRF list for the North Caucasus.

Elections that pit Dagestanis against other Dagestanis, as in the three single mandate districts, were usually relatively free and fair.[44] However, it appeared that Dagestani officials viewed federal elections as opportunities to demonstrate their fidelity to federal officials, while simultaneously placing the latter in positions of obligation. Hence, it appeared that elections in the territorial districts were fair because their outcome was a matter of relative indifference to federal officials. Conversely, one might hypothesize that the party list election was manipulated by local officials because it was of greater significance in Moscow. Yet if so, then Dagestani officials were likely interested in placating Kremlin leaders for the sake of Dagestani interests, or for the sake of Dagestani elites, that Moscow officials could later serve. This was suggested by the ways in which the results of the party list election apparently were manipulated to ensure the greatest possible number of Dagestanis in the Duma, even when that evidently meant inflated support for the KPRF.

It may be naive to suppose that any electoral fraud in Dagestan would occur in a simple top-down manner, on orders from the federal center. There may well be directives of some sort (perhaps subtle and informal) from the Kremlin to leaders in Makhachkala, but Dagestan's federal elections are more likely exercises in the mutual manipulation of central and local elites. From the perspective of some Dagestanis it may make little difference who runs Russia so long as Dagestan receives adequate financial support. Dagestan regularly receives more than 80 percent of its budget from Moscow. For their part, Kremlin officials use federal subsidies to purchase the loyalty of Dagestani leaders, on which they evidently expect delivery at times of federal elections.

Conclusion

As Soviet central authority disintegrated in the late 1980s, local groups in Dagestan began to cohere around specific shared agendas. When formal institutions of social order and adjudication neared paralysis, these groups sought to uphold and advance their interests by retaining, or acquiring, power and resources and by protecting their members. Thus when the Soviet federal center dissolved in the early 1990s leaving the people of Dagestan without a strong, bureaucratic administration, they drew upon indigenous political traditions in order to innovate viable institutions of executive and representative power that accommodated the tumult of Dagestani society.

For a decade after 1991, the activities of Dagestan's ethnoparties resulted in a fragmented structure of political forces, replete with its own complex of advantages and disadvantages. On the negative side, this fragmentation mitigated against the alleviation of any of Dagestan's most pressing problems. In addition to political corruption and economic stagnation, these included infrastructural exhaustion, organized crime (especially narcobusiness), and religious extremism. This was because Dagestan's fragmented political system prevented any of its leaders from consolidating the broad-based support necessary for an innovative, comprehensive, and therefore politically risky, approach to any major problem.

Yet, on the positive side, this political fragmentation had the benefit of successfully neutralizing the potential energy of the nationalist organizations that sprouted in the Dagestan of the early 1990s, while at the same time preventing the construction of a rigidly hierarchical power structure, by avoiding the concentration of power in the hands of any single group. Above all, these features provided Dagestanis with a unique and indigenous democratic pluralism, complete with its inherent set of constraints and counterbalances that sprang spontaneously from ancient traditions and internal political forces, without need of external institutional imports.

Dagestan's innovative democratic system was neither western, nor eastern, nor Slavic, nor traditional; it conformed neither to the Russian Federal constitution, nor to the expectations of Moscow political observers. It met nobody's preconceptions, and satisfied no one's ideals, because it aimed at not just a transition from one established political model to another, but a full-scale political transformation culminating in an unprecedented system that could not otherwise have been anticipated precisely because it was both uniquely Dagestani and uniquely a product of its time. The dynamic and continuing development of this system enabled Dagestan to negotiate the volatile decade that followed the collapse of the Soviet Union.

Yet for all their innovation and early indications of success, these political institutions never fully satisfied the democratic aspirations of the Dagestani people. Beginning in 1996, only two years after the adoption of Dagestan's first democratic constitution, the chief executive position was prevented from the rotation that the constitution required. Pluralistic access and political accountability were thereby thwarted almost from the start. Though many of Dagestan's local elections were notably free and fair, there were electoral irregularities and evidence of fraud from as early as 1995. If corruption was thereby on display at the highest levels of Dagestani politics, it soon permeated the system throughout. Faced once again with political disappointment, many Dagestanis turned, as had their ancestors, toward Mecca.

5

The Islamic Factor
Revival and Radicalism

World War II transformed relations between Russians and Muslims living within the Soviet Union. Seeking to drive a wedge between these groups, Adolf Hitler promised independence to those Muslims who collaborated with the German invasion. In response, Stalin promoted a supranational patriotism by relaxing antireligious policies and co-opting Christian and Islamic leaders. Three new muftiyats were established, one in Baku (to administer the Shia Muslims of the South Caucasus), and one in Tashkent (to oversee the Sunni Muslims of Central Asia).[1] The third new muftiyat, established in 1944, was the Spirtual Directorate of the Muslims of the North Caucasus (DUMSK), established to administer the Sunni Muslims of the North Caucasus. Originally headquartered in Buinaksk, Dagestan, it was soon moved to Makhachkala.

This combination of patriotic propaganda and pro-Islamic concessions effectively prevented large-scale collaboration between Soviet Muslims and German invaders.[2] The muftiyats called for jihad against German aggression, and were answered by military service and monetary contributions to the Red Army from millions of Muslims. On a per capita basis, the North Caucasus produced more heroes of the USSR than any other Soviet region.[3] Leaving aside the brutal, ethnic deportations of 1944 (which however devastating to other populations were marginal in their direct effects upon Dagestan), the legacy of the Great Patriotic War concluded with an enhancement of Muslim identification with Russia.[4]

Because Islam is not organized on a hierarchical basis, it was better prepared to endure the eradication of religious infrastructure than was the Orthodox Christian faith. According to Pilkington and Yemelianova, in the northeast Caucasus and the Fergana Valley, "practically every village had at least one unofficial mosque and in general, the number of unofficial mosques greatly exceeded the number of registered ones. For example, in the 1970s in Checheno-Ingushetia,[5] alongside five official mosques there functioned 292 unofficial ones. In Central Asia, 230 registered mosques co-existed with at least 1,800 unofficial mosques."[6] During Soviet repressions, underground Sufi orders kept Islam alive in Dagestani villages. During the 1980s, the Soviet war in

Afghanistan provoked Soviet Muslims toward greater political engagement. Soviet authorities responded by tightening their control of traditionally Muslim regions under policies that were surprisingly intensified during the perestroika period. Yet the Soviet withdrawal from Afghanistan revealed the weakness of the government, and the implosion of the Gorbachev regime issued in a period of erratic and inflationary and liberalization.

These years saw the emergence of the so-called young Imams, graduates of Central Asian madrassas "who criticized the 'old Imams' for their passivity, theological, ambivalence, low moral standards, and conformity with the Soviet establishment. They began a campaign for the restoration of the Islamic infrastructure on a pre-revolutionary scale, and for a wider involvement of Soviet Muslims in social and political life."[7] Soviet authorities responded with a series of concessions that included the establishment of dozens of new mosques in Muslim areas.[8] Prior to that time, Dagestan had a total of twenty-seven registered mosques. A single mosque in a low, nondescript building served the entire population of Makhachkala.

In the spring of 1989 there were conflicts over the leadership of a mosque that had been recently constructed in Buinaksk. In early May of that year Moslem activists, who would later be described as "Wahhabis" initiated a Congress of the Moslems of the North Caucasus in Makhachkala.[9] In the course of this Congress a group of Dagestani religious activists and their supporters from other republics of the North Caucasus, Tajikistan, Kyrgyzstan, Turkmenistan, and Kazakhstan leveled charges of bribery, moral degradation, and collaboration with the KGB against the mufti of the DUMSK, an ethnic Balkar named Makhmud Gekkiyev, and demanded his resignation. Despite support for the mufti from civil authorities, gunmen seized the office and residence of the DUMSK on May 13, 1989, and ejected Gekkiyev. The official newspaper of the republic wrote only that "in Makhachkala on the Lenin Square near the building of the Council of Ministers of the Dagestani Autonomous Soviet Socialist Republic (DASSR) over two hundred believers organized a meeting. The Chairman of the Supreme Soviet of the DASSR, M.M. Magomedov, the Chairman of the Council of Ministers of the DASSR, A.M. Mirzabekov, and other officials met with them. In the course of the encounter a constructive exchange took place and the demands of the believers received attention."[10]

In June 1989, Gekkiyev was succeeded by a young imam of the mosque in the village of Tarki, an ethnic Kumyk named Muhhamad-Mukhtar Babatov. Yet shortly thereafter Babatov was abruptly replaced by an ethnic Dargin alim named Abdulla-Hadji Aligadzhiyev, giving rise to strong indignation from the Kumyks. Indeed the string of religious disputes throughout 1989 tended to crystallize and exacerbate interethnic cleavages. These instabilities, together with those of the Soviet state, indicated that a regional Islamic organization was no longer realistic in the North Caucasus, and successor organizations began to emerge in each republic. In January 1990, the First Congress of the Moslems of Dagestan founded the Spiritual Directorate of the Muslims of Dagestan (DUMD), and elected as its mufti a Kumyk named Bagautdin-Hadji Isayev. On September 8, 1994, a few months following the adoption of Dagestan's democratic constitution, the DUMD received official recognition as a public organization under Resolution no. 161 of the Ministry of Justice of the Republic of Dagestan.

In September 1990, the Supreme Soviet of the USSR enacted legislation permitting greater religious liberty. This law catalyzed an Islamic revival that saw Soviets openly joining in a wide variety of Islamic ceremonies, rituals, and duties, including the hajj. At the end of that year there were 1,330 registered mosques in the Soviet Union, including 94 in Russia.[11] Mosques, madrassas, and Islamic institutions of higher learning were sprouting at an accelerating pace. The collapse of communism precipitated an Islamic revival with manifold repercussions, including: (1) a sharp increase in the observation of traditional Islamic rituals; (2) a revival and rapid development of *tariqat* orders; and (3) the proliferation of Wahhabi fundamentalism as a competing Islamic trend.

By 1996, Makhachkala's skyline was dominated by a beautiful new *djuma* (main) mosque, constructed with the aid of Turkish funding. By 1998 there were 1,670 registered mosques in Dagestan alone, with as many as 2,000 in Chechnya, and approximately 1,000 and 400 in Tatarstan and Ingushetia, respectively. There were 106 registered religious schools and 51 religious centers providing Islamic education. Dagestan alone had 9 Islamic universities, 25 madrassas, and 670 maktabs.[12] Nearly one in five Dagestanis was involved in Islamic education. Each year, about 20,000 Russians of whom more than half were from Dagestan, were making the hajj. Many Russian pilgrims received subsidies from the Saudi King, who also sponsored dozens of scholarships for Russian students studying in Saudi Arabia, Turkey, Jordan, Syria, Libya, Kuwait, the United Arab Emirates, and Malaysia. With partial Saudi support, Islamic literature was flooding into Russia from Saudi Arabia, Turkey, Pakistan, Britain, and several other points.[13]

Arrival of Wahhabism

From the latter 1920s to the latter 1940s, most Islamic practices were repressed by Soviet authorities. Those that survived were generally forced into the role of an underground opposition. Following the end of World War II, there were greater opportunities for Islamic practice, and these opportunities, gradually, if sporadically, increased up to the end of the Soviet period. The collapse of the Soviet Union inaugurated an Islamic revival in Russia's traditionally Muslim regions, during which forms of Islam that had once been repressed—for example, Sufism in Dagestan—became mainstream social and political forces. Islamic leaders sought, and frequently obtained, tangible forms of influence in the local post-Soviet political regimes. This left a vacancy in the traditional role of religious opposition to the government regime, and it was into this role that Salafism, known locally as Wahhabism, immediately stepped, beginning as early as 1989.

"Salafism," from *salaf* or ancestors, is a designation applied to those Muslims who subscribe strictly to the teachings of the Koran, the Prophet, his companions, and to those Islamic leaders and practices that were predominant within the next two or three generations. This interpretation is close to the puritanical teachings of an eighteenth-century Arab cleric named Mohammad Ibn Abdul Wahhab. Like Salafism, Wahhabism is a generic designation that is locally and loosely assigned to a variety of puritanical interpretations of Islam. The latter term is connotative of the links between Russian practitioners and Persian Gulf organizations that have provided educational, financial, and military support for the dissemination of their ideas among Islamic communities in Russia. Since "Wahhabi" is the term used by most Dagestanis, it will also be employed in the following discussion. However, neither of these terms is favored by Russia's salafist practitioners themselves, who prefer to describe themselves as "true" or "pure" Muslims.

Soviet repression paved the way for Wahhabism by undermining indigenous Islamic traditions, and leaving a residue of poorly educated and ill-prepared religious leaders. Thus, although it is a recent import, Wahhabism has rapidly proliferated because it has filled a series of spiritual and political needs that arose during the post-Soviet period in the traditionally Muslim societies of the North Caucasus:

- Along with other forms of religion, Wahhabism responded to the ideological void that was created by the collapse of socialism.
- In a similar way, Wahhabism responded to deficiencies in the preparation of traditional Islamic leaders. This is a role that foreign missionaries, foreign funding, and foreign educational institutions were primed to play.
- As traditional forms of Russian Islam were incorporated into emergent post-Soviet political regimes, Wahhabism filled the role of a repressed, religious opposition that had been previously established in Russia's traditionally Muslim societies. Moreover, this traditionally adversarial role was best suited to those radical Wahhabis who uncompromisingly rejected all forms of legitimate political activity.

- In this adversarial role, Wahhabism responded to the deficiencies of the corrupt and incompetent regimes that monopolized power in several of the traditionally Muslim North Caucasian republics. It did this by addressing a set of social, economic, and political problems.
- The latter problems have been connected with the proliferation of criminal activities in these same societies. Some forms of Wahhabism have been involved with criminal activities in ways that are complex, symbiotic, and mutually advantageous. Yet Wahhabism does not tend to support the corrupt, sometimes criminal, activities of established officials. Rather it tends to support those criminal activities that defy and subvert established authorities.
- In the criminal free-for-all of the North Caucasus, Wahhabism has provided its adherents with an organized and armed force for their protection against the opportunistic transgressions of predators and the arbitrary brutality of the police. Sharia has become a means of sustaining order despite the failures of law enforcement and government agencies.

Wahhabi Doctrines and Ideology

Rejecting the four established schools of *fiqh* (the juridical exegesis of sharia) and specifically rejecting both the Hanafi and Shafi'i schools,[14] Wahhabis insisted upon strict adherence to provisions of the Koran and Sunna regarding ritual, ceremony, behavior, and personal appearance, including beards and (sometimes) shortened trousers for men, and the veil for women.[15] They regarded all other practices as deviations from true Islam. Yet, by contrast, with respect to *muamalat* (social practice) they considered everything to be permitted unless it is specifically forbidden by the Koran or the Sunna.[16] Thus, whereas Wahhabis claimed strict obedience to the *zahir* (literal) provisions of the Koran and the Sunna, their project was closer to a constructed model of "purified Islam." Their construction was based upon an interpretation of sacred texts that was at once rigid and selective.

Wahhabism dispensed with many of the rituals that distinguished local Islam, along with the paternalism of traditional spiritual authorities. Wahhabism resembled other puritanical movements insofar as it denied the role of the sheikhs, and other professional "servants of Allah" in mediating the devotees' relations with God. Largely because of the teaching role of Sufi sheikhs, the radical Wahhabis rejected Sufism as *shirk* (polytheism), which is incompatible with Islam. Wahhabis sought to purify Islam of *bid'a* (unlawful innovations of Islam) and to revive the fundamental tenets of Islam with an emphasis upon *tawhid*, or monotheism.

Wahhabism was attractive not only to those who turn to religion out of spiritual concern for life's eternal questions but also to those with an ideological commitment to transform their societies within their lifetimes. It offered an approach to Islamic doctrine that was at once urgent, accessible, and rational. Hence, Wahhabism appealed to individuals from a wide range of educational backgrounds, and drew adherents from those whose objectives were spiritual, sociopolitical, and even criminal. This included the part of the intelligentsia that abandoned its connection to traditional Islam in Soviet schools and universities, and that subsequently found itself without ideological footing.

Wahhabis saw themselves as both spiritually and politically democratic, opposing inequity and elitism in social, political, and theological terms. They viewed their beliefs as being at once more accessible and more pure than traditionalist forms. They saw themselves as loyal at once to the ancient faith and to the more rational and streamlined needs of contemporary Muslim societies. At its best, Wahhabism offered many of the traditional appeals of Protestantism. It should not be forgotten that other protestant movements, for example, those of European Christianity of the sixteenth and seventeenth centuries, engaged not only in theological reform but also in violent political revolution, sometimes with egalitarian and democratic overtones.

Wahhabism's Ambivalent Appeal

Wahhabism appealed to some people in Dagestan on a number of different levels. The clarity and ideological simplicity of Wahhabism was appealing in its capacity to cut through the cumbersome, and often costly, pseudotraditions of both Central Asian and North Caucasian Islam, as, for example, the obligatory monetary gifts that have surrounded marriage ceremonies during the past six decades. Often these were grounded in traditional and pre-Islamic practices that became more costly as local standards of living improved in the later Soviet period. Under the conditions of post-Soviet economic depression, these same practices have imposed great financial hardship, for which Wahhabism provides spiritually sanctioned relief. Wahhabism dispenses with many of the rituals that distinguish local Islam, along with the paternalism of traditional spiritual authorities.

Yet its rejection of North Caucasian customs, particularly with regard to weddings and funerals, has tended to polarize its opponents, and has also been an obstacle to its spread. The rigid Wahhabi puritanism and veiled Wahhabi women were both alien and offensive to that freewheeling, hard-drinking, roughshod exuberance with which traditional North Caucasian Islamic authorities had long since learned to compromise. Yet Wahhabis nevertheless forced such issues through their inevitable zeal and spiritual resolve.

Some converts to Wahhabism experienced a sense of liberation in that its

exclusive devotion to Allah released the individual from the power of patriar-
chal clan traditions. Hence, it provided religious sanction for a young person's
search for autonomy and self-fulfillment within a framework of new, more
contemporary, forms of social solidarity.[17] Yet, Pilkington and Yemelianova,
also noted that Wahhabi *jamaats*[18] required discipline more exacting than
that of clan traditions, and that some individuals acquired the austerity of
the former while retaining the authority of the latter when an entire family
converted to Wahhabism.[19]

In the finest of protestant traditions, the spiritual egalitarianism of Wahhabism
was the logical antecedent to their calls for social justice. Thus Wahhabism also
offered an antidote to the gross economic disparities that arose in Russia in the
aftermath of the Soviet Union, and were sometimes pronounced most severely
against the comparatively higher poverty levels of Russia's Muslim republics.
Under circumstances of sustained and widespread unemployment, Islamic norms
concerning the male role as a provider combined with those that restrict alcohol
consumption to place young Muslim men under intolerable pressures, from
which the egalitarianism of the Wahhabi social critique and the more tangible
benefits of foreign funding provided welcome release.

In a similarly negative sense, the growth of Wahhabism may also be
viewed as a product of Western influences for it was a potent reaction against
the excesses of Western materialism and modernization. It sprang from a
deep disillusionment with the prospects for economic transition, and fed on
widespread despair over the myriad forms of moral and political decay that
rapidly overwhelmed North Caucasian society. Wahhabi puritanism provided
an ideological incentive and organizational impetus for the preservation of
civic conventions and traditional morality against degenerative influences of
the media, mass culture, individualism, and liberalism.

As North Caucasian governments grew increasingly corrupt, traditional
forms of Islam were sometimes seen to be compromised by their cooperation
with the political establishment. With its call to social and political activism,
Wahhabism was a natural response. In the North Caucasus, where ruling
elites effectively eliminated all legitimate forms of political opposition,
radical Wahhabism's uncompromising rejection of any form of political authority sometimes appeared to be the only realistic response. In view of the
further restriction of local political access and accountability that followed
from the federalized appointment of local governors in Muslim regions, the
uncompromising approach of radical Wahhabism seemed to some to be the
only rational response.

Whatever its virtues, Sufist introspection offered no immediate answers
for the critical social problems resulting from the period of sociopolitical
transition. And if the tariqah therefore seemed irrelevant to some impover-

ished mountaineers, there were other reasons why established Islamic orders appeared to be pernicious. These involved cooperation between religious and political establishments, since disillusionment with the former increased with the corruption of the latter. Wahhabite rejection of political authority was presented as a liberation from the bureaucratic constraints and political corruption of state officials. The Wahhabite critique of moral degradation, social irresponsibility, and the corruption of the religious and political establishment consequently found an eager audience among the least fortunate mountain villagers. Wahhabism lent dignity to the harsh austerity of their lives and provided spiritual sanction for their desperate resentment of the region's wealthy new leaders.

Unfortunately, Wahhabi ideology also appealed to criminal elements. According to Wahhabi strictures, any contemporary, or otherwise innovative, religious observance was evidence of a rejection of Islam, or *kufr*. Since the overwhelming majority of Russian Muslims (and, of course, all other Russians) fell outside of narrow Wahhabi interpretations, they were all regarded as *kuffar*, or infidels. For example, Walter Comins-Richmond noted that "in 1997, the Wahhabi Imam Salih Fauzan issued a fatwa on Sufism declaring that 'the polytheist stands outside the law, and it is therefore permissible to kill him and take his possessions in the name of Allah.'"[20] This provided justification for the extensive, sometimes horrific, criminal activities in which Wahhabis indulged, especially in Dagestan, Chechnya, and Ingushetia. It also justified Wahhabi terrorist atrocities. On the other hand, Wahhabi jamaats also offered an organized, and often well-armed, force that was capable of offering genuine protection to its members against the predations of criminals and the arbitrary, sometimes brutal, conduct of the police.[21]

Thus, while the arrival of Wahhabism led to deep divisions in North Caucasian societies, and while there were good reasons for its rejection, one cannot understand what occurred in the region after 1990 without appreciating the sociopolitical basis for its appeal:

- However radical they may have seemed, it was not possible to comprehend the appeal of Wahhabi doctrines so long as they were regarded as being merely virulent, aberrant, or irrational.
- Wahhabis did not simply "hijack a great religion."
- Wahhabis contested the future of their religion because many Muslim societies failed to resolve endemic problems of social injustice.
- Wahhabis offered a response to these problems that was clear, compelling, and rational.
- The Wahhabi response offered at least some of the traditional virtues of Protestantism.

- Within a broad historical context, their arrival was not more violent and uncompromising than that of some other forms of Protestantism.

Origins of Wahhabism in Dagestan

Salafism became an active force in the Soviet Union during perestroika when the Islamic Party of Revival (IPR) organized in Tajikistan and immediately attracted attention with its publication of an influential manifesto entitled "Are We Muslims?" A Dagestani Avar named Akhmed-Kadji Akhtaev, who was residing in Tajikistan, became the IPR chair. Akhtaev, who was a trained physician and a self-taught theologian moved to Dagestan, where he founded a spiritual and educational organization known as "Islamia."

Chechen political leaders regarded Akhtaev as a great religious authority. Akhtaev served as a deputy to Zelimkhan Yandarbiev in organizing the Caucasian Conference. He was also a deputy to Movladi Udugov in his movement Islamic Nation. On an invitation from Udugov, Akhtaev became head of Islamic Nation's Sharia Court.

The IPR was organized at the Union level in 1990 at a convention in Astrakhan, on the authority of Akhtaev and through the efforts of leading Dagestani Islamists, including the brothers Abbas (aka Ilyas and Bagautdin Kebedov). The organization was registered in Moscow as the All-Soviet Union Muslim Political Organization. Among its goals were the "spiritual revival" and the "political awakening" of Moslems, and the realization of their rights to construct their life on the basis of the Koran. The constitutive documents of the organization referred to the need for "the broad education of all peoples concerning the basis of the Islamic religion, the need for training of Moslem leaders who can understand the essence of Islam and are capable of giving answers to the vital problems of the contemporary world."

Akhtaev's program, in many ways, resembled that of the Muslim Brotherhood, which was moving into the South Caucasus at this time from North Africa and the Middle East. He practiced a "pure" form of Islam, regarding Sufism as a deviation, advocating the moral and spiritual superiority of Islam, and insisting upon its role in the economic modernization of Dagestan. Dagestan must become an Islamic state, he argued, because the interests of Russian Muslims required political support. Not unlike the UAM leaders some seventy years before him, Akhtaev believed that a united Islamic North Caucasus would gain greater respect from Moscow, along with greater economic and political autonomy. His calls for Russian devolution along confederal lines attracted the attention of Chechen separatists, who accorded him great respect and repeatedly offered him positions in the Chechen government. However, Akhtaev affirmed that Dagestan was situated historically in both Islamic and

Orthodox Christian civilizations and therefore rejected jihad against Russia. He sought a fundamental political transformation along Islamist lines, but he was prepared to work within established political structures, and he held political office in Dagestan. For these reasons, he was widely regarded as a "moderate Wahhabi," though he rejected this classification and viewed himself as a radical.[22]

From 1989 to 1992, Akhtaev worked with a group of "young Imams," as well as with ethnic Kumyk and Avar leaders to transform the official Islamic administration in Dagestan. Complex maneuvers led to the installation and removal of a series of muftis, and culminated in the "election" of an ethnic Avar tariqatist named Said Akhmed Dervish Gadjiev.[23] This result transformed tariqah Sufism from an underground, Islamic opposition movement in Dagestan to a position of institutional dominance. After 1992, the Spiritual Directorate of the Muslims of Dagestan was dominated by Avar tariqatists under the influence of Sayid-Efendi Cherkeyevsky, who joined in Dagestan's emergent power structure.

Having achieved this official recognition, the "young Imams" moderated their stance, combined with other Avar tariqatists, and achieved rapprochement with the Dagestani government. Thereafter they ignored Akhtaev's appeals for further cooperation toward a fully Islamic Dagestan, regarding him as a political opponent. Just as events were taking this turn in 1992, Akhtaev was elected as a representative to Dagestan's Supreme Soviet. In 1998, he entered the election for the chief administrative position in the Gunib raion. At this juncture, Makhachkala officials sought to discredit him by suggesting to Bagautdin Kebedov and the radical Wahhabis that Akhtaev was virtually conspiring with the government. At the same time, Akhtaev was subjected to a second smear campaign that accused him of ties to foreign Islamists. While these two charges would appear to have been aimed at separate audiences, they were equally alarming to the radical Wahhabis who rejected any cooperation with either the Dagestani or Russian governments, while seeking foreign funding for themselves. Thus Akhtaev appeared to them not only as a rival, but as a treacherous rival. This appearance may have undermined the wary peace that had characterized relations between these two branches of Dagestani Wahhabism. Thereafter the radicals sought to undermine the organizations that Akhtaev had created, including Islamia. Evidently, Kebedov feared that Islamia's operation as a quasi-political party would complicate his efforts at international fundraising.

By 1998, it seems that Akhtaev had fallen afoul of both the Makhachkala authorities and the radical Wahhabis. In Dagestan, either one of these difficulties is typically fatal. In the heat of the electoral race, Akhtaev suddenly died, amid widespread rumors that he had been poisoned.[24] In fact, he was a vigorous fifty-six-year-old. In that same year, foreign Islamist funding shifted from Akhtaev and Islamia to Bagautdin Kebedov and his jamaat. It was also in 1998 that Dagestani officials accused unspecified Persian Gulf organizations of waging jihad against Dagestan.

Akhtaev's death was effectively the end of moderate, intellectual Salafism in Dagestan. He was succeeded by his relative, Siradzhuddin Ramazanov (a previous head of the transport fleet), who soon succumbed to radicalism. After aligning himself with Bagautdin Kebedov, and the Chechen-Wahhabi invasions of Dagestan in 1999, Ramazanov was declared prime minister of the (virtual and ill-fated) Islamic Republic of Dagestan, and was thereafter incarcerated in Dagestan.

The demise of Akhtaev's moderate brand of Salafism left only two alternatives for the approximately 10 percent of the Dagestani population (see below) who sought an Islamist response to the corruption and incompetence of the Dagestani government: radical Wahhabism or ultraradical Wahhabism. An ultraradical Wahhabi fringe group was headed by Ayub Omarov (aka Ayub Astrakhansky), a Dagestani Avar from the Tsumadinskii raion. He resided in Astrakhan, and organized his ultraradical group among the Dagestani diaspora in that area. He was among the few who openly called himself a Wahhabi and who fully dressed the part with a long beard, trimmed mustache, and shortened, baggy pants. However, his geographical isolation combined with his counter-traditional practices to leave him with few followers inside Dagestan.[25]

An entirely different set of problems was faced by Bagautdin Kebedov, who led Dagestan's radical Wahhabis. Though Kebedov cooperated with Akhtaev in the early days of the IPR, and while they were similarly favored by Chechen separatists as late as 1993, their paths diverged as Bagautdin became immersed in the violence that overwhelmed Chechnya after the summer of 1994. Before the end of the first Chechen war in 1996, Bagautdin was organizing Wahhabi cells in Chechnya. Meanwhile in Dagestan he organized, and became the amir (spiritual leader) of the Jamaat ul-Islamiiun ad-Dagestaniia (Islamic Community of Dagestan).

During these years, Bagautdin was competing with Akhtaev to attract those Muslims who were alienated from Dagestan's political-religious establishment. Hence, he staked out a particularly uncompromising approach toward the new Sufi Islamic authorities. In a video recording of a sermon that he delivered in a Kiziliurt mosque in 1995, Bagautdin identified as many as 100 Sufi deviations from the shariat. In December 1996, Bagautdin published an article titled "We Call All Muslims to Monotheism" in a religious newspaper called *Nasha nedelya* (Our Week). In this article he identified the main difference between the Islamic dogma of the Wahhabis and the position of the Sufis. Since the original text was richly ornamented with quotations from the Koran and traditional, sacramental figures of speech after every mention of Mohammad, the text is not rendered verbatim, but is presented in its essence:

1. Sufis say that their *sheikhs-ustazes* (teachers-leaders) know sacramental mysteries. This contradicts the Koran. It would be enough just to mention all the *Ayats* (verses of the Koran) from the book of Allah, in which He, Himself, says that mysteries are known only by him, and that he owns them. There are many Ayats like this. Therefore, we declare that nobody knows the sacramental mysteries but Allah. The prophets can know only what Allah opens to them. Yet Sufis claim that their ustazes know everything, and even in their own homes are afraid to whisper about them for fear that others will hear them and learn about them. This means that Sufis falsely claim for their ustazes the qualities of Allah.

2. Sufis say that there should be a sheikh between Allah and his servants, as a communicator. This point is one of the fundamental ideas in tariqatist Sufism. We say that it contradicts Islam: there cannot be a mediator between God and man. Sufis make their sheikh a secretary, butler, or doorkeeper of Allah, claiming that a prayer to Allah sent through a sheikh would reach Allah faster. This attitude is more like Christianity, where there is mediation by priests with their rights to forgive sins, and so on.

3. Sufis claim that their sheikhs are insured from mistakes, that they do not commit sins, and that they are ruled directly by Allah. This contradicts the Islamic faith. We, of the Jamaat, say that Allah spared Mohammad alone from mistakes and sins, because Allah himself took the responsibility for the prophet's sinfulness.

4. We, of the Jamaat, call upon all the people not to fall into the trap of polytheism. We understand the ustazes' intention to lure as many people as possible under their influence in the name of earthly, material benefits. If the people would turn away from the ustazes, they would lose their authority and influence, based as they are upon a lie. In their attempt to avoid their fate, they fabricate an enemy from the Jamaat, call us Wahhabis, and fight against us.

5. It is characteristic that some branches of official power collaborate with the Sufis and prevent the Jamaat from appealing through the media to the wide range of the society, on the basis that the Jamaat is a derivation from the true Islam. In fact, the Sufis act outside the Koran and Khadises.

6. Another proof of the open war with the Jamaat is the statement of one of the Sufi-tariqat leaders, (Akhmed) Tagaev, on the first convention of Imams of Mosques, on November 5, 1996, in Makhachkala. He said, "Wahhabis should not be allowed access to the media under any circumstances. In that case, all Dagestan would follow them."

At the time of these statements, Bagautdin's involvement in the militant resistance in Chechnya and Dagestan, was indicative of doctrinal differences between radical Wahhabis and many other Russian Muslims concerning views of government authority and interpretations of the concept of jihad. Wahhabis believed that jihad was at the heart of Islam, but they took exception to the Sufi understanding of the term as the spiritual development of mankind. Instead, they interpret jihad as a campaign—and if necessary, as an armed campaign—to promote the international proliferation of Islam. Arms may be used not only for defensive purposes but also for the elimination of obstacles, such as those that were often presented by the existence of secular governments.

Thus the Dagestani Wahhabis rejected all official Islamic structures as complicit in the corruption of local government and the hegemony of the Russian state. They rejected all legitimate political activities, including the formation of political parties, and they ruled out any form of cooperation or compromise with officials in Moscow or Makhachkala. They were fiercely hostile toward Russia and were committed to the foundation of an Islamist state to span the North Caucasus as a prelude to its unification with the Muslim *umma*. They aimed to replicate the political ascents of Islamists in Afghanistan and Sudan. Yet the Jamaat never devised a political program, preferring to focus its efforts on religious propaganda and Islamic education, along with activities that were variously retributive, militant, and terroristic in their scope. Their efforts to implement sharia were mostly localized.[26]

Since Wahhabis are staunchly opposed to Sufis, the latter emerged as a bulwark against the former. Throughout the Soviet period, Sufism had endured in the remote villages of Dagestan as an underground, antiestablishment creed. Yet no sooner had it ascended to official preeminence in 1992, than it ironically found itself struggling against a new form of antiestablishment, underground Islam. In response to puritanical critiques of these radical Wahhabis, the tariqatist Spiritual Board of the Muslims of Dagestan claimed that the Wahhabis were guilty of apostasy. Some traditionalist leaders declared that paradise would be the automatic reward for anyone who killed a Wahhabi.

Yet by the end of the 1990s Dagestan's Wahhabis were flexing their muscles. With generous foreign assistance they built many of their own mosques and controlled no less than fourteen madrassas. They distributed religious literature from their own publishing house, and they operated a satellite uplink in

Kiziliurt (where Bagautdin was based) through which they communicated with one another, and with their supporters abroad. Each year, they sent dozens of young men to study in Islamic madrassas and universities in Saudi Arabia, Egypt, Algeria, Malaysia, Jordan, and Pakistan.

Moreover their political significance extended beyond their organizational achievements in at least three ways. First, they were often well-armed, and by their very presence they polarized village life, and provided an incentive for mountain populations to arm themselves for their own security. Religious schisms often occurred within a family, where children were at odds with parents or brothers were opposed to brothers.

Second, the Wahhabi critique of traditional clergy not only increased mutual enmity but also had a radicalizing effect upon the otherwise mild traditionalists. For example, in 1997, Dagestan's Spiritual Board of Muslims cited the Islamic prohibition against the realistic depiction of people in order unexpectedly to demand (by unanimous vote) an end to a project to erect a monument of Imam Shamil on the two-hundredth anniversary of his birth. Caught off guard, the Dagestani government canceled its decision to construct the monument to the leader of the emancipation movement of the Caucasian mountaineers.

Third, radical Wahhabism became the impetus for the rise of the "Islamic Djamaat" in Bagautdin's home village. The Islamic Djamaat first drew attention on June 21, 1996, when the administrative head of the Dagestani village of Kadar was murdered. Residents blamed local Wahhabis, who promptly fled to Chechnya. These events dramatically exacerbated tensions between Wahhabis and traditional Muslims in Kadar and in the neighboring villages of Karamakhi and Chabanmakhi, which historically have constituted a single djamaat. On August 8, 1996, villagers from the region hoisted placards reading "Death to Murderers" and "Down with Wahhabism" as part of a daylong protest on Makhachkala's central square. The protesters demanded a speedy investigation of the murder, accusing the authorities in the Buinakskii raion and the Office of Religious Affairs of conspiring with the Wahhabis. Even then it was clear that the local conflict was likely to acquire broader significance. In retrospect the incident foreshadowed events of summer 1999, for the traditionalists sought support in Makhachkala while the Wahhabis found refuge in Chechnya.

A serious conflict occurred in the same area on May 12, 1997, when Wahhabis and traditionalists clashed at a funeral in Chabanmakhi. The dispute began when Wahhabis insisted that mourners pray toward Mecca instead of toward the coffin of the deceased, in keeping with local tradition. Before it ended, two fatalities and two injuries had resulted from a melee involving no less than 450 armed individuals. Three hundred of these were traditional Muslims, who took up positions near Chabanmakhi, while 150 Wahhabis controlled a wooded area between Chabanmakhi and Kadar. Before dawn on May 13, a contingent of traditional Muslims captured twenty of the Wahhabis, with the intent of exchanging the hostages for particular Wahhabis whom they accused in the death of a traditionalist a few hours earlier.

Yet while shots were fired at the outset and while weapons were plentiful, gunplay was quickly terminated. Its prompt cessation was partly attributed to a rumor circulating through the crowd, which claimed that a thousand Wahhabis, heavily armed and seasoned in the Chechen war, were at the edge of the village and that further gunfire would provoke their advance.

In order to prevent further escalation, 170 police were dispatched from Buinaksk, along with an Interior Ministry special task force (OMON) equipped with armored vehicles. While 400 reserves stood by, OMON blockaded the villages of Kadar and Chabanmakhi to prevent outside supporters from joining the conflict.

Officials called to the scene included Said Amirov, who was then deputy prime minister (and later mayor of Makhachkala); Magomed Tolboev, the secretary of the Security Council of the republic; Mogomed-Salikh Gusaev, minister of Nationalities and External Affairs along with much of his staff; and Nadirshah Khachilaev, chairman of the Union of Muslims of Russia and Deputy to the Duma. Promising that the killer would be punished, Amirov managed to negotiate a three-way agreement, signed by the government and representatives from both of the opposing sides.

The agreement expressed condolences and regrets all around, and urged both sides to refrain from violence. The hostages were freed by OMON, along with representatives from the office of the public prosecutor and the Dagestani branch of the Federal Security Service. The government vowed to end the OMON blockade of the villages when the agreement was signed and it was quick to keep its promise. Criminal charges were filed and investigations were initiated by the Prosecutor's Office. Yet local tensions continued to mount.

As confrontations again began to escalate, surrounding villages were drawn into the conflict. Traditionalists raided a hospital where one of the Wahhabis was recuperating, and villagers formed roadblocks leading to numerous violent incidents. On the evening of May 14 the driver of a Kamaz truck was detained by a group of traditionalist vigilantes. When the driver refused their demands and attempted to drive through the barrier he was seriously wounded in a fusillade of automatic gunfire. Throughout the next day an anti-Wahhabi demonstration was well-attended by traditionalist residents of the djamaat and the surrounding area. Officials from as far away as Kaspiysk were joined by traditionalist clerics in attempting to calm the crowd, while 150 Wahhabis gathered in the town mosque. Against this backdrop, it is useful to consider a statement by the acting mufti of the DUMD, Akhmed-Khadzhi Tagaev to *Dagestanskaya pravda* on May 15:

> The conflict in Karamakhi has an especially religious character. The reason for this is that the conflict of the past several months of the two Islamic movements in the town and the district has been sharpening. Another reason for the tragic turn of events is the inactivity of the departments and power structures of the republic. It has been mentioned more than once that there will be a preparation of armed sympathizers in Chechnya. Karamakhi is becoming today's center of Wahhabism in Dagestan, where for a long time its illegal activities have been entirely conducted by citizens of Arabic states. . . . Unfortunately, it is impossible to say at this time that the conflict is reconciled. The representatives of the two conflicting sides signed a temporary agreement, which did not address the underlying causes of the clash. The agreement signifies only one thing: you sit with your own automatic weapons, but you do not shoot. . . . Since the reasons behind the clash were not resolved, Dagestan awaits more strife in the future. The influence of Wahhabism in the republic is strengthening. Their support for the partition of Russia by various powers attests that they are well organized, armed, and have access to satellite links and transport systems, despite their small number. In order to end the conflict we should judge by the full strictness of the law those who illegally bore arms and used them for criminal purposes. As to the eradication of the problem of religious extremism in the republic, it is necessary that the sanctioned Wahhabism and other extremist tendencies in Islam be prohibited.

In December 1997, an alliance was established by a "Military Mutual Assistance Treaty" signed by the Chechen commander, Salman Raduyev[27] and representatives of the Fighting Squads of the Djamaat of Dagestan. The treaty affirmed that Chechen government forces and the Islamic Djamaat of Dagestan were unified in the struggle for an independent Islamic Caucasian state.

On December 22, 1997, Wahhabis from this djamaat joined with Chechen and foreign fighters from Chechnya's International Islamic Battalion (comprising a total party of 30 to 120 gunmen according to various sources) to attack the 136th Armored Brigade based in the village of Gerlakh, near Buinaksk.

The International Islamic Battalion was commanded by a Saudi jihadist known locally as Emir al Khattab. He was born in 1969 to a Saudi father and an Adyghe mother who named him Saleh Abdullah Al-Suwailem. From the age of seventeen, he fought the Soviets in Afghanistan, where, by his own account, he came into contact with Osama bin Laden. From 1993 to 1995 he fought for the Islamist opposition in Tajikistan's civil war. He entered Chechnya in 1995 as a television reporter and pioneered films of the Chechen conflict that were used for purposes of international recruitment and fundraising. While acting as an intermediary for Islamist funding, he increasingly filmed his own military exploits. Khattab achieved notoriety in April 1996, when he led an ambush of a Russian armored column near the Chechen mountain town of Shatoi. By the end of the first Chechen war he was the commander of the International Islamic Battalion, consisting primarily of Arab and other foreign fighters. He married a woman from Karamakhi, where he resided intermittently.

The joint attack on the 136th Armored Brigade resulted in three civilian fatalities and fourteen casualties, though the raiders' claims were far higher. According to various Russian and Chechen accounts anywhere from 10 to 300 vehicles were damaged or destroyed. The Central Front for the Liberation of the Caucasus and Dagestan claimed responsibility for the incident, and the subsequent investigation placed the blame on Karamakhi Wahhabis in concert with their Chechen allies. At a session of Dagestan's People's Assembly, convened immediately after the attack, Wahhabism was roundly denounced and essentially outlawed through passage of a law "On the Freedom of Confession and Religious Organizations." On December 23, the chair of the Dagestani State Council, Magomedali Magomedov, emphasized the Wahhabi threat in his successful solicitation of 210 billion old rubles ($35 million) from the Russian Federation Council.

Yet the structure of political power in Dagestan was such that official proclamations, however resolute, were often ineffective. This was because Dagestani political institutions often operated in an authoritative vacuum, resulting from the fact that individual officials generally were held to be personally responsible for authoritative actions. Hence, individual officials bore responsibility for any government action against the Wahhabis. In a land where terrorist acts often were the means by which elites settled scores with one another, and where several high-ranking officials had been targets of multiple assassination attempts, no one wished to assume responsibility for actions against the Wahhabis. When legislative resolutions proved ineffective the prestige and notoriety of Karamakhi was further enhanced.

Such events thrust the Wahhabis into the public eye and provoked widespread public concern. The new political movement became a prominent feature of political discussion and press coverage, where it evoked commentaries both hostile and sympathetic. Increasing numbers of people were interested in Wahhabi beliefs. All the while, tensions mounted in the vicinity of Karamakhi.

On May 21, 1998, when gunmen under the leadership of the brothers Khachilaev seized the main government building in central Makhachkala,[28] a group of twelve to fifteen gunmen commandeered the police station in

Karamakhi. Breaking into the station and beating two militia men at gunpoint, the gunmen confiscated arms and radio equipment. On May 23, Dagestani Interior Ministry forces stationed in the Buinakskii and neighboring Levashinskii raions initiated punitive efforts. A police contingent of approximately 100 officers approached Karamakhi from two sides. Near Chabanmakhi the police were attacked by more than twenty gunmen, but they gained control of the road and began disarming all who passed along it. While searching passersby for weapons a police captain was killed, and later that day, two policemen were wounded in a skirmish near Karamakhi. At first the militia managed to disperse the gunmen in the nearby forest, but there the rebels were reinforced by approximately 200 more armed men. The larger force seized the road running between the village of Verkhnii Jengutai and "Wolf's Gates" (Volchyi vorota) pass. At the same time, the rebels surrounded forty-two policemen (twenty-five from Levashi and seventeen from Buinaksk) in the forest and demanded their guns. Militia reinforcements, sent to the aid of this beleaguered group, were detained by landmines in the road and sniper fire from the nearby heights. After dark, the forty-two policemen nevertheless escaped from the forest.

On the following day the confrontation intensified. A large group of residents from Karamakhi, Chabanmakhi, and Kadar emerged from their villages armed with automatic weapons, grenade launchers, mortars, and sniper rifles. On the same day, the chair of Dagestan's State Council, Magomedali Magomedov, consulted with executive administrators and law enforcement officials from raions and principal municipalities throughout the republic. Following these consultations the State Council determined to stabilize the situation in Buinakskii raion by political means.

At 10:00 PM that night, in the mosque of Nizhnii Jengutai, negotiations were conducted between the militants and government representatives, including the mayor of Buinaksk. The talks resulted in an agreement to separate the two sides, remove blockades on the road from Buinaksk to Levashi, and exchange prisoners. The roads were cleared at 3:00 AM, and the exchange took place on the following day. There could be no doubt that the government had abandoned control over the territory, thereafter known as the "Islamic Djamaat," at the very heart of the republic.

On July 5, a meeting of approximately 1,000 armed men took place in Karamakhi, which was variously advertised as the "United Congress of the Orthodox Muslims of Dagestan" and as the "Congress of the Military and Political Leadership of the Central Front for the Liberation of Dagestan." What was certain was their declaration of an independent political authority, the principal effect of which was to shift the forefront of anti-Russian agitation from Chechnya to Dagestan. Their demands included the resignation of the entire Dagestani government, union with Chechnya, and the withdrawal of all federal troops from Dagestani soil. In a published statement the Dagestani government responded that it would "do everything to protect the constitutional system, social rights, and freedom of the citizens."[29] Throughout the next month tensions continued to increase.

After July 14–15, when fighters from this self-styled "Islamic Djamaat" (or "liberated Dagestan") participated in an attack upon Chechen forces in the Chechen town of Gudermes, it was denounced by the presidents of both Chechnya (Aslan Maskhadov) and Ingushetia (Ruslan Aushev). Faced with intensified regional opposition, some Djamaat leaders indicated a new willingness to reconcile themselves with Moscow.

However, on August 10, the Wahhabis of Chabanmakhi and Kadar declared that they would henceforth control the roads passing through their region, which essentially threatened to separate Makhachkala in the east from the west-central portions of the republic. The situation was discussed on August 19, 1998, at a joint meeting of the State Council, People's Assembly, and Cabinet of Ministers. The meeting was addressed by Magomed Alkhlaev, chief administrator of the Buinakskii raion, Saidmuhammad Abubakarov, mufti of Dagestan, representatives of the assembly, high-ranking government officials, and law enforcement officers. According to *Dagestanskaya pravda,* the chair of the State Council, Magomedov, exhorted the participants "to give up their disagreements and think about the fate of the republic" (August 20, 1998). The meeting ultimately condemned the extremists, passed a resolution on measures for the normalization of the situation, and issued proclamations to the citizens of Dagestan along with an ultimatum to the "Islamic Djamaat." The proclamation declared that in case of further noncompliance with the demands of the "State Council and the People's Assembly, the Ministry of Internal Affairs is directed to use all necessary measures to prevent unlawful activity and reestablish constitutional order in the villages of Karamakhi and Chabanmakhi of the Buinakskii raion." The ultimatum was the result of a decision to prepare public opinion for a forceful conclusion of the crisis.

In fact, the government had resolved upon a strategy to begin ideological preparations for a possible deployment of force. Through its manipulation of the media the government sought to expand public awareness of the situation and to explain the measures that might prove necessary for its stabilization. The media were asked to initiate a discussion of the situation in Karamakhi and Chabanmakhi and to explain the previous attempts to normalize the situation.

On August 20, many political officials and opinion makers traveled to the villages of Dagestan to talk to people about the problem and explain the danger of religious extremism. The media devoted extensive coverage to these meetings, at which there was widespread condemnation of the Wahhabis, and numerous appeals that they avoid war by submitting to the laws of Dagestan and the Russian Federation.

The next day the mufti of Dagestan, Saidmagomed Abubakarov, and the chairman of the DUMD were killed in an explosion in the yard of the new djuma mosque (or main mosque) in Makhachkala. Though no one claimed responsibility, the attack was popularly attributed to the Wahhabis. The government issued a statement affirming that "Behind this terrorist act, there are political powers inside and outside the republic that wish to destabilize the situation in Dagestan and the entire North Caucasus at any expense." In a television appearance, Magomedov recalled the "insightful speech" of the *mufti* during the joint meeting two days before when he warned against the dangers that the Wahhabis presented for Dagestan. *Dagestanskaya pravda* reported that, in a meeting on August 22, the State Council passed a resolution emphasizing the urgent need "to fight decisively against terrorism and religious extremism."[30]

Yet that same August 22 meeting of the State Council, dedicated to the murder of the mufti, was the scene of other unexpected events. Without warning the vice-prime minister of the republic, deputy of the People's Assembly, and leader of the Avar national movement (the Imam Shamil Front), Gadzhi Makhachev, leveled accusations against Dagestan's two most prominent political leaders, Magomedali Magomedov and Said Amirov, both of whom were Dargins.

On August 25, at a crowded meeting of Avars in Khasaviurt, a "North Dagestan Coordination Council" demanded the resignation of the State Council and the Cabinet of Ministers, along with changes in procedures for the selection of the head of the republic. On the same day, the local television station broadcast Makhachev's denunciation of the two Dargin representatives to the State Council along with a statement by the mayor of Khasaviurt, an Avar named Saigidpasha Umakhanov, declaring that unless Magomedov and Amirov resigned, Umakhanov, along with the mayor of Kiziliurt and the chief administrators of Kazbekovskii, Gumbetovskii, and other raions would cease to recognize the authority of the government.

On August 26, Magomedov traveled to Buinaksk to negotiate with the rebellious Wahhabis, while, at the same time, a large contingent of Avars from the meeting in Khasaviurt, many of whom were heavily armed, set out for Makhachkala in order to demand the resignation of the government. They stopped near Kiziliurt for another meeting of Avars, which gathered between 700 and 1,000 people.

This event broke off the negotiations between Magomedov and representatives from Karamakhi and Chabanmakhi in Buinaksk. The prime minister, an ethnic Kumyk named Hizri Shikhsaidov, went to negotiate with the Avars meeting in nearby Kiziliurt. Shikhsaidov persuaded the Avars not to go to Makhachkala, where their presence would be likely to provoke armed clashes with supporters of Magomedov and Amirov, and possibly broader conflicts between Avars and Dargins.

Remarkably, at the same time, Amirov was making unexpected progress in a meeting with a delegation of his fellow Dargins from Karamakhi and Chabanmakhi. *Molodezh Dagestana* described this as a "constructive" exchange in which "both sides agreed that the highest aim is to preserve peace in Dagestan, and that all other problems can and should be solved by peaceful processes without recourse to violence and force."[31] Evidently, the imminent prospect of an ethnic civil war between Dargins and Avars temporarily trumped the temptations of political separatism in the service of religious extremism.

On August 29, an unprecedented Congress of the Muslims of Dagestan convened in Makhachkala. The meeting was formally dedicated to the commemoration of the martyred mufti and the condemnation of Wahhabism, yet its criticism unexpectedly turned against the government. The capital was patrolled, at that point, by reinforced militia, and the central square, which stands between the White House and other government buildings, was blockaded by special forces of the militia using large trucks filled with sand that closed one of Makhachkala's main thoroughfares. By the middle of the day the congress had passed a resolution containing three principal demands: (1) the resignation of the government of the republic, with its head, Magomedov; (2) popular election of an individual political executive (that is, a presidential system); and (3) the appointment of an independent commission to investigate the murder of the mufti. Their intent was that the Presidium of the Congress should present these demands to Magomedov.

On September 1, the situation shifted dramatically. Buinaksk was the site of a meeting between leaders of the republic and representatives of the Djamaat of Karamakhi and Chabanmakhi. Led by Magomedov, the government delegation negotiated a "protocol agreement," which was signed by Adilgirei Magomedtagirov, interior minister of Dagestan at the time, Magomed-Salikh Gusaev, minister of Nationalities, and M. Alkhlaev, head of Buinakskii raion. Signing for the Djamaat was Magomedshapi Djangishiev, head of the Islamic Cultural Center "Caucasus," and Mukhtar Ataev, self-styled "Amir of the Islamic Djamaat."

The first article of the protocol stated that residents of these villages promised to live according to the constitution and cooperate in the restoration of order and local administration. In other articles, the government agreed to permit Wahhabi leaders to enforce order in the villages, and guaranteed freedom for the confession of Islam according to personal preference. Government and media were further obliged to refrain from use of the word "Wahhabi."

Government officials further agreed to review a law "On the Freedom of Confession and Religious Organizations," that effectively constrained Islamic fundamentalist practice; to refrain from arresting Djamaat members on fabricated charges; and to permit Djamaat leaders to make television broadcasts.

On September 2, Sergei Stepashin, then the interior minister of the Russian Federation, began a visit to Dagestan at Karamakhi. Shortly thereafter, the Islamic djamaat began to receive supplies from Moscow, including building materials, appliances, and medicine for the local hospital. Surprised Dagestanis read newspaper reports about "humanitarian aid" for these villages with a reputation for relative prosperity.

Two days later there was an explosion in Makhachkala on Parhomenko Street that killed sixteen people, including four children. Houses nearby were completely demolished and twenty-two families lost their homes. No one took responsibility for the blast, which occurred 80 meters from Mayor Amirov's house and 100 meters from Prime Minister Shikhsaidov's residence.

Thereafter, the government's settlement with the Wahhabis diminished the level of tension in the republic, but it was widely viewed as a concession of official power indicative of an ominous enervation and indecisiveness. Throughout the autumn of 1998 and the spring of 1999, the authority of Makhachkala and Moscow sharply declined. Moreover, the capitulation of local and federal governments tended to undermine traditional Islam, while contributing to the prestige of the "Islamic Djamaat," and encouraging Islamic activism elsewhere in the republic. The latter sharply increased, especially in highland Avar villages of Botlikhskii, Kiziliurtovskii, Khasaviurtovskii, and Tsumadinskii raions.

Thus, by the beginning of 1999, on the eve of major conflict, Dagestan had become increasingly dominated by events in an independent territory at the strategic center of the republic, which was inspiring advocates throughout the raions, and especially in territories along the Chechen border. The growing urgency and complexity of the situation only served to underscore the dearth of information about Dagestani attitudes toward the crisis.

Wahhabism from a Dagestani Perspective

In the spring of 1999, our team received funding to investigate these issues.[32] Along with a team of Dagestani and German social scientists, we planned a study of Dagestani citizens and elites that would provide an opportunity to delve more deeply into Dagestani attitudes toward religion and politics. Unfortunately, warfare on Dagestan's western frontier in August 1999[33] made it necessary to postpone the start of the survey until March 30, 2000, after which it was conducted throughout Dagestan continuously until April 13.

The central part of this study, a formalized closed survey of 1,001 respondents from across the republic, involved the administration of a twenty-seven-question instrument. In accord with authoritative demographic data available in *Natsional'nosti Dagestana*, the sample was stratified, in the first phase of selection, with respect to ethnic groups, urbanites, and villagers. Villagers were further stratified among categories of lowlands, foothills, and highlands. In the second phase of selection, individual respondents were selected from voter registration lists in the sites that were chosen in the first phase.[34]

In order to provide a qualitative supplement to the quantitative survey data, as the second part of our study forty open-ended interviews were conducted from April 3 to May 22, 2000, with members of Dagestan's professional, scientific, and creative intelligentsia. Since sample selection was necessarily based upon accessibility and cooperation on the part of the prospective respondents, the interview results are more suggestive than conclusive. The interviews were conducted according to a prepared list of twenty-eight questions, and were recorded on tape with permission or otherwise stenographed. Both the survey and the interviews referred to "Wahhabis" and "Wahhabism" without attempt to specify these terms beyond common Dagestani usage. Indeed, we sought to learn what the terms meant to Dagestanis.

Of course, empirical research was particularly difficult in Dagestan at that time. Western survey methodologies were challenged by the extremity of the given cultural and infrastructural obstacles. Telephone interviewing was impossible as many Dagestanis and most villagers lacked telephones. Traveling for face-to-face interviews was difficult and often dangerous. Any tradition of interrogation on political issues for sole scientific purposes was lacking, and due to recent violence, people were sometimes afraid to speak out on issues as charged as Wahhabism. Therefore, political inquiry in Dagestan invariably encountered reticence on the part of some respondents to speak openly on issues of controversy. In addition, local cultures required consideration if responses were to be elicited at all. This sometimes raised conceptual and contextual, as well as linguistic, issues.

Discouraging as these difficulties may have been, it proved possible to surmount them to a great extent. However, the price was a rather inelaborate set of variables for which survey and interview data could be obtained. The results, in any case, were the best available data on Dagestani attitudes toward religious issues, and the exception to other reports, which were both rare and anecdotal in nature.[35]

How did Dagestani citizens see Wahhabism? In the population survey, respondents were asked to agree (1) or disagree (2) with each of the following three statements: (a) "Wahhabis are Muslims, and they should not be considered extremists," (b) "There are Wahhabis who are just simple believers, and

Table 5.1

Citizens' Perception of Wahhabism

Percentages of "agree" (based on whole sample)	(n)	Wahhabis are Muslims, not extremists		Some Wahhabis are just believers, others are religious extremists		Wahhabis are extremists behind a religious facade	
		Valid	Overall	Valid	Overall	Valid	Overall
Overall	(1,001)	11.4	9.1	39.3	30.1	87.1	77.0
Missing cases			20.5		23.6		11.7
Avars	(279)	12.4	10.4	48.6	36.9	80.4	69.2
Missing cases			16.5		24.0		14.0
Dargins	(172)	23.0	16.3	57.5	42.4	89.7	75.6
Missing cases			29.1		26.2		15.7
Kumyks	(134)	5.8	4.5	34.0	26.9	94.6	78.4
Missing cases			23.1		20.9		17.2
Lezgins	(130)	7.8	6.9	15.6	13.1	91.2	87.7
Missing cases			11.5		16.2		3.8
Laks	(50)	12.8	10.0	54.1	40.0	93.0	80.0
Missing cases			22.0		26.0		14.0
Russians	(71)	2.3	2.8	35.7	21.1	98.4	85.9
Missing cases			23.9		40.8		12.7
Chechens	(53)	14.9	13.2	31.3	28.3	54.9	52.8
Missing cases			11.3		9.4		3.8
Azeris	(39)	—	—	18.2	10.3	94.6	89.7
Missing cases			38.5		43.6		5.1
Tabasarans	(27)	4.3	3.7	8.7	7.4	100	96.3
Missing cases			14.8		14.8		3.7
Men	(486)	10.3	8.2	40.9	31.9	83.1	72.0
Missing cases			20.2		22.0		13.4
Women	(515)	12.5	9.9	37.8	28.3	90.9	81.7
Missing cases			20.8		25.0		10.1
Village	(496)	13.4	11.3	40.0	33.3	84.1	75.8
Missing cases			15.5		16.9		9.9
Town	(503)	9.3	7.0	38.5	26.8	90.3	78.1
Missing cases			25.4		30.2		13.5

other Wahhabis who are religious extremists," and (c) "Wahhabis are extremists that hide behind a religious facade." The results, displayed in Table 5.1, show that more than three-quarters of Dagestanis shared their government's assessment that Wahhabis are extremists behind a religious facade. Less than one-tenth thought that they were simply a variety of Muslims, but not extremists. However, it is remarkable that there were so many missing values, each corresponding to an individual who declined to answer the question. From this it may be inferred that there was remarkable reticence to disclose opinions on Wahhabism—suggesting that Wahhabism was a controversial and dangerous topic in Dagestan.

Wahhabis were seen as extremists especially by Tabasarans, Azeris, Russians, and Lezgins. Tabasarans are ethnic cousins to the Lezgins, though we had not anticipated that they would align with Lezgins on this issue. Azeris may have been suspicious of Wahhabis because they (along with a group of 5,000 Lezgins) are Dagestan's only Shiite Muslims. Since Wahhabis are Sunni Muslims, Azeris are a minority within the Islamic community who might therefore prefer a secular government. On the other hand, Chechens, and to a much lesser degree Avars and Dargins, tended to disagree that Wahhabis are extremists. These groups were above average in their assessment that Wahhabis are not extremists, but Muslims. Thus, whatever else it may have signified, the term "Wahhabism" denoted a genuine religious cleavage in Dagestani society, which had significant ethnic ramifications, and sometimes divided urban and rural residents. Clearly, it represented a significant threat to the stability of the republic.[36]

But exactly who viewed Wahhabis as extremists? To get an answer, we did a logistic regression analysis with the perception of Wahhabis as extremists being the dependent variable.[37] For this purpose, the answers of respondents calling Wahhabi extremists were coded one, and some of their characteristics were compared with those of all other respondents whose answers on the Wahhabism issue were coded zero. The results of a logistic regression analysis showed how many times more or less probable (odds ratio) it is for the dependent variable to occur if one specific characteristic is given. Table 5.2 summarizes such results. They make clear that the relation of Dagestan with Russia was the central determining factor in the evaluation of Wahhabism. Compared with Dagestanis who longed for a more independent Dagestan, those Dagestanis who wanted Dagestan to have closer relations with Russia were 2.7 times more likely to see Wahhabis as extremists. By the same token, those Dagestanis who desired to maintain the status quo were 2.6 times more likely to see Wahhabis as extremists than their fellow citizens who wished for a more independent Dagestan. In addition, those who were less inclined to see Russia as a threat to Dagestan, were 1.7 times as likely to see Wahhabis as extremists, than were those who saw Russia as a very serious threat to Dagestan. Dagestanis who did not see Russia as a serious threat at all were 2.6 times as likely to see Wahhabis as extremists than were those who saw Russia as a very serious threat. On balance, anti-Wahhabism, was positively correlated with a pro-Russia attitude. By the same token, Wahhabism was

Table 5.2

Logistic Regression for "Wahhabis Are Extremists Behind a Religious Façade"

	Odds ratio	Significance
Relationship of Dagestan and Russia:		
(reference c. = more independent Dagestan)		
closer to Russia	2.692*	0.000
status quo	2.565	0.004
Gender (reference c. = male)	1.848	0.004
Threat for Dagestan: Russia		
(reference c. = very serious)		
not so serious	1.716	0.098
not serious at all	2.651	0.002
Place of residence (reference c. = village)	1.057	0.794
Age (in years)	1.015	0.019
Educational attainment		
(reference c. = incomplete high school)		
high school, professional, technical	0.996	0.989
higher education, university student	0.651	0.152
Threat for Dagestan: Western countries		
(reference c. = very serious)	0.400	0.000
not so serious		
not serious at all	0.128	0.000
Trust in religious leaders		
(reference c. = not mentioned)	0.355	0.003
Cox and Snell R-quadrate	0.431	$n = 721$

*Read: Those who want Dagestan to have closer relations with Russia are 2.7 times as likely to see Wahhabis as extremists as those who desire a more independent Dagestan.

positively correlated with anti-Russia-involvement. This was particularly significant since other survey data showed that (a) Dagestanis strongly identified with Russia; 63.6 percent chose Russia as one of the two most important referents of their identification; (b) in case of an acute crisis more Dagestanis would trust "Russian Federal leadership" than any alternative, including "Dagestan's leadership" and private networks of relatives and friends (63.7 percent, 42.5 percent, and 42.6 percent, respectively); and (c) most Dagestanis (62.8 percent) wanted a closer relationship with Russia, as opposed to those who wanted more independence for Dagestan (14.8 percent). Thus, since support for Wahhabism correlated with negative attitudes toward Russia, and since attitudes toward Russia were consistently positive, it is not surprising that attitudes toward Wahhabism were overwhelmingly negative.[38]

In Table 5.2, the value of 0.4 for this variable indicated that those Dagestanis who did *not* consider Western influence as a serious threat to Dagestan were 40 percent more likely to see Wahhabis as a threat to Dagestan than those Dagestanis who actually did consider Western countries to be a serious threat.

In addition to those who were more sympathetic toward Western values, Table 5.2 indicated that town dwellers, women, and older people were more inclined to see Wahhabis as extremists. Islam played a greater role in the life of many villages than in city life, and therefore may have lent an atmosphere more conducive to the development of Wahhabism. Villagers also tended to be poorer and more isolated from economic and cultural benefits that may have derived from modernization. Since they were more likely to perceive the costs of transition than its benefits, and since some transitions were broadly associated with Western influences, villagers may have been more concerned about Western influences. On the other hand, city life encouraged toleration and cosmopolitanism, both of which were incompatible with rigid Wahhabi views. Islam had a wider appeal to Dagestani men than to women, perhaps because like other public religions it appealed to public inclinations that are often associated with men.[39] Traditionally, Dagestani women have taken a more moderate, less confrontational, approach to social and religious issues, whereas Wahhabism has sometimes been a focus of confrontational and extremist appeals. Moreover, the puritanical strictures of Wahhabism would place limits upon the social and political roles, as well as the attire, of women who enjoyed gender equality comparable to that in the West in Dagestan's larger towns. Older people, who were more likely to favor traditional North Caucasian Islamic practices, tended to be suspicious of recent spiritual imports. Generally, these results appeared to support anecdotal reports that many Wahhabis were young men from rural backgrounds.

Table 5.2 also raised questions concerning the relationship between education and Wahhabist proclivities. It appeared that Wahhabism was attractive to people, particularly young educated men, who were frustrated by a lack of economic opportunities, or whose education invited a critical attitude toward political realities. In Dagestan especially, significant numbers of influential young men were educated at universities elsewhere in the Islamic world where they were exposed to radical doctrines.

Elites' Views of Wahhabism

To explore Dagestani views of Wahhabism in greater depth, we asked members of the Dagestani professional, scientific, and creative intelligentsia about the factors that had contributed to the appearance and proliferation of Wahhabism in Dagestan. Elite opinions frequently echoed survey results, as for example, in the case of a Chechen-Akkin employed as a high level city administrator in Makhachkala:

So far, Wahhabism is only a cover-up. Those whom we call Wahhabis do not call themselves by this name. This name just covers up their real essence—banditry. They are anarchists, nihilists deep down. They are renegades who wish to realize their secret desires. Since they want to make it sound honorable they come forward with religious slogans. In the present situation it was a suitable slogan. If the situation changes they will choose a new slogan. In the twentieth century it was the slogan of the class struggle, expropriation of the expropriators. Both then and now active people were of the same kind: destroyers. I doubt that among the so-called Wahhabis there is even one person who would be able to conduct a three- or four-hour discussion on religion. They do not know half of what an ordinary mullah should know!

In addition, opinions regarding these factors could be classified into eight categories.[40] Among these, three factors stand out as being most significant:

- Fifteen respondents mentioned economic problems, including a low standard of living, unemployment, and poverty. Typical were statements similar to those of a sixty-two-year-old Avar employed as a physician in a municipal hospital: "Wahhabism, like any form of extremism, is based upon poverty and haplessness. The situation in Dagestan is staggering, so many unemployed."
- Fourteen respondents mentioned alienation resulting from political problems, including weakness, deceitfulness, corruption, and indifference to the lives of ordinary people on the part of leaders in Moscow and Makhachkala. Often they couched their assessments in terms similar to those of an Avar employed at the Dagestan Scientific Center: "The reason for the emergence of Wahhabism is the antiethnic politics of Russia; corruption, and deceit of top government officials, including those in Dagestan. And also the aspiration of people to improve their lives."
- Fourteen respondents mentioned various external factors, such as missionaries from Muslim and Western countries, their ideological pressure, and their finances. These references often resembled those of a Lak businessman: "Wahhabis appeared because of the money from abroad and the competition in the market of religious 'service.' One side called the other side 'Wahhabis.' Additionally, it is important that many people do not like the invasion of Western capitalism with its cult of money." These responses are significant particularly in highlighting the role of outside Islamist influence and funding in the spread of political Islam in the Northeast Caucasus. Many interviews suggested that external factors were important. For example, Protestant missionaries from the West

have had modest success in some of Dagestan's cities, while attracting local attention, and raising concern about converts drawn from among the Islamic faithful.

While these categories were most significant in terms of the number of responses, the reasons disclosed in the five additional categories are no less revealing:

- Seven respondents mentioned ideological factors occurring in the spiritual vacuum that emerged after the collapse of communism; the influx of Western ideology alien to Dagestani society; ignorance of the masses; and the spiritual searching that is characteristic of the youth. Such people often argued along the lines of a Lezgin government employee: "If Islam corresponded to its role and fulfilled its functions and tasks, there would not be any Wahhabism. It just proves that religion is weak and unable to fulfill its function of educating people regarding peace and love toward their neighbors." Four respondents mentioned a traditionally high level of Islamization among Dagestanis; their tradition of religious activity; and the historical role of Islam in Dagestan.
- Four respondents mentioned a traditionally high level of Islamization among Dagestanis, their traditional religious activity and the historical role of Islam in Dagestan.
- Four respondents mentioned an attraction of Wahhabism as an ideology of a clear and simplified Islam. One of the more complex arguments, which also includes reference to outside Islamist influences, was offered by a Kumyk who serves as the head of an educational institution:

Wahhabis are unhappy with the old religious leaders. Do not forget that the leaders from our past communist times are not the best people of this land. . . . The best people got educated and . . . moved to live in many parts of the Soviet Union. . . . They secretly believed in God, but did not stay in their high mountain villages yearning for education. . . . But those who served Allah officially were the ones who stayed in the mountains, wretched and embittered. They earned their bread by funeral services. . . . The religious renaissance began . . . during (the period of) Gorbachev. . . . The demand for religious people increased. In some villages the former leaders of the Communist Party started new careers in the Islamic business. . . . All authority had collapsed in the villages, so the religious way of solving local problems came to the forefront. Religion replaced the Communist Party. The people who could read the Koran in Arabic were advancing and competing among themselves. It was not easy for them to be overt social activists. . . .

Generally, they are deeply religious. They became firm in their faith in times when it was not encouraged and held no career prospects. Some of them are fanatics. . . . Old-fashioned religious leaders did not compromise their faith even if their new, wealthy sponsors from the Arab countries demanded it from them. They did not refuse financial help and the personal prosperity that came with it, and they were able to do so many things with money. But only on the condition that Islam would stay intact in the way they preserved it through generations in the hard conditions of the underground. But there are always people that are ready for reforms. The foreign Muslims certainly do not like the arrogance of our veteran Muslims, and their conviction that Islam is pure only here in Dagestan. They do not want to accept Dagestan as the center of orthodox Islam. Wahhabism is the new stream in Dagestani Islam that resists our traditional "catacomb" Islam. Many young people study abroad in Islamic universities. They are different Muslims already, not like our keepers of the ancient traditional Islam.

- Four respondents mentioned competition among religious activists leading to ideological divisions among them. The following, from a Lak journalist, is a representative statement, which also, once again, evokes themes of external funding, and of simplicity:

The problem of Wahhabism was artificially created by those pseudo-Islamists that go on the hajj with money from fraud and have nothing to do with true Islam. True Islam does not divide religion into Wahhabism and pure Islam, and so on. These people are far from Islam and just use it when drunks, thieves, and criminals started pretending to be saints, to go to the holy sites, do the hajj. They do not need the true Islam; they look for its simplified form. Pure Islam did not satisfy them. They promoted their own version of Islam, especially because it was generously paid for.

- Finally, two respondents mentioned the Chechen factor, that is, the influence of political-ideological processes in the neighboring republic.

According to Dagestani elites, therefore, Wahhabism seemed to be a problem stemming from a large variety of causes. The process of economic and political transitions shook the foundations of Dagestani society[41] and, by the same token, provoked a wide range of societal pathologies. As a reaction to it, a new interest in religion arose, filling the gaps of spiritual and ideological identification created by the demise of communism. The old, ill-educated, and traditional Islamic leadership was not sufficiently able to meet these challenges, such that there was room for a new course of Islamic revival. It came with funding from the

Persian Gulf and was by no means restricted to religious concerns, but served as a misleading label for political and criminal purposes as well. For Dagestan, Wahhabism was a problem with both domestic and foreign roots. Its economic and political features suggested the need for a government response.

The Dagestani government responded by banning Wahhabism through legislative action of Dagestan's People's Assembly on September 16, 1999. Fifteen interviewees saw benefits from this legislation, whereas sixteen respondents thought that the law would not help. Some respondents believed that Wahhabism was poorly defined by the law and therefore had no clear target. A young Lak technical specialist expected that, "This law will help to eliminate the word [Wahhabism] from use. But new words will emerge to define religious opposition." The Kumyk educator thought that the law would have even less effect:

> The anti-Wahhabi law does not work and cannot work. It is anticonstitutional, and the court cannot sentence anybody simply because he/she is a Wahhabite. If he is armed or breaks the criminal law, then the Wahhabi would be prosecuted on a certain basis in criminal law and not under our anti-Wahhabi law.

In addition, some expressed a general lack of confidence in Dagestani legislation and enforcement. A Kumyk arts employee confided: "None of our laws really work. Or they do not use them. They are written just to declare a wishful condition of life." Even proponents were skeptical in this respect. According to an Avar agronomist, "The law could help if it is used properly, instead of how it usually happens: they arrest someone for Wahhabite propaganda, keep him for a month, and then let him go. Same with militants. As a result, they [Wahhabis and militants] act aggressively and with impunity." A Lezgin economics professor summarized several common themes:

> It is very important that all the [Dagestani] people really want to get rid of this evil. I think there are still many people who sympathize with Wahhabis. So on the one hand its dissemination should be stopped, for which we need the law. And, on the other hand, we need to have well-planned ideological work, especially with young people whose searching leads them to be more interested in foreigners than in their own tradition.

Our survey results showed that Wahhabism appealed more to men than women, more to rural than urban residents, and more to the young than to the old, thereby supporting anecdotal observations that Wahhabism held particular appeal to young men from the villages.

We concluded that Wahhabism posed little immediate threat to Dagestan's stability because Wahhabism was rejected by an overwhelming majority of Dagestanis, and because it was identified by elites in terms of a variety of social pathologies rather than in terms of an authentic spiritual or ideological alternative. Moreover, because Wahhabism was correlated with respondents' attitudes toward Russia, its proliferation would be limited so long as Dagestanis retained their positive attitudes toward the federation.

Nevertheless, there were several reasons for concern over the longer term. First, support for Wahhabism clearly cut along, and potentially reinforced, ethnic cleavages. Thus, whereas Islam traditionally has cut horizontally across Dagestan's vertical ethnic segments, Wahhabism threatened to "verticalize" religious cleavages in a manner that reinforced ethnic divisions. Since the movement had greatest appeal among Avars, Dargins, and Dagestan's Chechen-Akkins, and since it had least appeal among Russians, Tats, Laks, and (for the most part) Lezgins, the numerous fears and controversies that it generated were ethnically divisive. Thus, on the one hand, support for Wahhabism might contribute to ethnic tensions, while, on the other hand, the latter might also augment the former. However, other survey data showed that the salience of ethnic differences tended to be overestimated by Dagestanis themselves, and that Dagestanis identified themselves most strongly, not in terms of their ethnicity, but in terms of their allegiance to Dagestan and to Russia, in that order.

Second, the study suggested that Wahhabism was feeding upon dissatisfaction with economic and political circumstances as well as upon cultural concerns about Western influences. All of these were long-term problems that proved difficult to resolve. Signs of economic growth remained marginal and were largely confined to population centers, whereas Wahhabism was most appealing in the countryside. While economic investment and growth seemed likely to limit Wahhabism, these proved difficult to cultivate in those sites where they were most needed.

Whereas Dagestan's political system was well-equipped to manage ethnic conflict, it had little experience with entrenched religious cleavages. This was dramatically illustrated by the fact that the "Islamic djamaat" managed to establish an autonomous region, as none of the national movements had ever managed to do. Its maintenance of this autonomy against government efforts to reassert authority continued to undermine popular perceptions of government legitimacy. Wahhabism's puritanical critique of corruption and social decay appealed to a population that had grown increasingly desperate in its poverty, disillusioned with its elites, weary with the stresses of democratization, anxious at the upheaval of modernization, and jaded with the promises of Westernization. At the same time, Wahhabism radicalized

Dagestan's traditional Islamic authorities and ensnared the secular government in religious controversy.

We concluded that the influence of Wahhabism upon Dagestan's stability was likely to remain limited if Dagestanis perceived tangible economic and political improvements, and so long as they continued to view Russia favorably. Therefore, the most optimistic scenario would involve sustained action on the part of the Russian Federation to remove corrupt Dagestani officials and promote economic development, particularly in the countryside. Unfortunately, this did not occur.

6

Conflict and Catharsis
Why Dagestanis Fought to Remain in Russia

There was a fateful inevitability to the military actions in Dagestan that began on August 2, 1999, and concluded on September 16. Dagestan was invaded by approximately 2,000 insurgents led by Chechen commander Shamil Basaev, and a Saudi jihadist known locally as Emir al Khattab. During the two preceding years, tensions within Dagestan's Islamic community had been building between fundamentalist Wahhabis and Muslim traditionalists. These tensions were exacerbated by Dagestan's sharp economic decline, which left unemployment at 80 percent in many rural areas. Some young men were attracted to military training camps operated in Chechnya by Khattab and Basaev with funding from abroad. In these camps rural Dagestani disaffection met Chechen militancy and the international jihadist movement. Meanwhile Wahhabism grew increasingly influential in Chechnya as rival political leaders appealed to puritanical Islam in order to transcend clan differences and to bolster their claims to authority.

In Grozny, on April 17, 1999, the second Congress of the Peoples of Ichkeria and Dagestan took place. In some circles the event was described as the "Congress of the Moslems of the North Caucasus." The Congress included 297 delegates from 25 Dagestani djamaats located in raions such as Buinakskii, Gunibskii, Tarumovskii, and Khasaviurtovskii. From Chechnya there were 195 official representatives plus over 200 invited guests. The most complete account of the proceedings at this congress was available in an article by E. Kozhaeva, the journalist for the Dagestani weekly, *Molodezh Dagestana*. Kozhaeva was invited to the Congress, and the following account is based largely upon her article, "Vainakhs and Us."[1]

The conference was opened by Shamil Basaev, who served as chair (*amir*) throughout. He declared the formation of a "military-political council" and a "security council," as well as an "Islamic legion" and a "peacekeepers brigade" comprised of a few thousand well-trained militants. According to Basaev, "these troops (were) needed for the implementation of the resolutions of the Congress, the major goal of which (was) the creation of an independent Islamic state.

In his report on activities during the preceding year, Basaev mentioned the measures that were conducted by the Congress. He called attention to the meetings of Chechen and Dagestani activists and intellectuals dedicated to the 100-year anniversary of Uzun-Khadji Saltinsky. This Avar sheikh from the village of Saltá, a distinguished leader of the civil war in Dagestan and Chechnya, effectively resisted Denikin's White Army forces in 1918, when the latter temporarily occupied the plains of Dagestan and Terskaya. Subsequently, in 1920, the uprising of the mountaineers of Dagestan and Chechnya flared up against the Communist authority, which was lead by "Imam" Nazhmutdin Gotsinsky and sheikh Uzun-Hadji. Following the suppression of this uprising, the Bolsheviks made a decision to give autonomous statehood to the North Caucasus mountaineers and to allow Islamic institutions to participate in the legal structures of the society and power.

Basaev noted that the Congress had sponsored a welfare assistance program for "brothers in need" and that there were plans to operate a television channel. He also announced plans to free 131 "brothers" imprisoned in Dagestan. Addressing the assembly, Basaev declared "we should strengthen our efforts to fight Russia, only jihad will help us to install an Islamic order. . . . I would like especially to emphasize that other public parties regard the Congress as a gathering of bandits. But we have a Congress here; we moved to the higher level. Today the entire Russian media and the leaders of Russia scold us, and this is good. It would be bad, if they would praise us. Today the entire world requires renovation, change. Today Islam attempts to arise from its knees. Let's take Kosovo, there is an open war against our brother Albanians. The Albanians have already begun jihad."

Basaev announced that he had founded the "peace-keeping Caucasian forces" that were amassing in training camps that he operated in conjunction with Khattab and Bagautdin Kebedov. In Basaev's words, "the military-political council and the security council are formed, as well as the Islamic legion and peacekeeping brigade, which consists of several thousands of well-trained soldiers." These forces, according to Basaev, "are necessary for the realization of the resolutions of the Congress, the main purpose of which is the formation of the independent Islamic state in the range of Chechnya and Dagestan. . . ." The same forces were among those that invaded Dagestan less than four months later.

Khattab was present at the Congress, along with Chechen leaders including Movladi Udugov, Abdulla Parkuyev, Isa Umarov, Abdulla Salgereyev. The Avar poet from Dagestan, Adallo Aliev, condemned current Russian occupation of the "Imamate," the so-called state that Shamil created during the Caucasian War and uniting the highlands of Dagestan and Chechnya.

Also among the Chechen leadership at the conference was Zelimkhan Yandarbiev, who sought to quell the animosity between *tariqahtists* and Wahhabis by calling upon all Muslims to "abandon their ambitions" and to "stop wasting their strength seeking for enemies among brothers in faith." Yandarbiev, who supported the Wahhabis, may have been directing his remarks, in part, to Basaev, who half a year earlier had declared that he was "disappointed in the Wahhabis." Yandarbiev also noted that the "establishment of the Shariat in Dagestan is impossible so long as the Russian troops are present there." A resolution of the Congress stated that the situation in the North Caucasus was "critical," and there was a need "to commence the process of the decolonization of Dagestan." Russian authorities were "offered the opportunity to start pulling their troops from the republic."

Beginning on August 2, and again on September 5, 1999, insurgents led by Basaev and Khattab invaded Dagestan from bases in Chechnya. In August they crossed the border into Dagestan's Botlikhskii and Tsumadinskii raions. On August 10, they declared the Independent Islamic Republic of Dagestan under the leader ship of Siradjin Ramazanov, a relative of Akhmed-Kadi Akhtaev who lacked the latter's propensities toward intellectualism and moderation. By that time they had seized the villages of Ansalta, Rakhata, and Shadroda and reached the village of Tando, close to the district town of Botlikh. The fighting in these villages endangered the entire population of Andis, an ethnolinguistically distinctive group of about 30,000 that is counted administratively, along with other small groups, as Avars.

To the evident surprise of the insurgents, their invasion was fiercely resisted both by the local villagers and by an overwhelmingly majority of the population of Dagestan, who spontaneously formed citizen militias. Dagestani officials repeatedly requested federal military assistance before the Russian troops were finally dispatched under the leadership of Colonel-General Viktor Kazantsev, commander of the North Caucasus Military District.

Faced with a hostile civilian population, an unanticipated counterattack from citizen militias, approximately 1,000 Dagestani OMON (special task force) troops, air-mobile Russian infantry, and a ruthless Russian bombardment that did not hesitate to obliterate Dagestani homes and that saw the introduction of fuel-air explosives, Basaev and Khattab withdrew on August 22. They declared that their subsequent efforts to unite Dagestan with Chechnya would be "political not military." By August 26, all fighting in the region had ceased.

Three days later Dagestani OMON troops initiated an offensive against the Islamist enclave in the villages of Karamakhi, Chabanmakhi, and Kadar. For a number of reasons, the attack upon these villages was accepted without protest by the people of Dagestan. First, Dagestani blood was initially spilled, not by federal troops, but by the Karamakhi militants who resisted an opening confrontation with Dagestani OMON forces. The militants were widely viewed as traitors for this reason, as well as because Wahhabis generally were viewed as aligned with Chechen invaders, and because the Wahhabis had attempted to import an alien ideology with foreign assistance. Second, the same Russian troops had already received strong popular support for their defense of the Dagestani border. Thus, in this case, the federal troops were viewed not as attacking Dagestani villages so much as defending Dagestan against a treacherous, and ultimately alien, presence. These events in some respects foreshadowed the initial Dagestani response to the subsequent Russian military operations in Chechnya, where federal forces were often regarded, not as outside aggressors, but as avenging allies.

During the night of September 4, as fighting raged in Karamakhi, a truck bomb ripped through an apartment block in Buinaksk, killing sixty-four people. Although the building was inhabited by civilians, it had previously housed military families.

The next day (September 5), Basaev and Khattab launched their second invasion of Dagestan in a month, this time further north, in Dagestan's Novolakskii raion. There is reason to suppose that this second invasion was intended to relieve the residents of Karamakhi from Russian attack. Yet there is no reason to rule out at least three other motives, including: 1) the recovery of historic Chechen territory in what had briefly been the Aukovskii district but which became primarily the Novolakskii raion of Dagestan following the deportation of the Chechens in 1944; 2) the conquest of a corridor to the Caspian Sea; and 3) the subsequent strategic division of Dagestan into northern and southern portions. Because these four potential objectives represent a linear eastward progression (from Novolaksk, to Karamakhi, to the Caspian shore), it is possible that Basaev may have entertained multiple motives and aspired to achieve as many of them as he could. Yet the only real consequence of the September 5 insurgency was the creation of a new theater of military action in Dagestan.

On September 9, 94 people died in their sleep when an explosion leveled a nine-story Moscow apartment building. Four days later, 118 died in another Moscow apartment blast. Just three days after that, 17 people died when a bomb exploded in a truck parked near an apartment building in the city of Volgodonsk. The recently appointed prime minister, Vladimir Putin, saw a Chechen connection in these explosions, though this was denied by Chechen president Aslan Maskhadov. Further doubts were raised after September 22 when another suspected bomb, discovered in the basement of an apartment building in Ryazan, turned out to be part of a "training exercise" sponsored by federal security services. The next day Russian aircraft bombed the Grozny airport, and a week later Russian troops reentered Chechnya.

Vladimir Putin's reputation soared on his hard-line prosecution of the conflict in the Caucasus, but there were lingering suspicions that the blasts had been the work of government authorities seeking to generate public support for an invasion of Chechnya. The Ryazan incident led to speculation that federal security services had planned an explosion there, and perhaps had planted the bombs in Moscow and Volgodonsk. Earlier questions had been raised when the speedy removal of rubble seemed to preclude a full investigation of the Moscow blast sites. Some observers noted that Chechen leaders such as Shamil Basaev and Salman Raduyev were usually quick to claim responsibility for their exploits. Would Basaev not have taken credit if the apartment blasts had been his work? Indeed why would any Chechen wish to enrage Russians by attacking civilians in their beds? And why did the explosions stop when Russian troops reentered Chechnya? If Chechens were behind the blasts then would the blasts not have continued after warfare resumed? In later years, two Russian legislators who were investigating the blasts died under questionable circumstances. A Russian lawyer, and former security agent, was arrested on a dubious weapons charge after inquiring about the case. Finally, in 2003, two Karachai men were convicted in the cases of the apartment block blasts. However, their closed trial answered none of the questions about the explosions, while raising new questions about the need for secrecy in a trial of great public consequence. These and other troubling ambiguities have been explored in a series of publications suggesting that Russian security services planted the bombs with the intent of blaming Chechens for the explosions and thereby mobilizing Russian society for a second war in Chechnya.[2]

Yet, pending further evidence, the simplest explanation for the apartment block blasts is that they were perpetrated by Islamist extremists from the North Caucasus who were seeking retribution for federal military attacks upon the Islamist enclave in the central Dagestani villages of Karamakhi, Chabanmakhi, and Kadar. There is much evidence for this hypothesis.

In an interview published in the Prague periodical *Lidove Noviny*[3] on September 9, 1999, Shamil Basaev said: "The latest blast in Moscow is not our work, but the work of the Dagestanis. Russia has been openly terrorizing Dagestan. . . . For the whole week, united in a single fist, the army and the Interior Ministry units have been pounding three small villages. . . . And blasts and bombs—all this will go on, of course, because those whose loved ones, whose women and children are being killed for nothing will also try to use force to eliminate their adversaries. This is a natural process and it is yet more evidence of Newton's third law, that each action generates a reaction. . . . What is the difference between someone letting a bomb go off in the center of Moscow and injuring 10–20 children and the Russians dropping bombs from their aircraft over Karamakhi and killing 10–20 children? Where is the difference?"

Among those whose women and children were in Karamakhi during the Russian assault was Khattab, who was married to a Karamakhi woman. On September 15, 1999, Greg Myre, an Associated Press reporter, quoted Khattab as saying: "From now on, we will not only fight against Russian fighter jets (and) tanks. From now on, they will get our bombs everywhere. Let Russia await our explosions blasting through their cities. I swear we will do it." Yet, in a subsequent interview with the Interfax news agency, Khattab denied that he had anything to do with the Moscow attacks. "We would not like to be akin to those who kill sleeping civilians with bombs and shells," Khattab was quoted as saying.

Khattab and other Wahhabis affiliated with the Islamic Djamaat clearly had a motive for blowing up Russian apartment buildings. In September 1999, when the Islamic Djamaat was being bombarded, their motive was somewhat more crystalline and immediate than were those of other suspects such as the Russian military and political establishments. Indeed, the last of the blasts, in Volgodonsk, occurred on September 16, the same day that fighting stopped in Dagestan. If the blasts were connected to the conflict in Dagestan, then one might expect them to conclude at the same time that the fighting did. Moreover, the Wahhabis would have had as much to gain from war as Russia's military and political leaders since warfare would also mobilize their own supporters and spur the international fundraising upon which they depended, much as did the Islamist attacks upon the United States two years later.

There is also much evidence that Dagestani Wahhabis are responsible for a long series of subsequent terrorist explosions in Dagestan. The best-publicized of these occurred at a parade in the Dagestani town of Kaspiysk on May 9, 2002, but there have been many other explosions. For many of these explosions, Dagestani officials have blamed Wahhabi gangs led by Rappani Khalilov and Shamil Abidov.

Proponents of the view that Russian security services were responsible for the apartment blasts, such as David Satter and Rajan Menon, have noted that the apartment block explosions involved hexogen, and have argued that hexogen is a highly controlled substance in Russia with availability tightly restricted outside of government circles. According to Menon, "the bombs used in Moscow and Volgodonsk were made with tons of hexogen, which is manufactured under tight security in very few locations in Russia; it would have been extraordinarily difficult to obtain it and transport it in such massive quantities."

However, Dagestani law enforcement officials sponsored a program for the voluntary surrender of arms from October 1, 2003, to December 1, 2003. Among the weapons that were surrendered were 1 ton, 877kg, 992g of explosives, including large quantities of hexogen and ammonite. Also surrendered were 57 artillery rounds and missiles, 3 guided antitank rockets, 6,807 grenades, 1,256 detonators, 1,151,033 bullets, 962 rifles and pistols, 291 grenade launchers, and 3 flame throwers.[4] Sizable amounts of hexogen and large quantities of weaponry, both familiar and exotic, were, and still are, readily available in Dagestan. Dagestani officials estimate that the surrender program recovered only a small fraction of the weapons, ammunition, and explosives circulating in Dagestan, since most of those wishing to dispose of these items would be better compensated on the black market. Certainly, the defenders of Karamakhi, Chabanmakhi, and Kadar, who were heavily armed and well fortified, had access to the full range of this ordinance.

In 2001, a Dagestani court convicted five local Islamists of the Buinaksk blast. One of them, who had previously worked as a cook in a terrorist training camp that Basaev and Khattab operated in Chechnya, described the transit of the explosives used in Buinaksk from Chechnya to Dagestan beneath a truckload of watermelons. In the autumn of 1997, the Karamakhi Islamists had signed a mutual protection pact with Chechen Islamist groups.

Hence, the simplest explanation for the apartment block blasts is that they were perpetrated by Wahhabis from Dagestan, and perhaps elsewhere in the region, under the leadership of Khattab, as retribution for the federal attacks on Karamakhi, Chabanmakhi, and Kadar. If the blasts were organized by Khattab and other Wahhabis as retribution for the federal attack on Dagestan's Islamic Djamaat, then this would explain the timing of the attacks, and it would explain why there were no attacks after the date on which the fighting in Dagestan was concluded. It would explain why no Chechen claimed responsibility. It would account for Basaev's reference to Dagestani responsibility, and it would be consistent with Khattab's initial vow to set off "bombs everywhere . . . blasting through their cities."

Yet if Khattab and other Wahhabis were responsible for the blasts then this would mean that the Chechens were blamed unfairly, and this injustice would have contributed to many injustices that followed. Vladimir Putin's suggestion that Chechens bore primary responsibility for the apartment block blasts appears to have been poorly grounded, and to have given rise to a dangerous and inequitable mythology of Chechen culpability.

At the same time, assertions that Russian security services are responsible for Russia's apartment block blasts appear to be at least partially incomplete insofar as they do not account for the preceding evidence. Conversely, the Ryazan incident is not addressed by the evidence above. Hence, a further possibility is that Khattab and his supporters (perhaps including Basaev or Raduyev) were responsible for the first blast in Buinaksk and for some or all of the following blasts, but Russian security forces, recognizing the utility of the blasts for purposes of social mobilization, were then preparing to follow Khattab's lead with a blast of their own in Ryazan.

In any case, resistance in the vicinity of the Islamic Djamaat was brought to an end on September 13, when the militants departed the ruined villages. Three days later, on September 16, the same date as the explosion in Volgodonsk, fighting ended in the Novolakskii raion. The Dagestani government counted 45,000 "victims of the war," including those who suffered property damage; 32,000 Dagestanis lost their homes or were otherwise displaced.

As the dust settled, it gradually began to appear that the conflict was nearly as cathartic for Dagestan as it was catastrophic for Chechnya. While the war led to further devastation of Chechnya, it stimulated a dramatic improvement in relations between Makhachkala and Moscow. Indeed, the war resolved the otherwise intransigent problem of a well-armed, well-fortified, militant Wahhabi djamaat, located at the strategic center of Dagestan near the main federal military base in Buinaksk. At the same time, Wahhabite insurgence in Tsumadinskii and Botlikhskii raions, resulted in their universal condemnation. Dagestani resistance was a genuine "people's war" that fused the interests of Dagestan's elite with those of the general population. In the months following the war, Wahhabis were treated as pariahs, their leaders arrested or driven underground. If only temporarily, Islamist radicalism was suppressed in a manner that not only avoided internal political and religious stress, but temporarily strengthened connections between rulers and ruled, and thereby, at least momentarily, addressed the political alienation that contributed to the appeal of the Islamists.

In a similar way, many complex problems that had emerged in Dagestan during the 1990s, and that had seemed to be nearly insoluble prior to the conflict, were in its aftermath, at least temporarily improved. These included problems resulting from: economic collapse, cross-border political realignment in Chechnya and Dagestan, and claims of the Chechen-Akkins in Novolakskii raion. Yet if the conflict strengthened the hand of the Dargin-dominated government in Makhachkala, it also gave rise to an Avar backlash that was focused at two new loci of power. These included a new and official recognition of the Avar-dominated DUMD (Spiritual Board of the Muslims of Dagestan.), and the rise of what came to be known as Dagestan's "Northern Alliance" under the leadership of Avars Gadji Makhachev and Saigidpasha Umakhanov. The remainder of this chapter considers data concerning Dagestani attitudes toward Russia and Chechnya in the aftermath of the 1999 invasion and then briefly surveys the shifting ethnopolitical cleavages of that period.

Dagestani Opinions

On the afternoon of August 4, 1999, one of us was boarding a flight to Moscow from New York's John F. Kennedy Airport. Around his neck was a pouch containing 200 $100 bills. We had received a total of more than $20,000 in grants from the National Research Council and the National Council for Eurasian and East European Research. With help from colleagues in Dagestan and Dresden, we planned to begin a population survey and a series of elite interviews throughout Dagestan in the following weeks. At the end of the jetway, he was handed a Moscow newspaper with a headline announcing that Dagestan had been invaded by a force of insurgents from Chechnya.

The fighting and subsequent population displacements and instability forced a delay in our research plans. However, our survey began on March 30, 2000, after which it was conducted throughout Dagestan continuously until April 13. Elite interviews were conducted from April 3 until May 22, 2000. To round off, event data were collected continuously from July 15, 1999, to April 15, 2001. The study was conducted according to the methods described in Chapter 4.

Survey respondents were offered a list of entities of reference that included Dagestan, Russia, the respondent's ethnic group, his or her religion, and his or her djamaat. They were asked: "If you had to choose from among these categories those that are most important to you personally, what would you choose? Please choose no more than two." Table 6.1 shows how often referents were chosen. The central finding was that three-quarters of the population identified themselves with Dagestan, and nearly two-thirds with Russia. Contrary to the conventional view that ethnicity was of paramount concern to Dagestanis, only 14.5 percent anchored their identity principally upon their ethnic group, even less on religion or djamaats.[5] Thus it appeared that one component of Dagestan's stability was this sense of integration as Dagestanis and as members of the Russian Federation.

Nevertheless, there were important differences in self-identification for members of different ethnic groups. The most notable exceptions were, on the one hand, Dagestan's ethnic Russians, for whom Russia was much more important than Dagestan, and, on the other hand, Dagestan's Chechen-Akkins, for whom Dagestan and Russia were weaker referents than for other Dagestanis. For these two groups, cross-border ethnic ties were of great importance. This was not as markedly the case for either Azeris or Lezgins, though both groups had large populations of ethnic kin in Azerbaijan. Yet, after Chechens, ethnic identification was most important to Azeris and Lezgins, respectively. For Chechens, ethnic identity, religious identity, and village identification were also of striking importance. This was Dagestan's least integrated ethnic group.

Table 6.1

Most Important Entities of Reference (Overall Percentages Based on Multiple Answers)

	N	Dagestan	Russia	Ethnic group	Religion	Djamaat
Overall	(1,001)	73.6	63.6	14.5	10.5	5.9
Avars	(279)	73.7	52.7	14.3	12.9	8.2
Dargins	(172)	77.9	63.4	9.3	6.4	5.2
Kumyks	(134)	73.1	68.7	12.7	10.4	6.0
Lezgins	(130)	83.1	73.8	15.4	4.6	3.1
Laks	(50)	76.0	64.0	12.0	10.0	4.0
Russians	(71)	59.2	88.7	12.7	0.0	0.0
Chechen-Akkins	(53)	47.2	22.6	39.6	50.9	11.3
Azeris	(39)	69.2	69.2	17.9	10.3	10.3
Tabasarans	(27)	96.3	85.2	0.0	7.4	0.0
Men	(486)	72.9	60.9	17.1	12.3	7.2
Women	(515)	74.2	66.2	12.0	8.7	4.7
Village	(496)	78.4	63.9	11.7	7.9	6.9
Town	(503)	68.7	63.4	17.1	13.1	5.0

Changes in sociocultural, political, and economic life were considered to be critical by many Dagestanis. Table 6.2 shows that respondents regarded the worst changes to have occurred in the economy, followed by politics and sociocultural life.[6] These results were not unique, and could be found in most of the successors of former socialist states.

Among different groups, Dargins, Kumyks, and Lezgins were more concerned than Avars and Tabasarans about the deterioration of the economy. Since life in many Dagestani villages was always impoverished, villagers were less concerned than townspeople about recent changes. The economic decline hit women harder than men, as is often the case in transitional societies.

Dissatisfaction with economic and political changes was consistent with a preference for socialism displayed by most Dagestanis in Table 6.3.[7] Predictably, those who saw changes for the worse favored a return to a socialist state. Less than a quarter of the population favored "Western democracy," only one-tenth would have chosen for Dagestan to become an "Islamic state"; and those, who would have so chosen also wanted to see Dagestan more independent (Spearman's rho: −0.34).

Again, differences between ethnic groups were telling. Chechens were least in favor of a socialist state (28.3 percent) and were the strongest supporters of an Islamic state (35.8 percent), but they offered nearly as strong support for Western democracy (34.0 percent). This suggested that Chechens, more than

Table 6.2

Perceptions of Changes in . . .

	N	Economy		Politics		Cultural Life	
		Mean*	Number of missing cases	Mean	Number of missing cases	Mean	Number of missing cases
Overall	(1,001)	2.56	45	2.45	136	2.26	73
Avars	(279)	2.41	17	2.40	26	2.13	11
Dargins	(172)	2.67	10	2.61	22	2.37	15
Kumyks	(134)	2.73	3	2.55	15	2.28	8
Lezgins	(130)	2.65	4	2.53	14	2.54	11
Laks	(50)	2.57	1	2.50	8	1.96	1
Russians	(71)	2.58	2	2.33	7	2.16	3
Chechens	(53)	2.55	4	2.47	14	2.33	10
Azeris	(39)	2.54	0	1.97	5	2.33	6
Tabasarans	(27)	2.42	1	2.27	1	2.54	3
Men	(486)	2.52	22	2.42	60	2.29	38
Women	(515)	2.60	23	2.49	76	2.23	35
Village	(496)	2.49	20	2.46	67	2.32	36
Town	(503)	2.63	25	2.45	69	2.20	37

*Calculation of means based on cases without missing values. Answers were coded as follows: changes for the better—1; no better/no worse—2; for the worse—3. Displaying only median values would hide much of the variation, which actually is in the data. Therefore, means are shown, although data have not been measured on a well-tested interval scale.

Table 6.3

Guiding Principles for a Dagestani State (%)

	Islamic state	Western democracy	Socialist state
Overall	10.9	22.5	63.4
Avars	13.7	30.1	53.8
Dargins	13.4	19.2	64.0
Kumyks	9.7	11.2	76.1
Lezgins	4.6	20.0	75.4
Laks	12.0	38.0	48.0
Russians	—	18.3	71.8
Chechens	35.8	34.0	28.3
Azeris	2.8	17.9	71.8
Tabasarans	11.1	18.5	70.4
Men	14.0	21.8	61.5
Women	8.0	23.1	65.2
Village	13.9	23.6	62.4
Town	8.0	21.3	64.6

any other group, were prepared to make a break with the Soviet past, but were divided on the choice of Eastern and Western paths. Comparatively low support for a socialist state was also to be found among Laks (48.0 percent) and Avars (53.8 percent). An Islamic state was especially unattractive for Azeris (2.8 percent) and Lezgins (4.6 percent). As Dagestan's only Shiite Muslims, Azeris had reason to prefer a secular government, and the Lezgin emphasis upon education had brought many into contact with Western secular values, whether in liberal or Marxist variants. Western democracy was most attractive for Laks (38.0 percent), though there was also significant support among Avars (30.1 percent). Kumyks were least interested in Western democracy (11.2 percent). Women favored a socialist state due to their disproportionate deprivation during the economic transition. Men were more likely to favor an Islamic state, as were villagers.

What of the established regime? Survey respondents were asked to evaluate Dagestan's political institutions, as displayed in Table 6.4.[8] Highest ranking among government institutions were the State Council and the Cabinet of Ministers (means 2.44). Next were the People's Assembly and the organs of law enforcement (means 2.46). Last was the Ministry of Economy (mean 2.59). This result, when compared with Table 6.2, shows how transitional problems led to low trust in local government institutions. Again, economic development proved to be of utmost importance.

Of greater importance, however, was the fact that very large percentages of the population were dissatisfied with all political institutions. This suggested that in Dagestan state institutions were not creating stability so much as consuming stability generated elsewhere. Nor was satisfaction higher with political parties and social movements. On balance, they were ranked low with a mean of 2.53. This underscored the significance of religion. Religious organizations received the highest evaluation with a mean of 2.11. Table 6.5 shows those ethnic groups that were either relatively high or relatively low in their rankings of these institutions.

Table 6.5 shows that some ethnic groups seemed to be comparatively less dissatisfied with Dagestan's political institutions (from State Council to Ministry of Economy). These groups included Tabasarans (noted 5 of five times), Azeris (5) and Avars (4). On the other hand, Lezgins were dissatisfied with the working of Dagestan's political institutions (noted 5 times of five times), and so were Chechens (4). Clearly, these groups were politically alienated. Unlike Lezgins, however, Chechens drew relative satisfaction from religious and social organizations.

What accounted for this alienation on the parts of Lezgins and Chechen-Akkins? In both cases there were complex cultural, historical, and political causes. Once again, many of Dagestan's Lezgins regarded themselves as

Table 6.4

Evaluation of Institutions (Means)

	State Council	People's Assembly	Government (Cabinet of Ministers)	Law-enforcement organs	Ministry of Economy	Political parties, social movements	Religious organizations
Overall	2.44	2.46	2.44	2.46	2.59	2.53	2.11
Avars	2.39	2.39	2.41	2.33	2.50	2.51	2.02
Dargins	2.45	2.52	2.44	2.45	2.63	2.58	2.12
Kumyks	2.45	2.46	2.40	2.64	2.66	2.52	2.07
Lezgins	2.64	2.59	2.62	2.65	2.73	2.61	2.40
Laks	2.52	2.43	2.55	2.40	2.60	2.72	2.02
Russians	2.39	2.48	2.38	2.47	2.62	2.58	2.21
Chechens	2.50	2.50	2.51	2.57	2.55	2.12	1.87
Azeris	2.21	2.30	2.22	2.29	2.47	2.54	2.12
Tabasarans	2.38	2.31	2.35	2.35	2.42	2.36	2.57
Men	2.44	2.42	2.44	2.45	2.59	2.55	2.07
Women	2.45	2.49	2.44	2.48	2.60	2.52	2.15
Village	2.40	2.46	2.40	2.48	2.57	2.45	2.11
Town	2.45	2.45	2.49	2.45	2.61	2.62	2.11

Answers were coded as follows: Performance of the institution is good (1), satisfactory (2), bad (3). Displaying only median values would hide much of the variation, which actually is in the data. Therefore, means are shown, although data have not been measured on a well-tested interval scale.

Table 6.5

Evaluation of Institutions (Differences Between Ethnic Groups)

Item (mean)	Better than average	Worse than average
Religious organizations (2.11)	Chechens (2.02) Avars (1.87) Laks (2.02)	Tabasarans (2.57) Lezgins (2.40) Russians/Cossacks (2.21)
Political parties, social movements (2.53)	Chechens (2.12) Tabasarans (2.36)	Laks (2.72) Lezgins (2.61) Russians/Cossacks (2.58) Dargins (2.58)
State Council (2.44)	Azeris (2.21) Tabasarans (2.38) Russians/Cossacks (2.39) Avars (2.39)	Lezgins (2.64) Laks (2.52) Chechens (2.50)
Government (Cabinet of Ministers) (2.44)	Azeris (2.22) Tabasarans (2.35) Russians/Cossacks (2.38)	Lezgins (2.62) Laks (2.55) Chechens (2.51)
People's Assembly (2.46)	Azeris (2.30) Tabasarans (2.31) Avars (2.39)	Lezgins (2.59) Dargins (2.52) Chechens (2.50)
Law enforcement organs (2.46)	Azeris (2.29) Avars (2.33) Tabasarans (2.35)	Lezgins (2.65) Kumyks (2.64) Chechens (2.57)
Ministry of Economy (2.59)	Tabasarans (2.42) Azeris (2.47) Avars (2.50)	Lezgins (2.73) Kumyks (2.66) Russians/Cossacks (2.62) Dargins (2.63)

arbitrarily and disadvantageously distinguished from Aguls, Rutuls, and Tabasarans. They also regarded themselves as unjustly separated from the Lezgin population of Azerbaijan. A combination of these culturally and historically affiliated groups would make Lezgins approximately as numerous as Avars with all the associated political strengths. Indeed, were the Avars distinguished from their fourteen affiliated groups, the Lezgins would be Dagestan's largest, and perhaps most powerful ethnic group. Thus, many Lezgins saw themselves to have been unfairly marginalized politically and relegated to an economic backwater in Dagestan's southernmost reaches.

At a time before the delineation of Dagestan from Azerbaijan, their villages in the hills and mountains around the Samur River valley constituted an independent Lezgistan, and before that the ancient Caucasian Albania, at an important crossroads, where the Samur River and the Caucasus Mountains met the West Caspian trade route. Moreover, with its emphasis upon education, Lezgin culture tends to produce more teachers, physicians, and engineers than political organizers and strongmen. For all of these reasons, Lezgins tend to be dissatisfied with their lot. Nevertheless, the ethnic repression confronting Lezgins in Azerbaijan leads Dagestan's Lezgins to a relatively strong identification with Dagestan and with Russia (Table 6.1).

Some of the causes of Chechen alienation are well known, but it would be impossible to overstate the significance of their brutal deportation to Kazakhstan in February 1944. They were not officially rehabilitated until 1957 and most were still not able to return to their historic villages in Dagestan. This is because Laks and Avars were forcibly resettled into those villages in March 1944, and they can no longer return to their remote and dilapidated highland homes. The Laks had agreed to move to less desirable land northwest of Makhachkala, but, ironically, the invasions of 1999 interfered with their relocation, and it is now uncertain that they will move (below). Since some Dagestanis regarded many Chechen-Akkins to have been complicit in those invasions, the latter had become an out-group. For all of these reasons, Chechens were unlikely to express satisfaction with their prospects in Dagestan or in Russia.

Moreover, Chechen social structure differs substantially from that of other Dagestani groups in the greater emphasis that it places upon kinship structures, and the relative weakness of political structures.[9] This helps to account for the greater emphasis that Chechens placed upon ethnic and religious referents in Table 6.6. Like Avars and Dargins, Chechens are also traditionally more likely to have deep attachments to Islam than are Dagestan's other Islamic ethnicities.

The survey asked respondents whom they would "trust in the event of an acute crisis," with more than one response permitted.[10] For a majority of Dagestanis, Russia was the second most important source of identity. Yet given the history of the Caucasus, it nevertheless seemed remarkable that in case of an acute crisis most Dagestanis said that they would trust in Russian federal leadership (Table 6.6). Indeed, during the invasions of 1999, this point seemed to come as a surprise to the Kremlin.[11] Yet it was placed in context by the fact that, on balance, Dagestani leadership did not even rank second overall as a source of critical support, but only third, after "myself, my relatives, and friends." On the one hand, this was evidence of the significance of informal structures such as family, tuhum, and djamaat. On the other hand, it was indicative generally of the extent to which Dagestanis were alienated from their own leadership, and particularly indicative of the perceived weakness and lack of resources of the Dagestani leadership in the case of an acute crisis.

Table 6.6

Trust in Case of an Acute Crisis

Valid = overall percent	Russian federal leadership	Dagestan leadership	Leaders of political parties and ethnic movements	Religious leaders	Myself, my relatives, and friends
Overall	63.7	42.5	8.0	7.8	42.6
Avars	61.3	31.5	8.6	7.9	43.4
Dargins	64.5	54.1	5.8	3.5	41.9
Kumyks	61.2	37.3	8.2	9.7	50.7
Lezgins	66.9	60.8	3.1	3.1	28.5
Laks	72.0	30.0	6.0	10.0	50.0
Russians	70.4	38.0	1.4	—	56.3
Chechens	15.1	30.2	45.3	45.3	45.3
Azeris	74.4	56.4	—	7.7	46.2
Tabasarans	81.5	66.7	3.7	—	25.9
Men	63.0	45.1	9.1	8.6	43.6
Women	64.5	40.0	7.0	7.0	41.6
Village	66.7	48.6	8.5	6.9	34.1
Town	60.8	36.4	7.6	8.7	50.9

Tabasarans, Azeris, Laks, and Russians were most likely to rely on Russian federal leadership; Chechens were least likely. Chechens, Laks, and Avars had the least trust in Dagestani officials. Tabasarans, Azeris, Dargins, and Lezgins had comparatively greater trust in the government of Dagestan. The level of trust in the latter group was remarkable given their relative disdain for Dagestani institutions. Chechens had unrivaled trust in their ethnic and religious leaders.

Whom did Dagestanis see as a major threat? Corresponding to the trust invested in the federation, Russia was seen as the least threatening of four possibilities in Table 6.7.[12] Chechnya was perceived as much more threatening, as the low mean of 1.27 suggests. Next in rank were the threats from Western and Eastern countries, respectively. However, different ethnic groups tended to see these threats in different lights. Chechens understandably feared Russia, but Avars and Kumyks also had greater than average reservations. Russians were understandably least concerned about a threat from Russia, followed by Lezgins, Tabasarans, and Azeris.

Especially Kumyks and Russians saw Chechnya as the most important threat to Dagestan, whereas Chechens were the only group that saw significantly less threat from Chechnya. For Chechens, the only serious threat was Russia, against which both Eastern and Western countries could be seen as potential allies.

Table 6.7

Threat to Dagestan . . . .

	N	Russia		Chechnya		Western countries		Eastern countries	
		Mean**	Number of missing cases	Mean	Number of missing cases	Mean	Number of missing cases	Mean	Number of missing cases
Overall	(1,001)	2.58	128	1.27	39	1.73	213	1.86	274
Avars	(279)	2.41	30	1.27	12	1.98	57	1.99	69
Dargins	(172)	2.68	26	1.23	10	1.61	45	1.76	49
Kumyks	(134)	2.46	13	1.13	2	1.69	34	1.90	45
Lezgins	(130)	2.85	18	1.23	9	1.40	21	1.80	36
Laks	(50)	2.67	11	1.22	0	1.74	16	1.65	16
Russians/Cossacks	(71)	2.72	7	1.06	2	1.60	9	1.65	11
Chechens	(53)	1.94	5	2.25	2	2.15	7	2.23	10
Azeris	(39)	2.91	7	1.36	0	1.71	8	1.86	10
Tabasarans	(27)	2.80	2	1.37	0	1.14	6	1.56	18
Men	(486)	2.59	45	1.33	18	1.74	82	1.91	117
Women	(515)	2.56	83	1.22	21	1.71	131	1.80	157
Village	(496)	2.62	56	1.29	23	1.72	88*	1.96	135
Town	(503)	2.54	72	1.26	16	1.73	124*	1.77	139

Notes:
*One case missing in calculation of the mean.

**Calculation of means based on cases without missing values. Answers were coded as follows: very serious threat (1), not very serious (2), and not serious at all (3). Displaying only median values would hide much of the variation, which actually is in the data. Therefore, means are shown, although data have not been measured on a well-tested interval scale.

Russians and Laks were especially likely to see a serious threat to Dagestan from Eastern countries. Again, Chechens were at the other end of the scale: no other ethnic group—with the possible exception of Avars—had less fear of Eastern countries. A lesser threat from Eastern countries was seen by men and villagers, both of whom tend to be more involved with Islam than women and urbanites.

The opinions of the interviewees, in many ways mirrored those of the survey. By far the greatest number of interviewees (fifteen) saw the primary threat as coming from Chechnya. An additional respondent described the principal threat as "attempts to separate Dagestan from Russia."

Five interviewees identified problems with Russia as the primary threat, but one of them was most concerned about the "lack of coordination between the federation and the republic," suggesting the need for closer relations with Moscow. On the other hand, two respondents saw "Russian instability" as the primary external threat; one focused upon the "politics of Russia"; one saw a threat in "Russia's mistrust of Dagestan's loyalty," and one saw the primary threat in "Russian chauvinism."

Three interviewees were most concerned about "Western influence," with one focusing upon "foreign culture, music, pornography," and another concerned about competition over Caspian oil. Some Dagestanis viewed Western culture and values as a threat to a traditional Islamic lifestyle. One interviewee was concerned that Western military or political adventures may destabilize the region by treating Chechnya like Kosovo.

Four interviewees were most concerned about threats that have come to Dagestan from Eastern countries. Three of these discussed "foreign Wahhabism," while one focused upon "foreign terrorism."

Three respondents did not think there was any external threat to Dagestan.

Most interviewees thought that the greatest internal threat to Dagestan's stability was economic. Three of these focused upon "poverty in Dagestan," while another described Dagestan's "economic backwardness," and two more were alarmed by "unemployment" and a growing "economic crisis." Six were most concerned about the increasing polarization of rich and poor.

Eleven respondents saw internal political issues as the greatest threat to Dagestan's stability. Five interviewees mentioned "corruption," "theft of power," or "bad leaders"; one described the "monopolization of power"; two concentrated upon the "struggle for power" or "change of leadership"; and two thought that the main problem lay in the imperfection of the electoral system.

Another ten respondents attributed the main problems to ethnic or kinship ties. Three of these talked about the "confrontation of clans"; three were most concerned about "ethnic nationalism"; one focused upon "ethnic separatism";

Table 6.8

Future Relations Between Dagestan and Russia

	N	Even closer overall	Status quo overall	More independent overall	Mean	Number of missing cases
Overall	(1,001)	62.6	22.0	14.8	−0.48	6
Avars	(279)	56.6	20.4	22.9	−0.34	0
Dargins	(172)	56.4	27.3	14.0	−0.43	4
Kumyks	(134)	76.1	15.7	8.2	−0.68	0
Lezgins	(130)	66.2	26.9	6.9	−0.59	0
Laks	(50)	64.0	18.0	14.0	−0.52	2
Russians	(71)	84.5	12.7	2.8	−0.82	0
Chechens	(53)	37.7	26.4	35.8	−0.02	0
Azeris	(39)	64.1	17.9	17.9	−0.46	0
Tabasarans	(27)	40.7	48.1	11.1	−0.30	0
Men	(486)	63.2	18.9	17.5	−0.46	2
Women	(515)	62.1	24.9	12.2	−0.50	4
Village	(496)	60.3	23.6	16.1	−0.44	0
Town	(503)	65.0	20.7	13.3	−0.52	6

Answers were coded: closer (−1), status quo (0), and more independent (1). So a negative value of the mean represents the desire for a closer relationship between Russia and Dagestan.

and one saw a threat in the "dominance of one ethnic group." Finally, one interviewee saw a threat in Dagestan's "lack of a national identity or concept."

Both Dagestan's invasion by Islamist separatists and the subsequent federal military buildup raised questions about Dagestan's relations with Russia. Should there be even closer relations between Dagestan and the Russian Federation or should Dagestan move toward greater independence? Table 6.8 presents the response to this question,[13] coded to maximize clarity in the following way: opinions favoring closer relations with Russia were assigned a value of minus one, preservation of the status quo was assigned a value of zero, and opinions favoring a more independent Dagestan were assigned a value of one. Thus, every mean below zero indicated that a group wanted a closer relationship between Russia and Dagestan; a group with a desire for a more independent Dagestan should have a mean above zero. The percentages for each answer are also shown.

Concordant with the their trust in the federal government, all ethnic groups preferred closer relations with Russia, or at least the status quo, in place of a more independent Dagestan. Though their interest in closer Russian ties was dramatically less than that of any other group, even Chechens did not want greater independence. Predictably, Russians were most in favor of closer ties with Russia.

Northern Exposure

Clearly, a key to the interpretation of these data was Dagestani perceptions of an ongoing economic crisis combined with the remarkable trust that Dagestanis were prepared to place in federal officials at critical junctures. Prior to 1990, Dagestan was dependent upon Moscow for 80 percent of its budget and upon the Soviet Union for 95 percent of its trade. The Soviet defense industry had a sizable presence in the republic and employed many Dagestanis, notably in the production of aircraft and torpedoes.

During the 1990s there was a decline in this support, and a consequent collapse of the Dagestani economy. In turn, the economic crisis exacerbated all of Dagestan's other problems. Moscow, which has chronically failed to understand Dagestan, evidently interpreted the republic's growing problems as signs of fundamental instability and a propensity toward separatism.

The conflict that came at the end of the summer in 1999 quickly reversed this situation. Suddenly, Dagestan appeared to be Moscow's anchor in the North Caucasus, with important economic consequences. On November 29, 1999, a session of Dagestan's People's Assembly discussed the third version of the republic's budget. Sergei Pinkhasov, who chaired a prominent Assembly committee announced that a tripartite commission composed of representatives from Makhachkala, the Federal Duma, and Ministers of the Russian Federation had resolved to focus maximum resources upon Dagestan's interests.

In 2000, Dagestan received 7.4 billion rubles from the federal budget, in contrast to less than 3.6 billion rubles in 1999. Direct federal transfers doubled in 2001 to 8.5 billion rubles. Dagestan has also received substantial economic support from throughout Russia (including 17 million rubles from the city of Moscow). Additionally, the federal center provided a 50 percent salary raise to Dagestan's state employees (including teachers, doctors, engineers, etc.). On the strength of increased support from the center, pensions were paid more regularly. Also in 2000, central political organizations increased their campaign expenditures in Dagestan, and the large influx of federal troops provided a sudden boost for the local economy. Meanwhile material aid was sent to Dagestan from cities and towns all over Russia.

Following the 1999 conflict, numerous small-scale industries and factories throughout Dagestan gradually began to revive. Soviet-era industries, including defense plants that were based in Dagestan, started receiving new orders. These plants began rehiring from the local skilled labor force, which was idled during the transition period.

Shortly thereafter construction was completed on the petroleum pipeline from Baku to the Russian port of Novorossiisk, bypassing Chechnya through Dagestani territory. According to Transneft vice president Sergei Grigoriev the development included a seventeen-kilometer link to Makhachkala's seaport designed "in connection with the uncertainty of deliveries from Azerbaijan to provide opportunities for the transport of Turkmen and Kazakh petroleum delivered from the sea."[14] This appeared to be a step in a sustained effort on the part of the Russian government to turn Makhachkala into a Northern Caspian oil terminal. Officials in Russia's Transneft oil organization urged transfers of Turkmen and Kazakh crude to Makhachkala facilities.

Moscow's development of Makhachkala as a petroleum port seemed to require explanation since it was, in some ways, a less obvious choice than a city such as Astrakhan. Historically, there are two principal means of access through which industrial infrastructure may be introduced to the North Caspian: the Volga Don canal system and overland routes. Both of these are dependent upon the Volga River system. Clearly, Russia sought to make the Volga cities such as Volgograd, Saratov, and Astrakhan major centers for energy-related transport, refining, freight transfers, and subsidiary economic development associated with the exploitation of Caspian reserves. Yet there also appeared to be at least three related reasons for Moscow's interest in Makhachkala's increasing hydrocarbon traffic.

First, it seemed that Moscow wished to support the Dagestani economy, and thereby contribute to the republic's political stability. There could be no question that this was part of Moscow's strategy given substantial increases in budgetary transfers from Moscow to Makhachkala in the early years of the twenty-first century. Moscow had concluded that economic development was the key to Dagestan's political future. Second, Dagestan's political stability was particularly important to Moscow because the latter recognized that the former was the key to its presence in the North Caucasus. Third, the maintenance of this presence was particularly important to Moscow because historically the Western shore of the Caspian is the north/south route of connection in the region. If Moscow was to maintain its influence in the Caspian and South Caucasus regions then it had to maintain a strong and vital presence in Dagestan. Were Dagestan to become a vestigial appendage, without real economic significance for the Russian Federation and without a role at the forefront of Russian strategy in these regions, then Russia would have lost its historic connection to the South Caucasus and beyond.

It seemed that federal assistance for Dagestan came from the top. When the conflict began on August 2, 1999, the Kremlin did not expect the overwhelming support of the Dagestani people. Even at the time that Putin assumed prime ministerial power, a week later, Russian leaders feared that they might find themselves facing a more or less united ethno-Islamic front in the Northeast Caucasus, or, at least, a civil war in Dagestan. Even after Makhachkala demanded federal military support, Moscow policymakers and military commanders moved slowly, fearing that they would encounter popular resistance in the Dagestani raions.

Hence, it would be difficult to overstate the surprise and relief among Russian officials as the breadth and durability of Dagestani loyalty became increasingly evident. In the countryside, federal troops were received as defenders and allies by people who historically had shown them little sympathy.

In the days immediately following Putin's appointment as prime minister in August 1999, he was widely dismissed by the Russian media, by the Russian public, and by other Russian leaders. Hence, it was his unexpected good fortune in Dagestan that signaled the real beginning of Putin's dramatic ascendance. As a result, Putin felt a sense of personal gratitude and attachment to Dagestan that could not be separated from his private aspirations. For example, he chose to celebrate the New Year in the republic, where he declared his "love" for "the Dagestanis." The latter event would have been entirely unprecedented for a Russian prime minister, even if it had not turned out to be the moment of Boris Yeltsin's emotional resignation and Putin's startling promotion to the Russian presidency. Here it was again auspicious for Putin, perhaps intentionally so, that in this moment of highest drama, he was seated not at Boris Yeltsin's feet but at the table of a people previously perceived as potential antagonists. Hence, Kremlin support for Dagestan seemed to emanate from the very top of the government, and other federal officials appeared largely to support a top-level policy shift. Our data showed that economic problems were paramount among Dagestanis, and, in the aftermath of the 1999 conflict, Moscow made renewed, if limited and ultimately ineffectual efforts, to ameliorate these problems.

Cross-Border Political Realignment in Chechnya and Dagestan

Our data also showed that many Dagestanis perceived threats from Chechnya. Prior to the conflict of 1999, this situation was rapidly deteriorating. During the autumn of 1998, Russia's first deputy interior minister, Colonel Vladimir Kolesnikov, arrived in Makhachkala to make selective purges among Dagestan's political elite. These purges appeared to focus upon challengers to Magomedali Magomedov's Makhachkala regime, and led to a confrontation between major political groups. These confrontations gave rise to two new trends: They strengthened relations between Chechen and Dagestani officials, while at the same time strengthening relations between opposition elements in Chechnya and Dagestan, as deposed Dagestani elites (such as Nadir Khachi-laev) sought refuge across the border. At the time, both of these tendencies seemed to point toward a possible unification of the two republics.

Indeed the year falling between Kolesnikov's purges and the subsequent conflict, from autumn 1998 to autumn 1999, had seen numerous negotiations between officials in Chechnya and Dagestan, particularly between law en-forcement agencies, which culminated in several joint operations. One such operation began in mid-April 1999, when law-enforcement agencies from Chechnya and Dagestan combined to prevent the illegal sale of petroleum products along their common border. Petroleum stolen from Chechnya's portion of the Novorossiisk pipeline was being smuggled into Dagestan and sold. Along with organized kidnapping, priority was assigned to the preven-tion of petroleum sales, as it was contributing to the financial strength of the opposition elements in both republics.

In Chechnya, approximately 160 armed groups had divided major sources of income among themselves. The largest of these groups controlled various segments of the pipeline, as well as petroleum products and arms smuggling. Other groups specialized in the kidnap and sale of human beings, including hundreds of Dagestani men, women, and children. Another large enterprise was the sale of nonferrous metals, acquired by dismembering Chechnya's industrial plants and other infrastructure, especially in Grozny, Gudermes, and Argun.

Transfer points were established for all such enterprises along the Chechen-Dagestani border. In a sense, Chechen gangs established a lucrative trade involving the regular export of pilfered mineral and metal products and the import of kidnapped human beings. The trade was profitable for individuals and groups on both sides of the border, including some law enforcement agen-cies. The year preceding the invasions saw an increase in official cooperation across the border in an effort to stem this cross-border traffic that tended to support opposition elements in both republics.

Yet such cooperation between the leaders of the two republics did not con-tribute to the stability of the region. Nor did this rapprochement initially affect the divergent long-range political orientations of the two republics. Chechen officials saw themselves firmly on a path toward sovereignty, while Dagestan was irrevocably part of Russia. Indeed, officials in both republics cooperated only on behalf of short-term objectives concerned with undercutting opposi-tion forces at home that were deriving support from their counterparts in the other republic.

Nevertheless, a reconfiguration of the political space in the northeastern Caucasus was gradually occurring between these two poles. At one end were the officials of Chechnya and Dagestan facing, at the other end, all of those forces, in both republics, who found themselves, for whatever reason, in opposition to their respective political establishments. Thus, whereas there had once been a vertical political division separating Chechnya from Dagestan along the border that runs between them, the political space was reconfigured in an increasingly horizontal manner. New linkages across the top were connecting political establishments in the two republics, while new linkages on the bottom were increasingly connecting a motley array of opposition forces.

As time passed, the authorities in both republics grew weaker while opposition elements throughout the Northeast Caucasus grew stronger. This was because the cooperation between Grozny and Makhachkala evoked retaliatory escalations on the parts of their opponents. As their struggle intensified, public opinion shifted increasingly toward the opposition in keeping with the traditional regional (and Russian) tendency to favor underdogs and outsiders.

Moreover, by means of their association the authorities of each republic risked the decline of their popular legitimacy since their respective constituents grew concerned that each would acquire the weaknesses peculiar to the other. Thus, to their coordinated efforts, Grozny brought a reputation for its failure to control its opposition, which was never one of Makhachkala's problems, while Makhachkala contributed its tradition of undeviating loyalty to the unpopular Moscow regime, which was not among Grozny's faults.

Thus, as ordinary Dagestanis watched their government growing closer to Grozny, they worried that Dagestan might be drawn deeper into the Chechen maelstrom. At the same time, ordinary Chechens were alarmed to think that Grozny's new ties to Makhachkala meant that it was only one step away from capitulation to Moscow. Whereas the growing cooperation between officials in the two republics was intended to weaken their respective oppositions, it had the unforeseen effect of undermining the support of their own constituencies.

At the same time, opposition forces grew stronger in the face of the growing pressure that was being placed upon them. Growing cooperation among the authorities provided both a focus for resistance, and an incentive for coordination among disparate opposition leaders on both sides of the border, including field commanders in Chechnya and disgraced ethnoparty elites in Dagestan.

As economies in the two republics declined through deepening poverty, growing unemployment, and concentration of capital, both republics were controlled by increasingly smaller circles, while growing desperation among populations on either side of the border prepared ordinary people in the republics to welcome any dislocation that might serve to change their lives.

Thus, whereas political power in both Dagestan and Chechnya is traditionally pluralistic, there began to emerge a sharply bipolar power structure, divided, in both republics, between regimes that were relatively conciliatory in their approach to Moscow and an opposition that turned increasingly toward political Islam in an effort to acquire legitimacy. This polarity could not be regarded as stable. Due to the deepening economic and political crises in both republics, and the deteriorating material resources of most people in the region, a growing variety of opposition groups gradually attracted more adherents.

As tension mounted, leaders of the opposition openly made personal threats against Dagestan's highest officials. Dagestani authorities clearly realized the growing danger in the republic, and official statements expressed concern about cooperation between opposition forces in Chechnya and Dagestan. Yet no precautionary measures were taken, and it appeared that no one knew what to do.

When it came, the war provided a swift, if also Draconian, solution to these problems. Relations between Makhachkala and Grozny were terminated. Dagestan's Wahhabis were defeated and Chechen militants were driven back by federal forces. Moscow abandoned the Khasaviurt Agreement between Russia and Chechnya, signed by General Alexander Lebed and Colonel Aslan Maskhadov in August 1996, and federal troops drove a wedge between the two republics. Dagestani officials were no longer threatened by the Chechen maelstrom into which they had been dragged by official cooperation between their capitals as well as by the combination of opposition forces in both republics. In this way, the war led to improvements in another problem that had seemed all but intractable only a few months before.

Claims of the Chechen-Akkins in Novolakskii Raion

The conflict also altered, if not fully alleviated, another complex problem involving territorial claims by the Chechen-Akkins (aka Aukhovs) of the Novolakskii (Aukhovskii) raion. The problem began in February 1944 when the Chechen population was brutally deported to Kazakhstan. In March of that year, entire villages of Dagestani highlanders, particularly Laks and Avars, were forcibly and hastily relocated to formerly Chechen villages and homes in order to occupy the land before spring agricultural work began.

Ironically, the Aukhovskii raion of Dagestan where the mountain Laks were moved was formed, in response to the Aukhov's desire to have a separate raion for themselves only two weeks before the Aukhovs were deported.[15] Immediately after deportation, Aukhovskii raion was abolished. One part of it with two large Chechen villages (Aktash-aukh, now Leninaul, and Yurt-aukh, now Kalininaul) was added to the neighboring Kazbekovskii raion, and was populated with Avars from the mountains. The rest of the Aukhovskii raion was renamed Novolakskii raion and was populated by highland Laks.

During the forcible relocation to this new territory, the Laks endured considerable hardship and repression. Until 1957 they did not make great efforts to settle in the new land, but rather remained painfully aware that they lived in the homes of others, that they cultivated fields that did not belong to them, and that the rightful owners remained alive.

In 1957, Nikita Khrushchev undertook a rehabilitation of repressed nations, including the Chechens. As Chechen-Akkins began to return to Dagestan from exile their housing became a central issue. At the same time, the Checheno-Ingushetia Autonomous Republic was restored (with modifications), and the highland Dagestanis who had been moved to the lands of this republic were returned to their old lands or to new lands on the plains of Dagestan. A decision was made that Laks and Avars who were moved to the Aukhovskii raion should stay there, and that Chechen-Akkins should get free land for housing in Khasaviurtovskii raion, neighboring their previous location in Aukh. At that time, this seemed a just resolution that would avoid territorial disputes between Laks and Avars, on the one hand, and Chechen-Akkins on the other. Following this accommodation, the Avars and Laks of the Novolakskii raion considered that they inhabited their own land, and the latter finally settled in, as they had not done before.

However, with perestroika in 1987–88, the Chechen-Akkins began to express their dissatisfaction at the loss of their primordial land. They set up pickets in front of government offices in Makhachkala and circulated petitions demanding the restoration of their "historic motherland." Yet they also wished to retain the new land that they acquired in Khasaviurtovskii raion after their return from exile.

In the early years of perestroika, mass protests made a deep impression upon the general public, as well as upon government officials, because they were unthinkable and unseen during the communist regime.[16] When Chechen-Akkins began to arrive from the Khasaviurtovskii raion, their assemblies in Makhachkala's central square were the first public expressions of dissatisfaction, and therefore had a resounding effect upon officials, who sought to pacify the protesters by any means available.

As a result, the Chechen-Akkins managed to secure the lands in Khasaviurtovskii raion, where they had been living for the preceding thirty years, while obtaining a guarantee that they would also be restored to their old territories, which had been populated for the past forty-four years by farming families of Lak and Avar ethnicities. Yet when this decision was made, it had not thus far been realized that problems no longer could be solved in the old Soviet style of either suppressing all concerned or ruthlessly resettling entire nations regardless of the suffering that would result. As the realities of post-Soviet life were gradually understood, it became clear that this decision has solved nothing while creating new problems.

These new problems began to appear as this victory of the Chechen-Akkins spawned a cascade of national movements, each one aiming to defend the interests of one of Dagestan's numerous ethnic groups against claims being made by newly formed organizations of other ethnic groups. As the situation in the Soviet Union began to spin out of control, ethnopolitical relations in Dagestan sank into a self-perpetuating maelstrom of increasingly complex problems.

In February 1989, the chairman of Dagestan's Cabinet of Ministers, a Kumyk named Abdurazak Mirzabekov, became the head of a newly formed committee charged with resolving the problem of the Chechen-Akkins. Predictably, the committee displayed the old Soviet mentality in its attempt to impose a solution. Yet, by that time, the Avar population of the raion had organized and was replicating the confrontational tactics of the Chechen-Akkins with equal efficacy on behalf of their commitment to remain in their homes. It was at this time that a Gadzhi Makhachev emerged as an effective agitator for Avar interests in the Kazbekovskii raion. Makhachev participated in the formation of the Avar national organization, the Imam Shamil Front, and quickly gravitated toward its leadership. Meanwhile, the Laks struck a more conciliatory posture that suggested they might agree to move under the right conditions.

Shortly thereafter, the political elite of the republic lost political support from the disintegrating Moscow regime, and the Dagestani government ceased to function monolithically. Since the Soviet central authority could no longer serve as the foundation for Dagestani politics, local leaders were forced to seek local political bases. Each leader started to play his own political game, seeking support at the roots of Dagestan's traditional social structure and among the newly emerging social organizations. As Dagestan's established political leaders turned to the newly formed ethnic organizations for support, the influence and prestige of the latter was dramatically enhanced. Thus, a local framework for Dagestani politics was reconstructed along ethnic lines. Yet these emergent ethnic structures were at least as much products of Soviet ethnic policies and contemporary political exigencies as they were of ancient social traditions.

Amid this confusion of crumbling and congealing political powers, consideration was given to the following possible solutions to the growing confrontation among groups representing Avars, Chechen-Akkins, and Laks:

1. *Conduct a reciprocal exchange of villages of the Novolakskii raion, plus Leninaul and Kalininaul of the Kazbekovskii raion, on the one hand, with*

Chechen-Akkin villages of the Khasaviurtovskii raion, on the other. This scenario was rejected by the Chechen-Akkins who insisted on retaining their new villages while also acquiring their old land.

2. *Sponsor the migration of Laks from Novolakskii raion to unpopulated land between Makhachkala and* Kaspiysk, *where a new town would be constructed for 6,000–7,000 people.* This approach was rejected by the Laks, at least in part, because the area is semiarid and unattractive, and because its suburban setting would likely prove unsuitable for agricultural purposes.

3. *Sponsor a return of the Laks to their "primordial" mountain territory.* This was also rejected by the Laks because their old villages had deteriorated through forty-five years of neglect, they were without electricity and other infrastructural development, and they were located far from population centers in rugged, nonarable terrain.

4. *Sponsor a migration of the Laks to land northeast of Makhachkala. There seven to eight villages would be constructed in a new "Novolakskii raion" to be formed from land to be taken from Lakskii, Gunibskii, and Sovetskii raions, along with land belonging to the Dagestan Scientific-Agricultural Institute, and the Makhachkala Forestry Center, which operates as a government-sponsored nursery for purposes of reforestation.* The proposal was accepted by the Laks.

At the time when this decision was made it was clear to all concerned that the republic lacked the funds to put it into effect, and that the solution therefore depended upon the highly unreliable federal budget. Yet a practical solution to the problem was among the least of the government's concerns. At best, political leaders were merely attempting to prevent an intractable problem from spiraling out of control. More often, political leaders were attempting to play these new political pressures to their personal advantage.

Since the Chechen movement was strongest at that point, the "solution" was skewed in its favor. Such an approach to decision making was itself an entirely new phenomenon, which demonstrated that a new political order had emerged in Dagestan. At the end of the 1980s and during the beginning of the 1990s, interethnic problems gave rise to ethnic organizations, which further complicated ethnic problems and produced ethnic clashes. This was precisely the development that followed in the problem of the Chechen-Akkins.

In the Novolakskii raion, clashes began between Lak and Chechen youths were followed by clashes between Chechens and Avars, who refused to move anywhere. Kumyks organized their own national movement, "Berlik," and began to protest that Laks would be resettled into their traditional territory.

Mountain villages that traditionally moved their livestock to certain pasture-lands in the plain north of Makhachkala refused to give up their grazing rights for purposes of Lak relocation. The process snowballed through a chain of ethnic disputes and the consequent organization of one ethnic movement after another. Chechen, Kumyk, and Avar ethnic organizations were followed by that of the Nogais, Laks, Lezgins, and so on. Soon these national organizations achieved official status, with recognizable leaders who began to climb the republics newly reconstructed political ladder. The consequent formulation of new concepts of ethnic interest preceded lists of grievances and demands.

In April 1991, Moscow accepted a law "On the Rehabilitation of Repressed Nations," ensuring the rights of Chechens and similar groups to return to their traditional lands. This law only served to aggravate the situation in Dagestan. Dagestani officials insisted on the application of a second federal law "On Deported Nations." The latter was intended to ease the adjustment of territorial claims through a more balanced consideration of counterclaims by groups, such as Avars and Laks, that had been relocated onto the land of the deported groups. However, this was not to be. Confrontations in Novolakskii and Khasaviurtskii raions intensified.

The Third Congress of National Representatives of Dagestan opened on May 12, 1991. At the same time, there were large-scale clashes between Avars and Chechens in the Kazbekovskii raion. The Congress was interrupted and a state of emergency was declared. Shortly thereafter a complex crisis ensued, during which a clash between thousands of Avars and Kumyks was narrowly averted.[17] Hence, it was not until June 23, 1991, that the Third Congress was reconvened and practical approaches to the Chechen-Akkin problem were discussed. It was decided that the Aukhovskii raion would be restored, though without the land that was apportioned to the Kazbekovskii raion in 1944, and that the Laks of Novolakskii raion would be moved to the land north of Makhachkala, where a new Novolakskii raion would be established.

Yet this decision was also problematic. In Novolakskii raion, the Laks lived on 25,000 hectares of good land. Following the decision of the Congress, they were expected to move to an area of 8,300 hectares of semiarid land, where few shrubs or trees were growing. Officially, 76 percent of this territory consisted of "salty soil," chiefly used as winter pastures for mountain livestock. Only 8 percent of the land could be used for crops.

At the time, it was expected that the relocation would require five years, with scheduled completion in 1996, and would involve the relocation of 3,300 farms with a population of more than 10,000 people. However, in the intervening years the number of prospective migrants increased as children reached maturity and began families of their own. Thus, by the beginning of 1999, the project had expanded to include the relocation of 4,000 farms.

During these same eight intervening years, new Lak families were unable to get land to build new homes.

Moreover, decisions of the Third Congress created further discontent among the lowland Kumyk-Tarkin population that previously claimed the land ceded to the Laks, as well as among the mountain villagers that traditionally used the winter pastures. Conflict was avoided through the establishment of a new Kumtorkalinskii raion near Makhachkala with a predominantly Kumyk population. Members of the Kumyk elite were guaranteed seats in the National Assembly.

The Novostroi construction company was formed to erect the new villages for the residents scheduled to move from Novolakskii raion. However, construction moved slowly due to shortages of funds and materials as well as because of corruption, and relocation was postponed. Yet even with all of these practical problems, the resolution of the Aukhovskii problem "in principle" had a stabilizing effect upon the situation in the Novolakskii raion.

The problem was pushed further to the side by the war in Chechnya from 1994 to 1996. At the time, Dagestanis tended to sympathize with the Chechens in their struggle with Russian troops. More than 130,000 Chechen refugees were accommodated by Dagestanis, frequently in their homes, including the homes of Laks in the Novolakskii raion. When the first Russo-Chechen conflict ended with the Khasaviurt Agreement in August 1996, the ethnopolitical situation in Dagestan was further aggravated. On the one hand, the Chechen victory had a considerable moral and political impact upon the Dagestani border population, among whom the Moscow regime lost all authority. On the other hand, constant conflicts, occurring almost daily, along the border of Dagestan and Chechnya increased anti-Chechen sentiments in Dagestan.

A considerable part of the problem arose from the fact that, after the war, many Chechen leaders believed that the restored Aukhovskii raion eventually should be annexed by the Chechen Republic. They considered that it had been "unjustly added" to Dagestan during the division of the Gorski and Dagestani republics in 1920.[18]

Chechen claims on Novolakskii raion were bolstered by a rapid increase in the Chechen population of the raion, which also contributed to Dagestani fears. At the beginning of the first Russo-Chechen conflict, in 1994, there were 62,000 Chechens in Novolakskii raion. Two years later, at the end of the conflict, there were 92,000. The situation was comparable in the formerly Chechen areas of Kazbekovskii raion (in Leninaul and Kalininaul), where the Chechen population also increased rapidly during the 1990s. Thus, by July 1999, problems in the Novolakskii raion were far from resolution, and tensions were rapidly increasing.

This situation was altered dramatically by events of August and September 1999. Along with the destruction of infrastructure, homes, and personal property, the militants who invaded Novolakskii raion from across the Chechen border robbed the local population and murdered some of them as their wives and children watched. In some cases, they did so with the help of local Chechen-Akkins, who placed ethnicity above any ties that they might have had to their neighbors in Novolakskii raion. The Chechens and their Wahhabi confederates were fiercely resisted by local Laks and many other Dagestanis, who came from throughout the republic to join the battle for the "liberation" of Novolakskii raion from the militants. In Kazbekovskii raion, well-armed contingents of local Avars managed to repel the invaders and to exert control over the Chechen-Akkin population.

As a result of these events there was a dramatic shift in Dagestani attitudes toward the Chechen-Akkins. The Laks asserted that Chechen rights to Novolakskii raion were forfeit. In the view of the Laks, they had now purchased the land with their blood. Powerful Lak leaders, such as Arsen Kamaev (deputy chairman of the National Assembly) and Magomed Ilyasov (chairman of the Central Bank of Russia in Dagestan) argued against a change in the resolutions of the Third Congress. Yet, at the time, there was little public support for this view.

Ironically, the new village being constructed near Makhachkala to satisfy demands of the Chechen-Akkins was used to shelter refugees from Novolakskii raion, who were almost entirely women and children. Local Chechen-Akkins, who were once better armed than their Lak and Avar neighbors, were entirely disarmed. Those Chechen-Akkin leaders who were neither in hiding nor in prison were compelled to affirm their loyalty to Dagestani law. The local Chechen population was diminished, as all Chechens without legal residence were deported from all of Dagestan's raions along the Chechen border. By agreement between Makhachkala and Moscow, Chechen refugees from the second Russo-Chechen conflict, which followed from the invasion of Dagestan and the apartment block explosions, were initially restricted from entering Dagestan.

Thus, once again, a seemingly intractable situation was altered by the conflict. The problem, in this case, had been deeply divisive for nearly fifty years and was rapidly growing worse up to the summer of 1999. The advantage that the Chechen-Akkins gained by being first to organize around ethnic grievances, and thereafter by exploiting confrontational tactics to manipulate an enfeebled political system, was lost to a dramatic moral shift along the Chechen border. By the end of September 1999, Lak and Avar grievances moved to the forefront, and Chechen-Akkins had lost moral footing for their claims.

Official Recognition of the DUMD

In addition to improving difficult situations and altering complex problems, the conflict in Dagestan also gave rise to other political developments that would later become problematic. Some of these developments were, in effect, aspects of an ethnic Avar backlash to the newly consolidated power of the Dargins in Makhachkala under Magomedali Magomedov and Makhachkala mayor, Said Amirov. This Avar backlash involved both official recognition of the Avar-controlled DUMD and the rise of Dagestan's Northern Alliance.

The conflict completely discredited Dagestan's Wahhabi movement. During the war, the National Assembly bowed to pressure from the DUMD and the Sufi tariqah, and urgently prepared legislation prohibiting Wahhabism in Dagestan. It gained considerable momentum in this regard from an Avar, named Surakat Asiyatilov. Asiyatilov was, at once, leader of the Islamic Party in Dagestan and head of the Assembly Committee on Civil and Religious Organizations and Affairs. He was strongly committed to the DUMD.

On September 16, the day the war ended, and after only one reading, the fourth session of the People's Assembly unanimously passed the law "On the Prohibition of Wahhabite and Other Extremist Activity on the Territory of the Republic of Dagestan." Generally, the law was not unique, as many of its restrictions were previously contained in the law "On Religious Organizations," which already carried prohibitions on extremism. However, it involved certain novelties.

First, the law specifically outlawed Wahhabism, a loose religious movement that did not necessarily involve extremism, especially of a political sort. Yet the law did not specify how, and by whom, it would be determined what would, and what would not, count as Wahhabism. The law did, however, designate the DUMD as the dominant Islamic spiritual organization in Dagestan. In effect, the law transformed the DUMD into a state organ for the regulation of religious affairs for Dagestan's Sunni Muslims.

The law contained seven articles. The first article reiterated existing restrictions on extremist activity and specifically added prohibitions on Wahhabism. The second article effectively established a "republican religious organization." It stated that the education of Dagestani citizens at religious universities outside of Dagestan and Russia is "allowed only under the direction of an organization for the administration of the republic's religious matters in conjunction with the State Organization for Religious Affairs of the Republic of Dagestan." No one in Dagestan doubted that the "organization for the administration of republican religious matters" was the DUMD. Thus, the law identified an ex-officio religious organization that would cooperate with the state in religious affairs. Through this organization the government could intervene directly in religious matters. At the same time, the law converted a religious nongovernmental organization into an organ of state control over the Islamic population. Since the DUMD would be able to oversee all Islamic education, whether domestic or international, the spiritual education available to those nine out of ten Dagestanis of Muslim heritage would be administered, at least in principle, by the government. This became explicit in the third article, which stated that "education in the republic's spiritual institutions must be conducted according to educational programs approved by the administrative organ of the republic's religious organization."

The fourth article required that all religious organizations in the territory of Dagestan "are subject to reregistration within a period of three months from the enactment of the law." Moreover, the same article required that the registration of religious organizations must be conducted by the Dagestani Ministry of Justice only with prior ("expert") approval from the "republic's religious organization," that is, the DUMD. The fifth article stated that those who violate articles 1–4 of the law, "if their actions do not involve an application of the criminal law, will be brought under administrative authority in the form of imprisonment for fifteen days or a fine from 100 to 500 times the minimum wage" (thereby adjusting penalties automatically for inflation). Hence, a Dagestani who committed no crime other than failure to submit to the DUMD could be punished by incarceration or a steep fine. The sixth article stated that the law was to be administered "according to the Codex of the Russian Federation on administrative offenses." Protocols for these "administrative" cases were usually compiled by administrators in villages, towns, cities, and militia units. For "timely and efficient preparation of the paperwork," the seventh article required that "expert councils be created within local administrations composed of local officials and representatives of the local religious organization," again the DUMD.

Thus, the law established an official religious organization with specified duties, sanctions, and connections with the governments of the republic and the localities. Essentially, it required that the DUMD create an internal organizational hierarchy, ironically reminiscent of the communist party, albeit without the ubiquity of the latter. Previously, the DUMD cooperated with Dagestan's political establishment. Its internal structure more or less paralleled that of the emergent political system, at least insofar as both were based in the djamaats. Previously, however, the government, while tending to favor the Islamic traditionalists, had sought to maintain a posture of neutrality on religious issues and had been reluctant to intervene in religious affairs.

All of this changed in September 1999. With the Mufti at its head, the DUMD began to monitor the "correctness" of Islamic spiritual life. "Incorrectness" with regard to issues such as domestic instruction or study abroad was rectified through government organs of enforcement, adjudication, and punishment. Ironically, the law inclined slightly toward an establishment of a kind of "Islamic republic," a concept strenuously resisted, in their struggle with the Wahhabis, by the vast majority of Dagestanis, and particularly by the authors of this law.

Given the traditional fervency of religious confession in Dagestan, given that different ethnicities tended to take different approaches to Islam, and given that differences in religious attitudes also distinguished urban and rural Dagestanis, the centralized regulation of faith, and especially of spiritual instruction, inevitably generated additional arenas of ethnopolitical cleavage, while also contributing to greater political alienation. Indeed, the DUMD soon came to be dominated by leaders connected with Avar tariqah orders associated particularly with Gunibskii raion.

Dagestan's "Northern Alliance"

Following the invasions of 1999, the "Northern Region" of Dagestan began to take on a more prominent political role. The region contains Nogaiskii, Kizliarskii, Babaiurtovskii, Khasaviurtovskii, Kiziliurtovskii, and Kazbekovskii raions, including cities such as Kizliar, Kiziliurt, Khasaviurt, and Yuzhnosukhokumsk. These areas are inhabited by many Avar highlanders who have migrated to the plains, often due to economic considerations. In these industrially developed regions of the republic, Avar ethnoparties played a significant role, and, following the incursions of 1999, consolidated their political opposition to the Dargin-led government in Makhachkala.

The war in Dagestan did much to legitimize private militias, which were quickly organized to defend the republic, but not so quickly disbanded. The fighting that began in the high mountains of Avaria provoked an especially powerful response among Avar migrants to the northern plains. The volunteer militias that they created played an important role in the August conflict in Tsumadinskii and Botlikhskii raions. Later, in September, when Chechen militants invaded the Novolakskii and Kazbekovskii raions to the north, the factor of "the Northern Territories" became especially important. Particularly prominent was the role played by the chief administrator—Saigidpasha Umakhanov—in charge Khasaviurtovskii raion, the largest and strategically most important raion of the region.

In the face of a surprise attack and widespread disruption, Umakhanov managed, not only to secure order in his own raion, in which Chechens are the most numerous ethnic group, but also to provide significant assistance to the people of Novolakskii and Kazbekovskii raions in "repulsing Chechen aggression." He also deported all Chechens residing illegally in his raion, and refused to grant refuge to Chechens fleeing the subsequent conflict in Chechnya.

Yet perhaps the most remarkable indication of Umakhanov's growing influence was an event that occurred, or rather failed to occur, on September 29, 1999. On that day, Magomedali Magomedov was supposed to meet, upon request of Prime Minister Putin, with Chechen president Aslan Maskhadov in the Dagestani border town of Khasaviurt. However, the meeting was prevented, evidently, by order of Umakhanov. Large groups of armed volunteers prevented Magomedov from entering the city. At the same time, Maskhadov's motorcade was stopped on the opposite side of town at the Gherzelsky Bridge. The incident demonstrated that, at least in his own region, Umakhanov had grown strong enough to defy the chief executives of Chechnya, Dagestan, and the Russian Federation in a single blow.

7

Russian Recentralization and Islamic Resistance

Stepping on the Same Rake

Following the military operations of August and September 1999, there was increasing federal intervention into Dagestani affairs. This contrasts sharply with the transitional period that followed the collapse of the Soviet Union, when there was minimal central influence upon events in the republic. Indeed there were times in the earlier period when it seemed that the influence and authority of the Azerbaijani leader, Geydar Aliev, was stronger than that of Russian president Boris Yeltsin.

The political latitude of this period is reflected in the constitution that Dagestan adopted in 1994. While Dagestan's unique political institutions were subject to some serious problems from the start, and while these institutions differed dramatically from those of any other Russian region, from those of the federation as a whole, and indeed from those of any other part of the world, they nevertheless proved to be both effective and resilient in managing and avoiding conflicts among its thirty-four ethnolinguistic groups.

However, beginning with efforts by the Kremlin to recentralize the Russian political system, these same distinctively Dagestani institutions became the focus of judicial and executive pressures applied upon Dagestani officials from the federal center. While the Kremlin demanded direct alterations of Dagestan's constitution, Dagestan's collegial executive and its ethnic electoral districts were challenged in Russia's Constitutional Court, and Dagestani officials perceived Moscow as signaling the modification of Dagestan's entire political structure.

Dagestan's democratic system was the result of a complex political evolution that had extended informally over centuries in response to constant power clashes and manifold counterbalancing forces that remained a part of Dagestan's political culture and that could not be readily eliminated from the political scene. Since Moscow could not hope to modify the localized internal pressures that produced this system and that had been successfully channeled within it, externally imposed modifications might have appeared to be counterproductive. Yet, beginning with the economic sphere, the federal center precipitously increased its control from 2000 on. Genuine federal principles were replaced by centralized, sometimes authoritarian, means of control, illustrated by the seven new federal districts patterned upon the top-down organization of the Russian military.

President Vladimir Putin had considerable support in Dagestan, and many ordinary Dagestanis welcomed external control with the hope that it would be sufficiently comprehensive and consistent to root out political corruption, institute the rule of law, and stimulate economic development. Yet in the absence of thoroughgoing improvements, an unceremonious, arbitrary, and partial alteration of political structures, including a cancellation of ethnic electoral districts and the forced implementation of a presidential system, had a destabilizing effect.

These elements of recentralization were of particular concern, not only because they eliminated features of the political system that provided for representation and proportionality but also because they occurred in concert with the contraction of Dagestan's local political elite. As late as 1998, Dagestani politics were controlled by approximately 200 families. Less than a decade later, the circle of genuine decision makers excluded all but members of five to ten families. The rapid contraction of elite circles created considerable insecurity and tension among Dagestan's leaders, as reflected in pernicious innuendo and incidents of intraelite violence.[1]

The scope of the recentralization effort was indicated shortly after Vladimir Putin's election to the Russian presidency in March 2000. That May, Russian officials announced the creation of seven Federal Districts. Under this new system Dagestan fell into the Southern Federal District, which was initially headed by General Viktor Kazantsev (from May 18, 2000 to March 9, 2004). General Kazantsev led the federal military response to the invasions of Dagestan in 1999, and was a participant in both Chechen wars. Later, in 2004, the Southern District was briefly headed by Vladimir Yakovlev (March 9 to September 13).

Initially the district was called "Northern Caucasian," but the name was changed at the request of General Kazantsev. Ostensibly, the name was altered to reflect the fact that in addition to traditionally North Caucasian republics (Dagestan, Chechnya, Ingushetia, North Ossetia, Kabardino-Balkaria, Karachai-Cherkessia, and Adygea), other southern Russian areas, such as Krasnodar and Stavropol krais, the Rostovskaya oblast and two other territories were also included. Indeed, Rostov was the administrative capital of the district.

However, the altered name also indicates an altered geopolitical orientation wherein Moscow serves as the point of reference. Thus the district may be north of the main range of the Caucasus mountains, but, more important, it is also south of Moscow. Analogously, the recent modification of some names in the region has reflected geostrategic changes following the collapse of the Soviet Union. Thus, the Moscow-oriented "Transcaucasus" has become the "South Caucasus," invoking Russia's separation from the region.

Dagestan's Ethnic Electoral Districts in the Russian Constitutional Court

The process of centralization arrived in Dagestan in the spring of 2000 by way of two ostensibly unrelated events. Federal officials initially requested that the attorney general of Dagestan, Imam Yaraliev, identify all articles of the Dagestani Constitution that did not match the Constitution of the Russian Federation. In early May 2000, Yaraliev appealed to the Constitutional Court of the Russian Federation to grant dispensation concerning disparities in many articles of the Dagestani Constitution with respect to its federal counterpart.

Yet before the court could rule on Yaraliev's appeal it had already begun to hear another case springing from an incident that occurred two years earlier in Dagestan's capital, Makhachkala. The latter case, which the court addressed on May 16, 2000, was filed by Isalmagomed Nabiev, the chairman of the Independent Trade Union of Entrepreneurs and Truck Drivers of Dagestan, who challenged the institution of ethnic electoral districts in the selection of local councils and the People's Assembly of Dagestan. Nabiev's challenge began in the Makhachkala City Council race of April 1998. Nabiev wished to stand for election in the district of his residence. In his complaint to the Constitutional Court of the Russian Federation, Nabiev wrote:

> On April 27, 1998, the Electoral Committee of Makhachkala denied my registration as a candidate in the 13th District when I submitted my petition with the requisite signatures. The basis for the refusal was my ethnicity (I am an Avar and the 13th District is "Lezgin"), and the norms of law (articles 11 and 34, point 18 of "The Law on Election of Representatives of Local Administration") allowing establishment of ethnoterritorial districts and prohibiting registration of candidates of other ethnic groups.[2]

Nabiev asserted that "the norms of the aforesaid articles contradict the Constitution of the Russian Federation and violate my electoral rights." Then he quoted his rights within the Constitution of the Russian Federation and added: "I am told that my rights are not violated, but only limited. I am told that I can be elected, but not in the district I want, where I live, where residents know me and ask me to run, rather in a district where some officials would allow me.[3]"

Though Nabiev was contesting only the law on the election to local councils, it was widely understood that a decision on this case inevitably would determine the constitutionality of ethnic electoral districts for the People's Assembly.

The leadership of the republic insisted that without these restrictions the local councils would not retain their legitimacy. It seemed possible that an abolition of ethnic districts would have a destabilizing effect, and might result in ethnic conflict because it likely would lead to over-representation of the larger ethnic groups. Election campaigns could revert to struggles between ethnic leaders, and the electorate might divide along ethnic lines without considering other characteristics of the candidates.

Prior to his appeal to the Constitutional Court of the Russian Federation, Nabiev's petition was deflected by the Constitutional Court of Dagestan. The Dagestani court ruled that "the norms allowing the establishment of ethnoterritorial districts, and disallowing the registration of candidates other than those of designated ethnic groups, are not considered as unconstitutional."[4]

The court's arguments were as follows: "The number of ethnoterritorial districts cannot equal the total number of electoral districts. The goal of the ethnoterritorial districts is to secure the representation of all ethnic groups, especially smaller groups. According to the Constitution of the Republic of Dagestan (Article 72b, part 1), the protection of the rights of minorities is the mutual responsibility of both the federation and the subjects of the federation. There are federal laws and other legal norms addressing the cooperation of the federation and its subjects (Article 76, part 2 of the Constitution of the Russian Federation). Thus, the subjects of the federation have legitimate right to accept their own normative legal acts to protect the rights of their minorities.

According to Articles 1, 2, 4, and 5 of the Constitution of Dagestan, the principle of the equality of rights of the people of Dagestan is the basis ... of the constitutional order. Since other constitutional policies may not contradict the foundation of the constitutional order, the legislature must coordinate the guarantees of the equality of electoral rights of the citizens with the principle of the equality of rights of the nations of Dagestan. Therefore, some restrictions are not excluded in the event that they are applied with the sole purpose of guaranteeing the principle of the equality of rights of nations of Dagestan, and protection of the rights of ethnic minorities.[5] The restriction does not lead to a violation of the rights of citizens to be elected to the representative organs of local government in open districts and in the ethnoterritorial districts corresponding to their ethnicity.

This conclusion is consistent with Article 4 of the Framework Convention on Protection of Ethnic Minorities of February 1, 1995 (ratified by federal law on June 18, 1998), which obligated parties to take necessary measures to encourage actual and complete equity between members of smaller and larger ethnic groups in all areas of economic, social, political, and cultural life. According to Article 4 (part 2) of the Convention, the parties should take into account the special situation of people that belong to an ethnic minority. In light of this article, the measures taken are not considered as discriminatory (Article 4, part 3). Analogous norms are contained in several international laws. . . .

[T]he legal position of the Constitutional Court of the Republic of Dagestan on this case is based upon the law of the Republic of Dagestan of November 30, 1998, in part regarding the establishment of ethnoterritorial electoral districts.

The Dagestani court concluded that Dagestan's electoral laws are not in contradiction to its constitution.[6]

However, just before the session of the Constitutional Court of Russia on May 16, 2000, Dagestani officials were informed that the Court tended to concur with the plaintiff that Dagestan's ethnoterritorial electoral districts contradicted the Dagestani Constitution. Dagestani officials urgently submitted a petition to postpone the session of the Russian Court on the ground that the republic's leadership regarded it as crucial that they should be present at the session, but that the complexity of the situation in Dagestan at that time did not permit them to do so.[7] After a two-hour debate, the Russian Constitutional Court decided to accept the petition of the State Council and postponed the session.

Thereafter Dagestan leaders urgently worked to modify Dagestan's electoral law. They introduced changes that would establish multimember districts open to candidates from any ethnic group. Ballots would list the candidates in ethnic categories, and a designated number of candidates from each of these categories would be elected. It was intended that this arrangement should preserve the ethnic balance of Dagestan's representative organs.

However, the problems that arose from this plan were no less significant than those of the preceding arrangement. For example, it was possible that a candidate from one district would be elected with fewer votes than an unsuccessful candidate from the same ethnic group running in a different district. Courts would be likely to encounter difficulties in such cases, compounded by the fact that they would be considered after the fact. Moreover, the new Russian passports did not designate ethnicity (as did their Soviet predecessors), and there were laws supporting citizens who declined to state their ethnicity. What would happen if a citizen declined to state his ethnicity in the registration of his candidacy? Indeed, the new passports could also present problems for the original ethnic electoral system.

Nevertheless, these modifications were accepted in their first reading by the Dagestani Assembly, thereby permitting Nabiev to withdraw his complaint to the Russian Court. Nabiev also may have fallen under pressure to withdraw.

Constitutional Amendments

Meanwhile the attorney general of Dagestan, Imam Yaraliev, had appealed to the Constitutional Court of the Russian Federation in May 2000, seeking dispensation concerning disparities in several articles of the Dagestani Constitution with respect to its federal counterpart. Documents submitted by Yaraliev noted that the Federal Constitution was contradicted at forty-five points by twenty-five articles of its Dagestani counterpart.

Without waiting for a ruling from the court, the Dagestani People's Assembly began changing the Dagestani Constitution to bring it into line with that of the federation. Table 7.1 shows the amendments to the Dagestani Constitution passed after their first reading at a meeting of Dagestan's People's Assembly on June 22, 2000.

There are points of the Dagestani Constitution that could be changed in the People's Assembly by two-thirds vote, and there are other points that could be changed only by Dagestan's Constitutional Assembly. The points shown in Table 7.1 were amenable to alteration by the People's Assembly. Dagestani officials successfully evaded other constitutional alterations demanded by Moscow on the ground that the latter changes required a meeting of the Constitutional Assembly. Nevertheless, the changes that occurred are indicative of the republic's decreasing autonomy vis-à-vis the federation.

Ethnic Rights

Throughout the summer of 2000, Dagestani officials either acquiesced or offered only passive resistance to federal pressures for the reform of republican political structures. Yet by that autumn Dagestani officials were beginning to mount a legislative and administrative defense of their constitution. At a meeting on October 18, 2000, the State Council considered the adoption of the federal law "On Guaranteeing the Rights of Small Native Ethnic Groups of the Russian Federation." Under this law, the designation of any ethnic group as "small," in addition to the advantages it provided in resolving socioeconomic problems, guaranteed a representative quota within state institutions. It was customary to define a "small" ethnic group as one that had no more than 50,000 members. In Dagestan at that time, eight of the fourteen major ethnic groups exceeded this number. Thus, in 2000, the republic contained

Table 7.1

Amendments to the Dagestani Constitution Passed by the Dagestan's People's Assembly on June 22, 2000

Original text	Amended wording
1. Article 65, part 6. "Action of federal laws and other legal enactments of the Russian Federation contradicting the sovereign rights and interests of the Republic of Dagestan, **can be suspended in the territory of the Republic.** These enactments can be protested in the order established by the law."	1. "Federal laws and other legal enactments of the Russian Federation issued in infringement of part 3 of the present clauses, **can be protested when due hereunder.**" Article 65, part 3 of Dagestan's Constitution says: "Outside of limits of jurisdiction of the Russian Federation and joint jurisdiction with the Russian Federation, the Republic of Dagestan carries out its own legal regulation, including enactment of laws and other statutory acts."
2. Article 65, part 8. "Creation and activity of federal bodies in the territory of the Republic of Dagestan **is presupposed on the basis of agreements.**"	2. "Creation and activity of federal bodies in the territory of the Republic of Dagestan **is presupposed in the order established by law.**"
3. Article 66. "The Republic of Dagestan **is an independent participant** in international and external economic relations and connections, **enters relations** with other states, **concludes contracts,** exchanges representations, and **participates in the activities** of international organizations."	3. "The Republic of Dagestan **has the right** to establish international and foreign economic relations **according to the Constitution of the Russian Federation,** federal laws and the present Constitution, to participate within the limits of the competence of performance of international contracts of the Russian Federation, in the formation and realization of a foreign policy course of the country on questions regarding interests of the Republic of Dagestan."
4. Article 70. "The Republic of Dagestan reserves the right to change its state and legal status **on the basis of the will of the Dagestani people.**"	4. "The Status of the Republic of Dagestan **can be changed by a mutual consent of the Russian Federation and the Republic of Dagestan according to the federal constitutional law.**"

5. Article 75. "Deputies of the Dagestan People's Assembly possess legal immunity throughout their terms of office. They cannot be detained, arrested, subjected to a search, except for cases of detention on the scene of crime, and also are exempted from personal inspection, except for cases when it is stipulated by the law for the safety other people."

6. Article 81, part 1, no. 5. "Jurisdiction of the People's Assembly includes: . . . 5) appointment and dismissal of Judges of the Constitutional Court of the Republic of Dagestan, the Supreme Court of the Republic of Dagestan, the Supreme Arbitration Court of the Republic of Dagestan, Judges of the raion and municipal courts."

7. Article 91, part 4. "The State Council of the Republic of Dagestan: . . . 4) proposes for [approval by] the People's Assembly, candidates for positions of Judges of the Constitutional Court of the Republic of Dagestan, the Chairman and Judges of the Supreme Court of the Republic of Dagestan, the Chairman and Judges of Arbitration Court of the Republic of Dagestan, the Judges of raion and municipal courts, and the Public Prosecutor of the Republic of Dagestan."

8. Article 91, part 7. " appoints and dismisses after consultations with appropriate committees of the People's Assembly **the diplomatic** representatives of the Republic of Dagestan."

5. Second sentence: "They cannot be involved in criminal or administrative responsibility **imposed by judicial order**, nor detained, arrested, subjected to a search or interrogation **without the consent of the People's Assembly**, except for cases of detention at the scene of a crime, and also subjected to personal inspection, **except for cases when it is stipulated by the federal law** for the safety of other people. **The specified restrictions are not applied to actions of the deputies that are not connected with their official duties.**"

6. "Appointment and dismissal of judges of the Constitutional Court of the Republic of Dagestan, appointment of social judges [*mirovye sud'i*], **approval for an appointment** of judges of the Supreme Court of the Republic of Dagestan, the Supreme Arbitration Court of the Republic of Dagestan, judges of raion and municipal courts."

7. "The State Council proposes for [approval by] the People's Assembly candidates for the positions of the Judges of the Constitutional Court of the Republic of Dagestan, social judges [*mirovye sud'i*], and approves candidates for appointment of the Judges of the Supreme Court of the Republic of Dagestan, Arbitration Court of the Republic of Dagestan, raion and municipal courts, and proposes a candidate for the position of the Public Prosecutor of the Republic of Dagestan."

In part 7, to exclude the word "diplomatic."

(continued)

Table 7.1 (continued)

Original text	Amended wording
9. Article 91, part 13. **"carries out the pardon of the persons condemned by courts of the Republic of Dagestan."**	Part 13 to exclude.
10. Article 112, part 3. "establish the judicial system of the Republic of Dagestan, the Constitutional Court of the Republic of Dagestan, the Supreme Court of the Republic of Dagestan, Supreme Arbitration Court of the Republic of Dagestan, regional and municipal courts."	"The judicial system of the Republic of Dagestan is a component of the judicial system of the Russian Federation and includes the Constitutional Court of the Republic of Dagestan, the Supreme Court of the Republic of Dagestan, the Arbitration Court of the Republic of Dagestan, regional and municipal courts, and the social judges [*mirovye sud'i*]."
11. Article 113. "The Constitutional Court of the Republic of Dagestan is **the supreme judicial** body for the protection of the constitutional structure."	"The Constitutional Court of the Republic Dagestan is a **judicial** body for the protection of the constitutional structure."
12. Article 113, part 5, no. 2. The Constitutional Court of the Republic of Dagestan "draws conclusions about [i.e., is the final authority on] the conformity of the Constitution of the Republic of Dagestan to laws and statutory acts of the Russian Federation in questions concerning the joint operation of the Republic of Dagestan and the Russian Federation."	To exclude.

Note: Bold font indicates text showing relevant changes.

577,000 Avars, 333,000 Dargins, 268,000 Kumyks, 250,000 Lezgins, 150,000 Russians, 100,000 Laks, 95,000 Tabasarans, and 90,000 Azeris.

Nevertheless the State Council determined that all native ethnic groups in Dagestan were "small." This should not be dismissed as a disingenuous political maneuver, since Dagestan's ethnic electoral districts originated through efforts to avoid an outcome in which only Avars and Dargins had been elected and to ensure that the smaller groups were also represented. Thus, Dagestan's ethnic electoral practices were truly intended to protect the 35,000 Nogais, the 18,000 Tats, the 17,000 Rutuls, and the 16,000 Aguls. Indeed, they protected the 6,500 Tsakhurs who were given their own electoral district. Since the existing system represented the smaller groups, and since any other system could jeopardize that representation, the decision of the State Council was supported by a compelling argument. Russian Prime Minister Mikhail Kasyanov was informed of this decision in a letter that asked him to include all of Dagestan's titular ethnic groups in the federal registry of small ethnic groups.

Additionally, throughout November 2000, Dagestani representatives raised this issue in a series of parliamentary hearings in the State Duma. In earlier meetings, not attended by Dagestani representatives, the Duma determined to eliminate such districts in order to bring local legislation in line with federal norms. Yet, as of November, the chair of the People's Assembly of Dagestan Mukhu Aliev, Dagestan Duma deputy Sergei Reshulsky, head of the Dagestan State Assembly Judiciary Department Magomed Khalitov, and head of the republican electoral commission Siyabshak Shapiev began participating in the discussion.

At that time, Dagestan's State Council was the only collegial executive in the Russian Federation, and the only executive that was not chosen by direct election. Its fourteen members each represented one of Dagestan's principal, recognized ethnic groups: Aguls, Avars, Azeris, Chechen-Akkins, Dargins, Kumyks, Laks, Lezgins, Nogais, Rutuls, Russians, Tabasarans, Tats, and Tsakhurs. Because the State Council ostensibly provided representation for all, most Dagestanis favored this arrangement for its protection of the smaller ethnicities, and therefore thrice rejected referenda that would have established a presidential system. Hence, it was ironic that these arrangements were jeopardized by a federal law providing a "Guarantee of the Rights of Indigenous Small Ethnicities in the Russian Federation."

Enacted on April 30, 1999, the law obligated parties to take necessary measures to foster equity between members of smaller and larger ethnic groups in all areas of economic, social, political, and cultural life. This legislation was particularly significant for Dagestan given that its population comprised thirty-four ethnolinguistic groups, many of whom were subsisting in highland regions under conditions of near total economic collapse. Yet whereas this legislation was intended to assist such groups throughout the federation, the peculiarities of Dagestani society were such that the law effectively threatened viable institutions and established political processes upon which these groups depended.

The law defined "small ethnic groups" as those whose membership did not exceed 50,000. In Dagestan, only four ethnic groups officially met this definition: Aguls, Rutuls, Tsakhurs, and Tats. Yet other groups had bases for claiming on ethnocultural, and more important, on linguistic grounds that they qualified for consideration as "small ethnic groups."

For example, in addition to those "proper" Avars, who speak the Avar language, fourteen other linguistically independent ethnic groups were also considered administratively as "Avars." These groups, which tended to be compactly accommodated in high mountain villages, were as follows: (1) Andis, (2) Archins, (3) Akhvakhs, (4) Bagulals, (5) Bezhtins, (6) Botlikhs, (7) Ginukhs, (8) Godoberins, (9) Gunibs, (10) Didois, (11) Karatins, (12) Tindals, (13) Khvarshins, (14) Chamalals. Similarly, two small and linguistically distinct groups had been counted administratively as ethnic Dargins. These are: (15) Kubachins, (16) Kaitags.

Several of these groups, especially those living along Dagestan's rugged southwestern border, found themselves economically, politically, culturally, and infrastructurally isolated. Having lost the material benefits and ideological assurances of socialist society they were also entirely without the opportunities that had accompanied socioeconomic transition and sometimes lent encouragement to residents of Dagestan's larger towns. In the face of this plight, some of them also believed that they lacked adequate political representation since, in their eyes, they were not genuinely Avars or Dargins.

While their classification as such derived in part from traditional affiliations among ethnolinguistic groups, it also resulted from peculiarities of Soviet ethnography in the 1920s. On the one hand, the first fourteen of these groups were classified as Avars. On the other hand, Lezgins were distinguished administratively from Aguls, Rutuls, Tsakhurs, and Tabasarans, all of whom had traditional affiliations with Lezgins that resembled the affiliations between groups like the Andis and the Avars. Yet while Andis were counted as Avars, Aguls were distinguished from Lezgins.

The law of the Russian Federation "Guaranteeing the Rights of Small Minorities" aggravated nationalist sentiments among these Dagestani groups particularly because their recognition as independent ethnic groups would have entitled their leaders to seats in the cabinets of power. Hence, questions arose concerning changes in the number of seats in the State Council of the Republic of Dagestan and ethnic quotas in the legislative Assembly. For example, the law precipitated demands for an expansion of the State Council from fourteen ethnic representatives to include sixteen new representatives from Dagestan's smaller groups. Some of these demands were credible. For example, the Tsakhurs, who were represented in the State Council, had a population of 6,500, while the 30,000 Andis, who were classified as Avars, did not have a separate representative. Any consistent policy for the determination of independent ethnicity would have expanded the State Council to thirty members. Yet since exactly half of these would be representing groups that were previously regarded as Avars, and that did in fact have affiliations with Avars, Dagestan's other ethnic groups would find this result difficult to accept.

Many of these problems arose from the fact that the true ethnic structure of Dagestani society is constituted, not by ethnicities, but by those smaller structures known as djamaats. Historically, Dagestani djamaats were compact, densely populated, well-fortified hamlets that controlled their surrounding countryside. These separate "city-states" had their own distinctive civil laws, know as *djamaat adati*. In the nineteenth century there were approximately 350 to 400 djamaats.

The traditional "free societies," "principalities," and "khanates" that were described by Russians when they first arrived in the region were generally "molecular" aggregations of Dagestan's "atomic" sociopolitical units, or djamaats. In some cases, these unions among djamaats were voluntary, and in some cases they were forced. The form of local government often varied with the geography. In the mountains "federal republics" or "unions of free societies" were the norm, whereas the plains and foothills were often home to more authoritarian regimes.

Such traditional aggregations of djamaats could make credible claims for independent ethnic status. They display various degrees of linguistic differentiation, from dialects to genuinely separate languages. Additionally, the members of each occupy a compact, well-delineated territory. They share a common political history and distinctive cultural traditions of both a material and spiritual nature. Most important, they share an explicit identification with their society or community, which members retain even when they depart their djamaat for the life of the cities.

In light of these considerations, the law on small ethnicities appeared as a throwback to the traditionally minute, prerevolutionary fragmentation of Dagestani society. For instance, if, according to the law, djamaats of Rutuls and Tsakhurs were granted certain privileges, then what would be the reaction of their neighbors, living under corresponding circumstances in Lezgin, Lak, and Azeri djamaats? Though they lived in the same raion under similarly deprived highland conditions, the latter groups would not be extended the special privileges of small groups. If Andis and Botlikhs acquired the special cultural and economic privileges of small ethnic groups then what would happen in the neighboring Avar djamaats? Dagestan's 3,000 to 4,000 Tats, almost 90 percent of whom enjoyed the relative ease of Dagestan's urban areas, would be granted special privileges that would be denied to the 100,000 Laks, 28,000 of whom subsisted on the rocky and barren land of Lakskii and Kulinskii raions.

The legislation gave rise to numerous comparisons of a similar nature, all of which created problems for Dagestani society. If the law were to have gone into effect it would likely reorganize the ethnic self-identification of Dagestanis. Rather than the fourteen principal ethnic categories that serve as a basis for representation and proportionality in Dagestan's political institutions, and rather than the thirty-four Dagestani ethnic groups that are identified by ethnographers, there would be sixty or seventy djamaat-based ethnic identities.

Dagestani leaders recognized these problems early on and therefore actively objected to the law from the earliest stages of its preparation. Initially, the resistance of Dagestani representatives in the Russian State Duma appealed to the fact that such legislation was not applicable in the Caucasus, and could serve only to help Russia's northern ethnicities. At each successive reading in the Duma, Dagestani deputies tried to block the legislation by explaining the potentially disastrous implications for Dagestan.

From the beginning Moscow was cognizant of such concerns. On two occasions (August 25 and October 15, 1995), and with President Yeltsin's support, the Duma rejected a law on "The Basis of the Legal Status of Small Ethnicities of Russia." On each of these occasions, it was determined that certain articles of the proposed law failed to comply with the Constitution of the Russian Federation. A year later, on May 22, 1996, the State Duma accepted the law after the third reading. But on June 5, it was rejected again, this time by the Council of the Federation, ostensibly on the ground that it granted special privileges to small minorities, which effectively established ethnic discrimination, and thereby contradicted general rights that were guaranteed by the Federal Constitution. Dagestani leaders such as Magomedali Magomedov and Mukhu Aliev, who are members of the Council of the Federation, had worked behind the scenes to defeat the law.

Despite these difficulties, work on the law continued. The law was backed by members of the Committee on the North, a powerful and effective group that is generously supported by corporations interested in northern resources. On March 5, 1999, the State Duma finally accepted the law under the title of "Guarantees of Rights of Indigenous Small Ethnicities of the Russian Federation." On April 30, it was ratified by the Council of the Federation, and was signed by President Yeltsin with an attachment titled "The Comprehensive List of Indigenous Small Ethnicities of the Russian Federation." The law was intended to apply only to those ethnicities on this list.

The final version of the law recognized its implications for Dagestan. The first article of the law stated that "in view of Dagestan's unique ethnic diversity, and with regard to the number of ethnicities accommodated therein, the State Council of the Republic of Dagestan shall determine the quantitative requirements and other details of its indigenous small ethnicities as well as establish the list of such ethnicities for inclusion in the 'Comprehensive List of the Indigenous Small Ethnicities of the Russian Federation.'"

In light of this mandate, Dagestan's State Council issued an executive protocol on October 18, 2000, announcing the only policy that seemed viable under these circumstances. It established that the indigenous small ethnicities of Dagestan were Aguls, Avars, Azeris, Chechen-Akkins, Dargins, Kumyks, Laks, Lezgins, Nogais, Russians, Rutuls, Tats, Tabasarans, and Tsakhurs. In short, they were the same fourteen principal ethnicities that were represented by seats in the State Council and by ethnic electoral districts in the People's Assembly. This meant that the classification of the ethnicities was unchanged, and that the list of "the small ethnicities" included not only some of those with populations of less than 50,000 (such as Tats, Aguls, Tsakhurs, and Rutuls) but also those Dagestani ethnicities that had significantly greater populations (such as Avars, Dargins, Kumyks, Lezgins, Laks). Indeed the list included groups that defy classification as "small ethnicities" such as those Azeris, Chechens, and Russians who reside in Dagestan. In this way, the State Council exploited a loophole in the Federal law in order to preserve the republic's status quo and to avoid the potentially destabilizing inconsistencies and inequities that might have resulted from other interpretations of the law.

Yet this interpretation clearly involved inconsistencies of its own. The State Council had flagrantly violated quantitative restrictions on the determination of small ethnicities, and had not offered any sort of gesture toward the general spirit of the law. Moscow sought to achieve a compromise solution through the offices of the Institute of Ethnology and Anthropology of the Russian Academy of Sciences, under the leadership of Valery Tishkov. On the one hand, Tishkov insisted that Avars, Dargins, Kumyks, and Lezgins should be excluded from the list. Yet at the same time he accepted that relatively small ethnicities, such as Laks, Tabasarans, and Nogais, could be included, even though their populations exceed 50,000. Institute representatives were adamant that Russians should be excluded from the list because of the "total absurdity" of presenting them as a small, indigenous ethnicity. Yet they allowed that Dagestani Azeris and Dagestan's indigenous Chechen-Akkins could be included on the list "if they decide to declare themselves ethnic groups independent from other Azeris and Chechens."

Nevertheless, following numerous protests in Dagestan, and following

Magomedov's visit to Putin in the spring of 2001, Moscow finally accepted Dagestan's principal fourteen ethnic groups on the official list of small indigenous ethnicities. Through their sheer persistence, Dagestani officials successfully evaded central pressures that threatened to undermine their chief executive body. The fact that the threat was posed by a law intended to protect small indigenous ethnicities is a measure of the complexities posed by Dagestan's position in the Russian Federation.

Dagestan's National Assembly Election: March 16, 2003

Dagestan's third National Assembly was chosen on March 16, 2003, according to modified electoral procedures. The procedures according to which previous assemblies were selected in 1995 and 1999 were altered to conform to the federal constitution. In Moscow, liberal democratic norms of juridical thought could not be reconciled with mandatory ethnic representation.[8] Federal officials demanded an end to Dagestan's system of ethnic representation. Yet the realities of Dagestan's ethnic heterogeneity demanded that ethnicity play a genuine political role. Would it be possible to find a middle path between these opposing sets of demands, or would one be sacrificed for the sake of the other? Dagestani leaders worked with Moscow experts to develop a compromise solution for Dagestan's electoral system. This scheme was tested during Dagestan's election of its third National Assembly. Its essence was as follows.

In the highland electoral districts where residents were of a single ethnicity, the single-member districts were left unchanged. These accounted for 61 of the total 121 seats in the assembly. In the multiethnic localities of Dagestan's cities, lowlands, and some foothills, multimandate districts were introduced in a manner that allowed for ethnic considerations. For example, in the capital city of Makhachkala, five mandates were allotted to a central district, known as Leninskii raion. The ballot for this district included five separate lists, four of which were restricted to candidates of one specific ethnicity. These were candidates who were respectively Avar, Dargin, Kumyk, and Russian. The fifth seat for the district was declared a "free mandate," for which candidates of all ethnicities were able to register. Every multiethnic district had one "free" list, in which candidates of any ethnicity might compete.

Upon receiving this ballot, a voter had the right to select one candidate from any of these lists, but not one from each list. For example, a voter who chose a candidate from the Avar list could not select a candidate from any other list. The winners were the five candidates who received a majority of the votes, each on their own lists, whether ethnic or "free."

Those who devised this system hoped that it would preserve the ethnic proportionality of representation in the National Assembly, while at the same time relieving those problems that had led to "the restriction of the rights of citizens," when prospective candidates had been barred from running in specific districts. Under this scheme anyone could run in any district, whether on an appropriate ethnic list, on a "free" list, or in the highland districts, where there were no formal restrictions, but where ethnic homogeneity guaranteed a predictable result.

As a consequence of these new multimandate districts, only 83 electoral districts were established for the election of 121 Assembly representatives in the election on March 16, 2003. Of these, 61 were simple single-mandate districts, and 22 were multimandate districts, which included both ethnic lists and "free" lists. In all cases, the highland single-mandate districts produced the anticipated ethnic results, as illustrated in Table 7.2.

Since the results of the elections in these sixty-one districts were predictable, they allowed for the design of the ethnic mandates in the multiethnic regions and cities of the republic. Twelve two-mandate districts were formed, each of which had one ethnic and one "free" mandate (Table 7.3).

Seven regions were established as three-mandate districts. Each of these had two ethnic lists and one "free" list (Table 7.4).

In the capital of Dagestan, Makhachkala, there were, in addition to the three-mandate districts described in Table 7.3, three five-mandate districts, each of these featuring four ethnic lists and one "free" list (Table 7.5).

Analyses of this electoral scheme and its results indicated that it was possible to control the ethnicity of 99 out of 121 cases. This was because (1) there were sixty-one mandates open to all candidates, but located in monoethnic districts where the electoral outcome could be reliably predicted; (2) twelve two-mandate districts, each with twelve guaranteed ethnic representatives; (3) seven three-mandate districts with another fourteen guaranteed ethnic seats; and (4) three five-mandate districts with twelve ethnic mandates. These accounted for a total of ninety-nine mandates or 82 percent of the elected National Assembly representatives.

Besides these guaranteed ethnic quotas that were formally incorporated into the electoral scheme, there were also other informal, and in some respects, hidden mechanisms for the management of the electoral process with regard to ethnicity. In some regions, the ethnic content of the population allowed for predictions as to ethnicity of the representative chosen from the "free" mandate. For example, in the highland Rutulskii raion, a two-mandate district was established: one list for Tsakhurs and the other list "free." Yet because of the ethnic composition of the local population there were no doubts that this "free" seat would be filled by a Rutul, thereby completing the quotas for these two groups. Moreover, in the twenty-two multimandate districts with twenty-

Table 7.2

Monomandate Electoral Districts in Regions with Monoethnic Populations Guaranteed Election of Representatives with Each of These Ethnicities

No.	District	Guaranteed election of a representative of this ethnicity	No.	District	Guaranteed election of a representative of this ethnicity
1.	Agulskii	Agul	32.	Kurakhskii	Lezgin
2.	Akushinskii	Dargin	33.	Lakskii	Lak
3.	Muginskii (Akushinskii raion)	Dargin	34.	Levashinskii	Dargin
4.	Akhvakhskii	Avar	35.	Urminskii (Levashinskii raion)	Dargin
5.	Akhtynskii	Lezgin	36.	Tsudakharskii (Levashinskii raion)	Dargin
6.	Lutkunskii (Akhtynskii raion)	Lezgin	37.	Magaramkentskii	Lezgin
7.	Andiskii (Botlikhskii raion)	Avar	38.	Sovetskii (Magaramkentskii raion)	Lezgin
8.	Botlikhskii	Avar	39.	Samurskii (Magaramkentskii raion)	Lezgin
9.	Kazanishenskii (Buinakskii raion)	Kumyk	40.	Novolakskii	Lak
10.	Gergebilskii	Avar	41.	Tlyaratinskii	Avar
11.	Gumbetovskii	Avar	42.	Untsukulskii	Avar
12.	Gunibskii	Avar	43.	Zarechenskii (Khasaviurt City)	Chechen
13.	Chokhskii (Gunibskii raion)	Avar	44.	Kharakhinskii (Khunzakhskii raion)	Avar
14.	Dagogninskii	Azeri	45.	Kharakhinskii (Khunzakhskii raion)	Avar
15.	Kishinskii (Dakhadaevskii raion)	Dargin	46.	Khunzakhskii	Aar
16.	Urkarakhskii (Dakhadaevskii raion)	Dargin	47.	Tsumadinskii	Avar
17.	Dokuzparinskii	Lezgin	48.	Tsuntinskii	Avar
18.	Izberbashskii	Dargin	49.	Charodinskii	Aar
19.	Zavodskii (Izberbash raion)	Dargin	50.	Golotlinskii (Shamilskii raion)	Avar
20.	Guniyskii (Kazbekovskii raion)	Avar	51.	Hebinskii (Shamilskii raion)	Avar
21.	Dylymskii (Kazbekovskii raion)	Avar	52.	Yuzhnosukhokumskii	Avar
22.	Barshamaiskii (Kaitagskii raion)	Dargin	53.	Nogaiskii	Nogai
23.	Madzhalisskii (Kaitagskii raion)	Dargin	54.	Sergokalinskii	Dargin
24.	Gubdenskii (Karabudakhkentskii raion)	Dargin	55.	Urakhinskii (Sergokalinskii raion)	Dargin
25.	Kakashurinskii (Karabudakhkentskii raion)	Kumyk	56.	Gereikhanovskii (Suleiman-Stalskii raion)	Lezgin
26.	Karabudakhkentskii	Kumyk	57.	Kasumkentskii (Suleiman-Statskii raion)	Lezgin
27.	Stalskii (Kiziliurtovskii raion)	Avar	58.	Ortastalskii (Suleiman-Stalskii raion)	Lezgin
28.	Askerkhanovskii (Kiziliurtovskii raion)	Avar	59.	Ersinskii (Tabasaranskii raion)	Tabasaran
29.	Gamzat Tsadasa	Avar	60.	Tininskii (Tabasaranskii raion)	Tabasaran
30.	Kulinskii	Lak	61.	Hurinskii (Tabasaranskii raion)	Tabasaran
31.	Kumtorkalinskii	Kumyk			

Table 7.3

Two-Mandate (Ethnic and "Free") Electoral Districts of Dagestan in the Election of the National Assembly of Dagestan on March 16, 2003

No.	District	Guaranteed ethnic list	Ethnicity of candidates running on the "free" list
1.	Babaiurtovskii	Nogai	All Kumyks
2.	Khalimbekaulskii (Buinakskii raion)	Kumyk	1 Dargin, 2 Avars
3.	Hazarskii (Derbentskii raion)	Azeri	2 Lezgin, 1 Kumyk
4.	Terkemenskii (Derbentskii raion)	Kumyk	All Azeris
5.	Kaiakentskii	Dargin	1 Kumyk, 1 Azeri
6.	Primorskii (Derbent City)	Russian	All Lezgins
7.	Zubutli-Miatlinskii (Kiziliurtovskii)	Kumyk	All Chechens
8.	Rutulskii	Tsakhur	3 Rutuls, 1 Lezgin
9.	Tarumovskii	Russian	All Avars
10.	Aksaevskii (Khasaviurtovskii raion)	Kumyk	All Chechens
11.	Muzalaulskii (Khasaviurtovskii raion)	Avar	All Kumyks
12.	Bamatiurtovskii (Khasaviurtovskii raion)	Chechen	4 Avars, 1 Russian

Table 7.4

Three-Mandate Electoral Districts During Dagestan's Election of March 16, 2003

No.	District	Designated ethnic and "free" lists
1.	Derbentskii	1 Tabasaran, 1 Tat, 1 Free
2.	Kaspinskii	1 Lezgin, Russian, 1 Free
3.	Buinakskii	1 Dargin, 1 Kumyk, 1 Free
4.	Krainovskii (Kizliarskii raion)	2 Russian, 1 Free
5.	Kizliarskii	2 Russian, 1 Free
6.	Dagestanskii (Makhachkala City)	1 Dargin, 1 Lak, 1 Free
7.	Khasaviurtovskii (Khasaviurt City)	1 Chechen, 1 Kumyk, 1 Free

Table 7.5

Five-Mandate Electoral Districts During Dagestan's Election of March 16, 2003

No.	District	Designated ethnic and "free" lists
1.	Kirovskii (Makhachkala City)	1 Avar, 1 Dargin, 1 Kumyk, 1 Russian, 1 Free
2.	Leninskii (Makhachkala City)	1 Avar, 1 Kumyk, 1 Lak, 1 Russian, 1 Free
3.	Sovetskii (Makhachkala City)	1 Avar, 1 Lezgin, 1 Tabasaran, 1 Russian, 1 Free

two "free" seats, twelve of these twenty-two "free" seats were contested by candidates from a single ethnic group, though in principle candidates might have registered from any ethnic group (see Tables 7.3 and 7.6).

Table 7.6 indicates that from a total of 121 seats in the National Assembly, 111 seats were predictably "guaranteed" for a representative of a specific ethnicity. Since these "guaranteed" seats accounted for 92 percent of the seats in the assembly, the ethnic composition of Dagestan's legislature was almost as readily controlled as it ever had been.

During the first round of the election on March 16, 2003, ninety-eight representatives were elected. By the time the second round was finished, two weeks later, nearly the entire National Assembly had been chosen. Ethnic representation in the assembly was closely matched to ethnic proportions in the republic (Table 7.7).

The election campaign was difficult because a decision had been made to undertake the simultaneous election of (a) 121 representatives to the National Assembly; (b) 50 local representative organs in cities and raions, totaling 1,205 representatives; (c) 613 village councils, totaling almost 7,500 representatives; and (d) elected heads of local administrations[9] in 432 populated areas. The multiplicity of ballots for all of these different political levels caused great confusion among the voters. Yet this worked to the advantage of Dagestan's highest leadership since it effectively dispersed the energies of local political leaders, who therefore were less able to control the electoral outcomes in their areas at any given level.

Four hundred sixty-five candidates contested the 121 seats in the National Assembly. However, for various reasons 53 of these were not successfully registered, leaving 412. From this number, 40 withdrew their candidacies, usually to throw their support to another candidate. Hence, the election fielded 372 candidates competing for 121 seats, for an average of 3 contestants per seat.

The monomandate districts contained only 7,000 or 8,000 voters, permitting considerable candidate contact. Yet there were significantly more voters in the multimandate districts. For example, in one of Makhachkala's five-mandate districts there were 65,000 voters choosing five representatives. In principle, every candidate in this district was obligated to work with all of the potential voters. Thus candidates in monomandate and multimandate districts faced significantly different types of campaigns, though in each case the campaign conditions that they faced were identical to those of their local electoral opponents.

During the campaign some "dirty tricks" appeared to have been imported from Russian elections elsewhere. For example, in some cases "candidates" who had surnames similar to those of sincere competitors were encouraged

Table 7.6

Representative Seats Effectively Guaranteed to Specific Ethnic Groups by the Structure of the Electoral Districts During Dagestan's Election of March 16, 2003

	Type of district (according to the number of mandates they contain) Number of districts of each type Number of seats guaranteed to any specific ethnic group					
Ethnicities	1 mandate 61 districts 61 seats assured	2 mandate 12 districts 12 seats assured	3 mandate 7 districts 14 seats assured	5 mandate 3 districts 12 seats assured	Free mandate districts 22 districts seats that were assured because all candidates turned out to be from same group	Total
1. Avars	22	1	0	3	4	30
2. Dargins	14	1	2	1	1	19
3. Kumyks	4	4	2	2	2	14
4. Lezgins	11	0	1	1	1	14
5. Laks	3	0	1	1	1	6
6. Russians	0	2	5	3	0	10
7. Tabasarans	3	0	1	1	0	5
8. Chechens	1	1	1	0	1	4
9. Azeris	1	1	0	0	2	4
10. Nogais	1	1	0	0	0	2
11. Rutuls	0	0	0	0	0	0
12. Aguls	1	0	0	0	0	1
13. Tsakhurs	0	1	0	0	0	1
14. Tats	0	0	1	0	0	1
Total	61	12	14	12	12	111

Table 7.7

Ethnic Representation in Dagestan's Third National Assembly

No.	Ethnicity	Absolute number	Percentage
1.	Avars	33	27.3
2.	Dargins	21	17.3
3.	Kumyks	15	12.4
4.	Lezgins	14	11.6
5.	Russians	10	8.3
6.	Laks	6	5.0
7.	Tabasarans	5	4.0
8.	Azeris	5	4.0
9.	Chechens	5	4.0
10.	Nogais	2	1.6
11.	Rutuls	1	0.8
12.	Aguls	1	0.8
13.	Tsakhurs	1	0.8
14.	Tats	1	0.8
	Total	121	100

to enter the race in order to split the vote. In some cases, when candidates concluded that one of their rivals was significantly more popular than the rest, all of the latter withdrew in order to deny the popular candidate competition and thereby delegitimize his election. This occurred in the town of Kizliar, where the director of the Kizliar Electromechanical Plant, I. Akhmatov, was nominated along with D. Dzhambuev and A. Mutalipov. When the latter two candidates withdrew from the race, the consequent lack of competition led to the postponement of the election in that district for six months.

Voters were also bribed, in many cases, with payments of 300–500 rubles. It was difficult to investigate or expose these cases, since Dagestan lacks any tradition of reporting such infractions to authorities. Vote buying was therefore an effective campaign tool in Dagestan. Moreover, Dagestan once again saw a form of collective "bribery" that was not so different from some Western campaign practices. Voters sometimes supported the candidate who promised to perform a communal service such as repairing a road, a bridge, or a water system. Campaign promises of this sort were often effective.[10] In some cases, voters threw their support behind candidates who performed these good deeds prior to the election.

The election also saw minor incidents of conflict and confrontation. On April 2, approximately 1,000 residents of the villages of Leninaul, Kalininaul,[11] and Almak in the Kazbekovskii raion, blocked the "Caucasus" federal highway at the bridge over the Sulak River in the Kiziliurtovskii raion. They were protesting the second round of the National Assembly election, which was lost by A.S. Satiraev, and demanded that the election results be declared to have been falsified. The incident was "resolved" by 215 policemen.

Arsonists were blamed when the campaign headquarters of I. Abudullaev were destroyed in the village of Beledi. Elsewhere, a thousand ballots were destroyed on the night before election when almost 400 supporters of A. Gamzatov, the head of the Buinakskii raion, broke into a local club that was to be used as a polling station in the town of Chirkey.[12] Gamzatov's supporters were prevented from further mischief by the entire contingent of raion police bolstered by fifty Interior Ministry troops, but there were three additional incidents in Chirkey involving injuries and deaths.

On election morning in the *kutans*[13] of Tsuntinskii raion and Babaiurtovskii raion, about 250 rural residents started a fight in the polling station, assaulted M. Magomedov, who was in charge, and destroyed 163 ballots. The protesters were unhappy that members of the electoral commission were related to one of the candidates, V. Abdurakhmanov. Eight people were arrested, and the election resumed at noon. However, the election was stopped in the village of Ingishi of the Gumbetovskii raion after an incident between supporters of two candidates competing for the local council.

There was also an effort to destroy ballots in the village of Kuletsma of the Levashinskii raion. Someone attempted to steal 179 ballots in the village of Chapaevka of the Kumtorkalinskii raion, but the perpetrator was apprehended and the ballots were returned.

There was a conflict in Makhachkala at polling station no. 84, during which an unknown individual fired two shots into the air. At Kaspiysk's polling station no. 1, an unknown person broke the Panasonic television camera belonging to the TVS Moscow station.

The day after the election, 2,000 people gathered in the central Dagestani town of Kiziliurt. The protesters, who hailed from the villages of Aknada, Kirovaul, and Sovkhoz Komsomolskii, were unhappy with the local results of the National Assembly election, and attempted to force their way into the administration building. More than 570 policemen responded to the incident, which left only a few broken windows. The protesters were met by A.M. Gadzhiev, head of the local administration, who promised to investigate their concerns.[14]

Molodezh Dagestana[15] reported that the new electoral system led to frustrations in Rutulskii raion where, "introduction of the multimandate districts simply confused the local voters, inexperienced in political nuances. As it turned out, not only ordinary voters but also many members of the electoral commissions are not familiar with the new law. . . . It led to numerous irregularities and breaches of the law."

There was also "confusion" at the Shinazskii polling station, where the initial results reported I. Yakubov with 249 votes, and H. Radzhimov with 14 votes. However, the results were changed to 122 votes for Yakubov and 134 votes for Radzhimov, following a "recount" that was not attended by members of the election commission or observers.[16]

Other details emerged after May 12, when there was an attempt to assassinate Magomed Omarov, a major-general in the militia and the deputy interior minister of Dagestan. An explosion occurred as General Omarov's car passed beneath a bridge on Lenin Avenue, wounding the general and his driver. During his hospitalization, General Omarov gave an interview to *Dagestanskaya pravda*[17] in which he revealed that

> people with criminal pasts had been identified among the candidates. I would not be mistaken to say that up to 30 percent of the candidates at all levels are such people, including some who are currently suspects or fugitives in serious cases. We are now prevented from arresting those who obtained mandates.[18]

Officially, candidates could spend 225,000 rubles for their campaigns regardless of the size of the electorates to which they were appealing. Realistically, however, many candidates spent well beyond this limit.

Much was left to the heads of local administrations, who were responsible for organizing local electoral commissions and counting votes. Under the new laws, these individuals could not be elected to the National Assembly, and therefore largely devoted their efforts to the election of their family members, friends, and supporters. The editor of *Molodezh Dagestana* wrote, "Our Dagestani political elite has very well-known names."[19]

The following well-connected individuals were elected to the National Assembly: (1) the son of the chair of the State Council (SC), Magomedali Magomedov; the son of Dagestan's prime minister, Hizri Shikhsaidov; the brother of the mayor of Makhachkala, Said Amirov; two brothers of Duma representative, Gadzhi Makhachev; the brother of the mayor of Khasaviurt, Saigidpasha Umakhanov; the brother of the mayor of Buinaksk, Abankar Akaev; the brother of the mayor of Kizliar, M. Palamarchuk; the brother of the Azeri member of the SC, Kurban Kurbanov; the brothers of the vice-ministers, G. Gamzaev and A. Amuchiev; the brothers of the ministers of finance, A. Gamidov, and agriculture, Umalat Nasrudinov; the brother of the head of the Kazbekovskii raion, A. Azaev; the daughter of the well-known businessman, head of a large winemaking operation, and an Assembly representative in his own right, Nariman Aliev; the brother of Assemblyman Magomed Saidov; and the son of the late businessman, Magomed Charfaev.

Parties and Presidents

The recentralization of the Russian state inevitably affected the structure of Russia's political parties. In 2002, the passage of a federal law "On Political Parties" essentially annulled local parties, and extended recognition to only those parties that were registered with the Ministry of Justice and organized federally with local branches. These provisions essentially supplemented those of another federal law enacted in 2001, and titled "On the Principal Guarantees of Electoral Rights for Citizens Participating in Referenda of the Russian Federation." For each of the federal subjects, this latter law required that not less than half of the legislative seats be distributed to candidates elected from the lists provided by the local branches of the federal parties. The law required that changes in the local legislatures should have been made before July 14, 2003. These requirements were enacted with a view toward Dagestan where legislative districts were strictly territorial.

The election of Dagestan's third National Assembly was scheduled to take place in March 2003, just four months prior to the time that these new requirements went into effect. Candidates were consequently selected for a four-year term according to the modified version of the preceding territorial scheme (outlined in the preceding section), and not according to party lists. When some local political activists called for the introduction of electoral procedures in accord with the new federal laws, Dagestani authorities countered that "Dagestan is not prepared for this."

However, at the end of May, a month and a half after the election, and after the newly elected Assembly began its work, the same Dagestani officials decided that the republic should comply with the new federal laws. By this timing the officials ensured that the new regulations would not have take effect until four years later, at the end of the third Assembly in 2007. Concurrently, Dagestani officials announced that federal requirements also mandated that the republic's highest executive authority should be determined on the basis of a general election. However, this reform would not take effect until the end of the current term of the State Council in June 2006.

Clearly, the highest leadership of the republic had been preparing for these reforms, but decided to enact them after allowing the March Assembly election to proceed according to the old constitution. Indeed, the plan was probably in the works prior to the SC election in June 2002. Yet officials waited until after the conclusion of both elections to announce their plans to the population.

Though there may have been marginal costs to this approach in terms of democratic culture and institutional legitimacy, there were also clear benefits in terms of the deferral, and probable minimization, of turmoil associated with these constitutional changes. On the one hand, the timing of the official announcements regarding institutional reforms was in the Dagestani style of avoiding confrontations by dealing obliquely with issues. It had the effect of preserving the old institutions for the longest period possible under the new federal regulations, while maximizing the interim for public education and preparation regarding the institutional transition.

On the other hand, the timing of the announcement was also in the tradition of self-serving maneuvers on the part of Dagestan's highest leadership. It gave Dagestani officials ample opportunity to organize party structures that would represent their interests in the subsequent election based upon party lists. Indeed, some Dagestani observers suggested that all of this was but a smoke screen for what is essentially a political coup d'état. They argued that the predominant result of these changes would be a presidential system that shifted the basis of Dagestani politics from ethnicity to personality. In effect, it would institutionalize and legitimize a shift that had already occurred on an informal basis through personal power amassed, particularly by Magomedali Magomedov, but also by Said Amirov, the Dargin mayor of Makhachkala, and to a lesser extent by other Dagestani politicians.[20]

Prior to the SC election in June 2002, it became clear that while Magomedali Magomedov would certainly hold on to the chair, this would be his last term in that position. Though he has been astute in manipulating the Dagestani Constitution to permit himself extra terms in office,[21] federal law would not allow him another election. From early 2002, this circumstance inspired extensive maneuvering on the part of Dagestani politicians. New prospects for Dagestan's chief executive position began to put themselves forward, and Dagestanis started paying attention to what they were saying and doing. Political rivals negotiated among themselves and began to create alliances. There was much popular speculation about Magomedov's eventual successor.[22] Tensions mounted among the highest political elites. Inevitably, the March 2003 election of Dagestan's National Assembly became an arena for this long-range competition, as several leaders sought to bring their allies into political office.

All of this was in anticipation of Magomedov's forced retirement at the end of his term in 2006, and all of it changed with the announcement of Dagestan's transition to a presidential system. With the announcement of this transition, it became clear that the seventy-three-year-old Magomedov would have another three years of power as chair of the SC, and would then have a legal right to seek election to the head of the republic under the rules of the newly revised Constitution of the Republic of Dagestan.

When it finally occurred, this political transformation was accomplished in a brisk and well-organized manner. On May 30, 2003, the headline in *Dagestanskaya pravda* proclaimed "Constitutional Reform Is Beginning."

From this newspaper article, the people of Dagestan first learned that the SC had met on May 29 to discuss the realignment of the republic's electoral practices in accord with the federal requirements "regarding the election of no less than half of the representatives of the republic, or one of its chambers, according to the proportional system of election." The newspaper reported that during discussion of this question the SC had determined that the new federal requirement "leads to the necessity of constitutional reform, including reformation of the organs of executive power of the republic." The article did not clarify the "necessity" of a connection between reforms in Dagestan's legislative elections and the fundamental transformation of its executive branch, noting simply, if obliquely, that the State Council had concluded that its own constitutional foundation "does not correspond to the new political situation," and that it was therefore necessary to establish a new individual executive officer chosen by a general election. Essentially, the article explained that the SC had decided to disband itself, perhaps at the end of its current term in 2006, in favor of a presidential system.

At the same meeting, the SC recommended that Dagestan adopt a two-chamber National Assembly, in place of its current single chamber, evidently to provide a new organ of ethnic representation in compensation for the loss of ethnic representation at the highest executive level. It was suggested that the upper chamber should be composed of "representatives of raions and the cities," which would convey some features of ethnic representation since many raions and some towns are dominated by particular ethnic groups. It was recommended that the lower "legislative chamber" contain thirty representatives, half to be elected from party lists, and the other half from territorial electoral districts.

On June 10, a third session of the recently elected National Assembly took place to consider constitutional changes that were being proposed by its own Constitution Committee. During the preceding three years, when Dagestan had been under federal pressure to revise its constitution, the assembly's Constitution Committee had been considering various proposals.

The assembly accepted the committee's draft of the new constitution with discussion that focused on only a few of its provisions.[23] The draft constitution proposed the post of "head of the republic, elected for four years by the citizens of the Russian Federation permanently residing on the territory of the republic of Dagestan based on the general, equal, and direct electoral right by secret ballot."[24] It described a single-chamber Assembly with sixty representatives, half to be elected from party lists. Some of these procedures remained ambiguous, but Dagestani observers assumed that party organizations participating in the election would have to surpass a 10 percent barrier. The other half of the representatives were to be elected from monomandate and multimandate territorial electoral districts.

The June 10 Assembly meeting featured controversy regarding the number of seats in the new Assembly. This was not surprising since there were, at that time, 121 seats in the assembly, and any number less than that would ensure the exclusion of some of those who were considering the composition of the new body. Some of the representatives argued that sixty representatives were too few, and that as a result "some ethnicities, and whole raions, w[ould] not be represented in the [new] assembly." There were various suggestions of larger bodies, seating 80, 120, and even 242 representatives. Representative Magomed Magomedov, who suggested the latter number, stressed that a small assembly would lead to situations in which residents of small communities[25] would go without representation. Therefore, in his opinion, the current 121 territorial representatives should remain and the same number should be added, based upon election from party lists.[26] However, the majority of the assembly favored a body with 60 seats.

Several of the objections to committee proposals for the new constitution that surfaced during the assembly discussion were deflected with a standard phrase: "The [federal] center recommended it."[27] In his presentation on the topic, Mikhail Gashimov, who chaired the assembly Committee on Legislative, Judicial, and Executive Institutions, said, "We accept these laws not because we want them, but because we have to be within the same judicial sphere as Russia."

Some members of the assembly also supported the view that "ethnicity is not important anymore." With reference to the number of seats in the assembly, Gashimov said, "We . . . calculated and reached the conclusion that no matter how many representatives are in the assembly, even 240, it is impossible to represent all ethnicities proportionately, as it is impossible to represent every raion. Dagestan needs people who will think about the future of the whole republic independently of their ethnicity. We do not need quantity; we need quality."[28]

Still the context, and occasionally even the logic, of these arguments demonstrated that Dagestani politics still took place within ethnographic parameters. For example, Assemblyman Ibrahim Ackhmadov, who directed the largest plant[29] in Kizliar said that, "some representatives are pushing the ethnic question for the sake of their personal interests, being afraid that . . . they will not be able to secure a position for themselves in the new assembly. If we continue to look at each other through the prism of ethnicity we will never build a lawful or righteous society"[30] Yet those who were present could not forget that Ackhmadov was a representative of Dagestan's largest ethnicity, the Avars. No less important were the facts that he was one of the most influential people in Kizliar, a city that was, in the recent past, predominantly ethnic Russian in its population, and that his plant served as the widest gate through which

Kizliar had been accepting immigrant Avars from the hardscrabble mountain villages of the republic. Representative Suleiman Uladiev, who edited the newspaper *Novoye delo,* said that it was time to reconsider whether the basis of Dagestani politics should be defined in ethnic or civil terms:

> If we follow the first principle, then not only in the organs of the executive power, but in all organizations and enterprises we would also have to follow the principle of ethnic representation, and then we would have to create a special instrument for the measurement of its exact proportionality. . . . We should immediately stop filling Dagestanis with the idea that we are so different. We are a united people, we should not fix on the ethnic ideal.[31]

Then, in a tone of political realism, the chair of the State Council, Mago-medali Magomedov, rebuked the representatives for their concern with the number of seats in the assembly, and brought the discussion to a close by declaring that he was not going to ask Moscow to grant Dagestan special considerations. "Previously," he said, "we were surrounded by a circle of separatists, and could not hope for the support of the center because it was weak. . . . Now if we make a mistake we will be corrected by the center, and will be shown to our place."[32] Later he explained that previously

> The center was weak, and in Makhachkala people came out on the square, armed groups of people captured this building.[33] . . . Now we have a different situation. The center is strong. We have a president [Vladimir Putin] who completely controls the situation. . . . Now it is not dangerous for us to act as other subjects of the federation act.[34]

In the end, the assembly passed a draft constitution and the first reading of a new electoral law. These envisaged Dagestan having a popularly elected leader serving out a four-year term, and a new one-chamber sixty-member parliament replacing the current 121-member chamber.

Dagestani law required that proposed constitutional changes be published, and that the public be provided with an opportunity for discussion and for consultation with their representatives. Therefore, proposals of the Constitution Committee were circulated on the following day, June 11, and the committee formed a working group, or Constitutional Commission, to be charged with revision of the draft constitution in accord with the preceding discussion in the assembly, and with that of the public discussion that was to follow. The announcement of these procedures invited Dagestani citizens to contact members of the Constitutional Commission regarding their concerns. By June 20, elections were to be held by local representative bodies of the raions and the cities to choose the second half of the Constitutional Assembly that was empowered to make the final decision on constitutional reforms. The Constitutional Assembly was to meet on July 10, 2003, for the special purpose of approving the new constitution of the Republic of Dagestan.

On July 1, the Constitutional Commission settled all the outstanding issues. The new head of the republic would be called president and the parliament would have seventy-two members, of whom half would be elected from party lists and the other half from twelve regional three-member constituencies in which ethnic quotas would be introduced. On July 10, the Constitutional Assembly adopted the new constitution in a little over an hour so that it could come into force in two weeks, just in time for Dagestan's Constitution Day, July 26, which was the day that the previous constitution was ratified in 1994.

One local observer described this process as a "blitz-reform." Radical alterations in Dagestan's political system were first introduced on May 29, accepted by the SC on June 4, confirmed in the National Assembly on June 10, published on June 11, and finally recognized as the law of the land on July 26, precisely nine years to the day from the enactment of Dagestan's preceding constitution, but less than two months from the start of the reform process.

Yet none of this had an immediate effect. Since the State Council was elected only a year before, and the National Assembly was elected only three months earlier, Articles 4, 5, and 6 of the old constitution (regarding the formation of the State Council as a collegial executive, the National Assembly, and the government of Dagestan as a Cabinet of Ministers) remained effective until the expiration of the concurrent terms of office. That was to be 2006 for the SC and 2007 for the National Assembly. At those times a president and a new National Assembly would be chosen according to the requirements of the new constitution.

Thus did Moscow dismantle Dagestan's previous political structure, based on principles of consociational democracy. From this point forward, Dagestani political authority gradually shed the strong connections that drew support from Dagestan's traditional social structure during the chaotic period of regime transition following the collapse of central power. Power in the republic slowly turned away from the ethnoparties,[35] which provided the Dagestani political system with an internal dynamism and flexibility, promoted a constant process of corrective balancing, prevented any segment of Dagestani society from acquiring dominance, and provided the inherent resilience and stability that underwrote Dagestan's fidelity to Moscow. Dagestan's new constitution reoriented its political focus from this internal "force field" and located its center of gravity outside of the republic at the federal center. Personal political power was no longer based upon internal political conditions, but upon the bureaucratic authority of official functionaries, leaning for power on higher-level administrative organs that are connected ultimately to the Kremlin.

The appearance of ethnic parity would be preserved through proportional representation, since without this appearance no authority could maintain political legitimacy in Dagestan. Yet electoral processes would shed their genuinely popular basis and would tend to function largely as confirmation for administrative decisions. To the extent that this approximated the old Soviet power structure, Dagestani elites were prepared to apply it, and Dagestani citizens were conditioned to accept it. The very manner in which the new constitution was imposed suggests that nothing from that earlier period has been forgotten.

Previously the various groups that were competing in Dagestan sought support from Moscow, which acted as a political ballast to stabilize the republic amid their fluctuations. Yet with the new constitution, all that occurred in Dagestan would be directly sanctioned by the Kremlin. Moscow had become the guarantor of Dagestan's stability, instead of Dagestan's own internal social parameters. The local political elites would consider the views of Moscow leaders ahead of local social moods and the needs of their local supporters. As a consequence, the ruling elite might become further alienated from local needs and demands. Up to this point, those Dagestani elites who were offended, defeated, or otherwise aggrieved could seek Moscow's support and mediation. Henceforth, those who were aggrieved would likely grow in number, and could only seek supporters and allies who cast themselves in opposition to Moscow.

Terrorist Attacks and Assassinations

Throughout the period in which these changes were being instituted, Dagestan became the scene of an intensifying terrorist campaign. Following is a partial list of terrorist attacks from the beginning of summer 2002 to the end of summer 2003:

- On the morning of May 9, 2002, an explosion killed 42 people, almost half of them children, and injured more than 150 others in the town of Kaspiysk, near Makhachkala on Dagestan's Caspian shore. The blast occurred at a Victory Day parade commemorating the defeat of Germany in World War II. Elderly veterans and families lined the parade route down Kaspiysk's main street. A group of children ran just ahead of a military marching band. At the moment the band struck up the Victory Day tune an antipersonnel mine was detonated by remote control. After the blast the street was filled with battered musical instruments, body parts, and streams of blood.

- Exactly two years earlier, on May 9, 2000, a trained detection dog found a powerful explosive device hidden in bushes near a platform that was to be used by most of Dagestan's highest ranking officials to address a crowd in Makhachkala's Lenin Square that day. Had the device not been discovered it could have decapitated Dagestan's government and killed or injured thousands of citizens.
- On September 27, 2002, the chief of the Department to Combat Extremism and Criminal Terrorism, Colonel Akhberdilav Akilov, was killed in Makhachkala.[36]
- In Makhachkala, on February 20, 2003, an attempt was made on the life of Arip Kurbanaliyev, deputy chief of the section to combat banditry of the Organized Crime Department in the Dagestani Interior Ministry. Kurbanaliyev was hospitalized in Moscow with a head wound.[37]
- In Makhachkala, on July 28, 2003, police captain Magomed Mekhtalov, chief of the Department to Combat Extremism and Criminal Terrorism, was killed outside his house. The body of the officer was riddled with bullets from a Kalashnikov assault rifle. Thirty 7.62 mm caliber cartridge cases were collected from the scene of the murder. "The Wahhabis killed him," said an employee of the Kirovsk Internal Affairs Department. "He had tackled so many of them, and so many of them were then acquitted! It is those who were 'acquitted' who killed him."[38]
- On August 12, 2003, assassins murdered Major Tahir Abdullayev, a senior officer in the Department to Combat Extremism and Criminal Terrorism, outside of his Makhachkala home.
- Less than half an hour after the murder of Major Abdullayev on August 12, Nadirshah Khachilaev, leader of Dagestan's Lak people and the Union of Muslims of Russia, chairman of the Dagestani branch of the Russian Peace Foundation, and former State Duma deputy, was killed in Makhachkala. The attack appeared to be professional, and resembled the attacks on some of the police officers.
- Magomed-Salikh Gusaev, Dagestan's popular minister for Nationalities, Information, and External affairs was killed on the morning of August 27, 2003, as he was being driven to his office from his apartment building Akushinskii Prospect in central Makhachkala. He was fifty-two. Two unknown assailants fled after placing a magnetized mine to the roof of his Volga sedan when it slowed along Akushinskii Prospect. Moments later the device was detonated. It was not the first attempt on his life.
- As Gusaev left his apartment building on June 8, 2001, a bomb exploded beneath the metal grating that is used to clean shoes.
- On August 7, three weeks before his death, Gusaev published a commentary about the war on terrorism in *Dagestanskaya pravda*.[39] In the

article titled "The Globalization of Terror," Gusaev argued that the war on terror was becoming so politicized that it might lose the support of the international community. On the one hand, he said, the United States sought international cooperation against terror, but, on the other hand, the United States was not prepared to revise its long-standing geopolitical interests in order to facilitate cooperation with other states. Gusaev argued that a unilateralist approach based upon American military strength could not defeat global terrorism. He insisted that the only antidote to global terrorism was an international order grounded upon international law and institutions. He criticized the double standard that had been applied by Western countries toward Russia's antiterrorism efforts in the Caucasus, and provided an analysis of the introduction and proliferation of terrorism in the Caucasus-Caspian region, with a focus on Islamism in Chechnya. Gusaev argued that the terrorists sought to destabilize the Caucasus/Caspian regions for several reasons, including the control of natural resources, and observed that this was contrary to the interests of local people, of Russia, and of the West. He argued that a center to combat terrorism should be founded in Dagestan, and implied that this center should be coordinated with, and at least partially funded by, Western antiterrorist efforts. In the article, Gusaev asserted that the emergence and development of Muslim extremism in the North Caucasus were the results of a global Islamist plan.

- On August 28, 2003, a car bomb exploded in central Makhachkala near the offices of the organized crime department and the Department to Combat Extremism and Criminal Terrorism.[40] It appeared that the driver of the car intended a suicide-style attack, but that he leapt from the car moments before the explosion when he saw the newly installed concrete barriers around the buildings. Soon thereafter, a similar explosion occurred outside the Internal Affairs Department building for the Khasaviurt raion, near the Chechen border.
- August 2003 also saw numerous unsuccessful attempts on the lives of law enforcement officials. For example, in Makhachkala, an attempt was made on the life of Mali Safarov, a staffer in the Department to Combat Extremism and Criminal Terrorism. Safarov was hospitalized with bullet wounds, and survived. That same month the car of another staffer in the same office was blown up immediately in front of the ministry building. At the time of the blast, the car was unoccupied. "There are dozens of such examples," said an Interior Ministry spokesman.[41]
- On September 3, 2003, multiple shotgun blasts killed Salikh Shamkhalov, police driver of the Extremism and Terrorism Control Department of the Dagestan Interior Ministry. His twenty-year-old pregnant wife also died

of shotgun wounds. The attack occurred in Makhachkala as the couple was returning home in their private car. Thirty-three empty cartridges were found at the scene of the crime.

- In late September, two policemen and two police probation officers were killed in a gun battle on the outskirts of Makhachkala. They were shot by the owner of a car carrying explosives and weapons.[42]
- On September 30, five officers of an Interior Ministry in the Khasavi-urtovskii raion were killed in a car on their way to work. Investigators believed that the primary target was the criminal investigations officer Zaur Bekbulatov, who worked for the Interior Ministry Department to Combat Extremism and Criminal Terrorism.

That same day in Khasaviurt, Russian deputy general prosecutor Vladimir Kolesnikov stated that investigators were operating on the theory that the officers were murdered for their involvement in the investigation into the Dzhannat (Paradise) Islamist group. Nine members of the gang were arrested during the six weeks preceding this attack. According to Kolesnikov, the gang operated in Dagestan on orders from Rappani Khalilov,[43] an ethnic Lak, and his lieutenant Shamil Abidov.[44] Kolesnikov claimed that Khalilov was responsible for an underground Islamist organization that exacted retribution on government and law enforcement officials who attempted to eliminate Wahhabism. Kolesnikov blamed Khalilov for the Kaspiysk blast, and stated that while several members of his organization has been apprehended, Khalilov himself had eluded Dagestani investigators by taking refuge in Chechnya.[45]

Altogether, the summer of 2003 saw the murders of more than ten Dagestani law enforcement officials who were engaged specifically in the struggle against terrorism and extremism. Their deaths brought to nearly twenty the total number of Dagestani law enforcement officials murdered in the preceding twelve months.[46] All of them were working in the Department to Combat Extremism and Criminal Terrorism, the Administration for Combating Organized Crime, the Criminal Investigation Department, and other law enforcement agencies combating local religious extremists.[47] The same period had seen assassination attempts on other Dagestani officials, including Dagestan National Assembly chairman Mukhu Aliev, State Duma deputy Gadzhi Makhachev, and Makhachkala mayor Said Amirov. Both Aliev and Makhachev issued statements blaming Islamist extremists for the spate of violence.

One of the division heads in the Sovetskii raion Organized Crime Division, described a vendetta against government and law enforcement officials involved in the elimination of Wahhabi Islamists in Dagestan following the military operations in August–September 1999. "At that time," the source said, "the suspicion of guilt alone was enough for the police to 'concoct' a case against a religious extremist or one of his followers. Now these people, who resent authority, have served their terms and are being released." The source stated that Chief Akilov of the Organized Crime Division had cautioned officials of an Islamist retributive campaign shortly before his death.[48]

There were also reasons to suspect that the minister of nationalities Magomed-Salik Gusaev was killed by Wahhabis. When Dagestan was invaded in 1999, Gusaev organized an information bureau to combat the propaganda of Chechen leader, Movladi Udugov. Thereafter he emerged among the most influential proponents of the campaign to eliminate Wahhabism from Dagestan. According to Dagestani police spokesman Abdulmanap Musaev, Gusaev "was the one who almost single-handedly organized a campaign against religious extremists in Dagestan. In terms of influencing people's minds and ways of thinking, Gusayev was probably the No. 1 person in the republic."[49] For his efforts, Gusaev was sentenced to death by a sharia court in Chechnya in 1999, according to Dagestani police records. Shamil Basaev, who led the invasions of Dagestan, was affiliated with the court. A website operated by Chechen militants published occasional references to the death sentence.

According to Ali Temirbekov, a spokesman for the Dagestani General Prosecutor's Office, Wahhabism was being actively exported to the region from Saudi Arabia: "Unfortunately there are many rich people there with radical ideas and more money than they know what proper use to put it to," he said. "So they try with their money to build a base for radical Islam in the Caucasus. Gusayev was their ideological enemy No. 1 in Dagestan, and they must have been waiting only for a suitable moment to settle their score with him."[50] The Prosecutor's Office stated that at the time of his death Gusaev "was actively engaged in the campaign against extremism and Wahhabism."[51] Dagestani authorities classified Gusaev's death as political.

The pace of these attacks accelerated during the remainder of 2003, 2004, and 2005. As high-ranking officials augmented security precautions, the attacks focused increasingly on ordinary law enforcement officers, especially in the vicinities of Khasaviurt, Makhachkala, and Kaspiysk.

In March 2004, Rappani Khalilov, who styled himself the "Amir of Dagestani Mujahedeen," released a statement claiming broad responsibility for these attacks. The statement, which attracted widespread attention following its circulation on leaflets that were distributed in several Dagestan cities during the latter half of the month, claimed that Dagestan's pro-Moscow officials had launched a war against Dagestani Muslims and against the "Islamic Djamaat."[52] According to Khalilov's statement, the victims of this official crackdown "undergo severe tortures, their human dignity is humiliated, their religious principles are . . . mocked . . . , and they are beaten into confessions of crimes that they did not commit, when any methods of physical violence and suppression of personality are used, which even butchers at fascist concentration camps were not even thinking about." The statement went on to warn police and security officers that any "participation, whether direct or indirect, in the war against Muslims makes them enemies and retribution will inevitably catch up with them." In the statement, Khalilov also claimed that neither he nor his organization targeted civilians. He specifically denied responsibility for the Kaspiysk blast.

Despite their rhetorical tone, Khalilov's claims of police brutality, like his warnings of further retaliation, were largely credible. From 2000 onward there was considerable anecdotal evidence from victims and witnesses of brutal police tactics against young Muslim men who sometimes seemed to have little or no connection to Islamist extremism. Often these tactics appeared to have a radicalizing effect upon these young men, who swore retribution against the police in what promised to be a vicious cycle of brutality.

After Beslan

On September 1, 2004, a group of militants under the direction of Shamil Basaev commandeered School No. 1 in Beslan, North Ossetia. They held over 1,000 hostages under unspeakable conditions in the school gymnasium. Following events that remain controversial, more than 330 hostages died, more than half of them children. The episode shocked the world, convulsed Russia, and altered the course of Islamist militancy in the North Caucasus. Though his invasions of Dagestan had not substantially discredited Basaev outside of Russia, the events in Beslan were condemned across the Muslim world, and he was blamed even by some of his militant Chechen supporters.

On September 13, 2004, President Putin cited this security crisis in the North Caucasus as a reason for his appointment of Dmitri Kozak, one of his staunch supporters, as "presidential plenipotentiary envoy to the Southern Federal District." At the same time, and also with reference to the crisis, Putin cited the need for a stronger central authority in Russia. Toward this end, he announced sweeping electoral changes in Russia's eighty-nine regions. The plan would strengthen federal control by giving the Russian president power to nominate regional governors with the "endorsement" of regional legislatures. In line with this proposal, current regional leaders could serve out their terms and term limits would be scrapped. According to Putin, these arrangements would strengthen the executive chain of command.

At the same time, Putin expressed support for a Central Election Commission proposal to eliminate the single mandate constituencies that then accounted for half of the seats in the Russian State Duma, thereafter requiring that all Duma representatives should be seated from lists compiled by the national parties. This move would effectively eliminate independent deputies in the Duma, would strengthen party control of the body, and would eventually reduce the number of viable federal parties. At the time of the announcement, the pro-Kremlin, United Russia Party enjoyed a two-thirds majority in the Duma, sufficient to initiate changes to the constitution. Proponents of these changes argued that they would reduce local corruption, streamline decision making, and strengthen government control in response to threats such as North Caucasian terrorism.[53]

Yet in Dagestan there were reasons for concern. Because of Dagestan's ethnically segmented, and traditionally pluralistic, political system, Moscow's appointment of any head of state could immediately alienate many of the local political elites. In one possible scenario, some of these alienated elites could appear to acquiesce while quietly working to sabotage the system.

The further implementation of national party lists in the Duma elections raised other concerns in Dagestan. If one were prepared to overlook blatant vote buying by all sides and occasional incidents of violence, then elections among Dagestani candidates have tended to be relatively free and fair. Electoral irregularities have been few, and when they have occurred they have generally been identified, protested, and investigated. However, in Dagestan, there has also been evidence suggesting that federal elections among national political entities have been characterized by significant irregularities.[54]

In the context of Putin's proposed electoral reforms, the point is that whereas Dagestanis are less likely to manipulate single-mandate district races among Dagestani candidates (where a Dagestani is certain to be seated regardless of the outcome), they may be more likely to manipulate party list elections to the Duma in a manner that satisfies the expectations of Moscow leaders and maximizes the number of representatives from Dagestan who are seated from various lists. Hence, the shift of subsequent Duma elections entirely away from single-mandate districts, increasing the role of party lists, could increase the degree of federal electoral fraud in Dagestan, and perhaps in other North Caucasian republics. At least in Dagestan, these irregularities have usually benefited the party of power. After the Russian presidential elections of 2000 and 2004, there were claims that Vladimir Putin had benefited significantly from massive electoral fraud in the North Caucasus. Further electoral reforms may benefit the party of power.

The Federal Report on Conditions in Dagestan

While continuing his predecessors' efforts to increase security and decrease terrorism, the new presidential envoy to the Southern Federal District gradually shifted the focus of his office toward economic development. The shift was underscored in Dmitri Kozak's 2005 report to President Putin. During the preparation of this report, the situation in Dagestan was scrutinized by analysts working for Russia's Southern Federal District under the leadership of Alexander Pochinok. The result was a 117-page document titled: "Report on Conditions in the Republic of Dagestan and Measures for Its Stabilization."

Although the report was classified for Kremlin use, it was discussed in June at a special session of Dagestan's State Council, and was "leaked" to the Russian media in July. A complete draft was published in the only Dagestani opposition newspaper operating at that time: *Chernovik,* no. 28, July 22, 2005. An attempt to destroy this issue of the paper was only partially successful. The report made for interesting reading in Dagestan because of the stark contrast that its somber tone and disquieting data presented to the optimism of official pronouncements and publications that had appeared in Dagestan during the preceding four years.[55]

According to the report, Dagestan had become a severely depressed region with an adverse investment climate. The downturn had resulted from numerous political, social, and economic problems, most of which afforded the preconditions for the further deterioration of the situation. In particular, the report noted that the increasing influence of religious associations on political processes had become an additional source of instability. Local Islamic practices had become steadily politicized. Religious communities had been actively participating in elections of government bodies, and religious authorities were exercising increasing influence over heads of municipal administrations in mountainous areas of the republic.

These chronically unresolved problems had opened a credibility gap between the authorities and the citizenry, and had culminated in a political crisis. According to the report, the proportion of Dagestanis with a positive view of Dagestan's State Council, which was already abysmally low, had dropped by half in the five months of 2005 that preceded the report's completion: from 9.9 percent in February to 5 percent in June. Tables 7.8 and 7.9 are taken from the report.[56]

The same survey showed that more than 65 percent of the population of Dagestan thought that their courts worked badly, while only 21 percent took a positive view of the courts. The activities of Dagestani law enforcement bodies were viewed negatively by 63 percent of the respondents. A six-month content analysis of the Dagestani media indicated that officials almost never recognized their own mistakes, and that they avoided self-criticism even when it was obliged by obvious errors. Official corruption permeated every sphere of Dagestani life, having reached a level at which some government sectors effectively ceased to function, except for purposes of private appropriation. Corruption, nepotism, and cronyism perpetuated backwardness and illiteracy

Table 7.8

Replies to the Question: "How Would You Evaluate the Activity of the State Council of the Republic of Dagestan?" (%)

	June 2004	October 2004	February 2005
Generally positive	38.6	19.0	9.9
Indifferent	9.3	22.5	5.3
Generally negative	23.3	35.6	72.8
Know nothing about its activity	13.3	7.3	6.8
Do not know what to say	15.6	16.0	6.3

Table 7.9

Replies to the Question: "How Would You Evaluate the Activity of the State Council of the Republic of Dagestan?" (%)

	February 2005	June 2005
Generally positive	9.9	5.0
Indifferent	5.3	8.5
Generally negative	72.8	67.2
Know nothing about its activity	6.8	2.8
Do not know what to say	6.3	16.6

among the bulk of Dagestan's bureaucrats and civil servants. Problems in social services were chronically unaddressed, and since government, for the most part, no longer aimed at service to the public, the report characterized the continuing growth of police repression as an inevitability.

All together, an astonishing 96 percent of the population stated that they were prepared to take some sort of antigovernment political action. According to the report, 52 percent of Dagestan's population was ready to participate in authorized protest actions, and 29 percent were ready to participate in unauthorized protest actions. Fifteen percent were prepared for direct action, with 8 percent ready to seize buildings and to block transportation, and 7 percent were prepared to use weapons.

In 2004, Dagestan's overall volume of production had declined. The report estimated that 44–49 percent of Dagestan's economy was operating in the shadows, as compared with 26 percent for the Southern Federal District and 17 percent for the Russian Federation. Side by side with Chechnya, Dagestan led the federation for unemployment, with an average per capita income of $120, half of that for Russia as a whole. Although federal subsidies were increasing, they were not effectively employed to expand the taxable economic base and to improve the living standard of the general population. Tax revenues were falling even though potential sources of revenue were found to be significantly underestimated. Dagestan's economic potential remained largely unexploited.

Anticipated income from the management of state property was not reaching the republic's budget. Either the revenues were being plundered, or investments were managed so inefficiently as to yield no return, or, most probably, some combination of the two. Embezzlement of budgetary funds was prevalent at all levels of government. Funds from federal programs that targeted specific problems in Dagestan were dissipated without appreciable effect. Disaster relief funds did not reach victims, in part, because there was particularly massive and systematic corruption in the construction industry. Large agricultural enterprises that remained under state control were being intentionally bankrupted so that they could be acquired cheaply when they were subsequently privatized. The fishing resources of the Caspian Sea were being plundered. Tourism remained stagnant, and the Soviet recreational infrastructure was rapidly deteriorating.

The report placed Dagestan's socioeconomic problems within a quasi-traditional ethnopolitical context. Though ethnic aspects of Dagestani politics had gradually begun to fade over the preceding decade, the recent power struggle (see below)[57] had brought some of them back into contrast, particularly insofar as Avars and Dargins are concerned. The report suggested that if Dagestan's trajectory of social disintegration remained unchecked over the following five to ten years, it was possible that the republic would undergo a process of fragmentation. Fragmentation could acquire quasi-federal features with de facto statelets emerging in southern, central, and northern Dagestan, the latter perhaps strengthening its affiliation with the Grozny regime as its ties to Makhachkala gradually weakened. Simultaneously, the growing influence of local religious communities could lead to the emergence of "sharia enclaves" in mountainous areas of the republic, with a corresponding de facto contraction of Russia's genuinely sovereign space. The report suggested that this process of disintegration into local Islamic enclaves was already under way. These were the main points of the report.

Despite its overall tone of solemn realism, it appeared that high-ranking Dagestani officials were able to exercise some influence in the preparation of the report. For example, the report placed the blame for the situation in Dagestan primarily upon Hizri Shikhsaidov, the former prime minister, and serving prime minister Atai Aliev—both ethnic Kumyks—while Magomedali Magomedov evaded responsibility.

However, this assignment of responsibility was clearly misleading. It was true that Shikhsaidov was corrupt, though no more so than many of his government colleagues. Yet, Shikhsaidov's influence in the affairs of the republic was marginal compared with that of Magomedov, Amirov, or Makhachev. Shikhsaidov was forced out of power[58] at the end of summer 2004, and was clearly being used as a scapegoat in the report. He was replaced by the little known Atai Aliev, who lacked real power, and who had been responsible for relatively little, good or bad, during his year in office.[59]

Two other points in the report were also strangely misleading. First, it stated that Sadval, the Lezgin national movement, "essentially influenced events in the republic." Yet, in actuality, Sadval had only a nominal existence and influenced nothing. Second, the report claimed that Dagestan's internal migration of high-land populations to the plains was "destabilizing." Migration from the highlands did in fact pose problems for Kumyk livestock breeders, who had complained of mountaineers moving onto their lowland pastures. Most recently, internal migration had also posed problems for the ethnic Russian population, especially in the Kizliar area of northwestern Dagestan. Russians had fled northward as mountain Avars moved in and took Russian jobs. Yet while internal migration had not been favorable for the Kumyk and ethnic Russian populations it was far from destabilizing in its effects.

The final chapter of the report, which offered conclusions and recommendations, was also disappointing. The data and analysis throughout the body of the text offered a sobering tour de force, yet the report culminated in a series of empty gestures concerning, for example, the advancement of the Russian language as a medium for multicultural communication, and gradual preparations for the reduction of federal subsidies to the republic. Clearly, the authors of the report were not prepared to offer any real solutions for the numerous pressing problems that they identified.

Regime Change

On February 15, 2006, the seventy-five-year-old chair of Dagestan's State Council, Magomedali Magomedov, unexpectedly resigned, and was quickly replaced by Mukhu Aliev, the sixty-five-year-old chair of the Dagestani legislature.

In the spring of 2005 there were rumors that the Kremlin would finally push Magomedov aside. However, that July, on his seventy-fifth birthday, Magomedov was awarded a medal by Putin's regional envoy, Dmitri Kozak, who announced that Moscow had no intention of replacing Magomedali.

Nevertheless, Magomedov announced his resignation upon his return from Moscow, where he came under pressure during his visit to the Kremlin on the afternoon of February 15, 2006. It was also announced that Magomedov's son, Magomed-Salam, would replace Aliev as chair of the People's Assembly. Since Magomedali would attempt to exert influence through Magomed-Salam,

Magomedov and Aliev had once again effectively traded places. Evidently, this was part of the deal that Magomedov cut with the Kremlin prior to his departure. Magomedov may have been hoping that he could subsequently maneuver his son from the chair of the legislature into the chief executive position, just as he had maneuvered himself from the former position to the latter in 1994.

Indeed, there were rumors that Magomedov similarly outmaneuvered the Kremlin that July when he received his medal. Reportedly, Magomedov had told Kozak that he would accept a high honor from the Kremlin as an opportunity to make a graceful departure from office. Yet when Kozak bestowed that honor, Magomedov announced that he had been "reenergized" by the Kremlin's support, and that he was therefore able to continue in office. If true, this would be essentially the same maneuver that Magomedov used on Aliev in 1996, when Magomedov declined to honor his agreement to step down after a two-year interim term as chair of the State Council.

When the change of leadership came, it was clear that it had been prepared by Moscow cautiously and in complete secrecy, providing an indication of the seriousness with which Moscow leaders viewed the situation in Dagestan, and their recognition of the dangers that the situation entailed. Their meticulous arrangements for the political transition were evident in the precise moment that they chose to enact their plan, the sequence of events that followed, the speed with which the operation was completed, and the selective release of information. Up to the moment that Magomedov officially announced his resignation, nobody in Dagestan knew for sure what was going to happen. Almost uniquely in the life of this republic—where rumor and innuendo are regular political fare and official secrets are rarely kept—no one had correctly anticipated the course of events. Crowning it all was the unexpected means by which the federal center shrewdly chose to ensure the continuing presence of the departing leader through the proxy of his son.

Immediately after his Kremlin meeting of February 15, 2006, Magomedov told members of his entourage "everything is fine." Those accompanying Magomedov interpreted these words to mean that the results of the meeting were favorable for Magomedov, and by that evening the Makhachkala political elite was absolutely certain that Magomedov would remain in power. On the next day, February 16, Magomedov returned to Dagestan, and promptly convened a lengthy airport press conference in which he outlined his meeting at the Kremlin. By Magomedov's account, he had requested the meeting with President Putin in order to report the results of his economic program during the past five years. Magomedov said that he "stressed that the results of the socioeconomic development of Dagestan are among the best of the subjects of the Russian Federation in the Southern Federal District."[60] Magomedov reported that Putin had responded with praise for Magomedov's successful stewardship in Dagestan. Thus Magomedov's speech to the media assembled at the Makhachkala airport appeared to be a preamble to an announcement of his retention of power. After his lengthy speech about the "success" of Dagestan's economic development, a reporter for *Novoye delo* remarked that "the news of (Magomedov's) resignation came at a moment when absolutely nobody expected this outcome."[61] Magomedov suddenly announced:

> At the end of my [economic] report I informed the president of my decision to resign from the post of chairman of the State Council of Dagestan prior to the end of my term. Vladimir Vladimirovich responded that as president he was happy with my work and that he did not have any problems with my staying [in power]. He also said that he would not mind if I decide to run in the presidential election. But I am seventy-five [years old]. Lately, the condition of my health has not permitted me to fulfill all of my duties as chairman of the State Council. The president supported this decision . . . though not immediately and only after [my] persistence. . . . [and my insistence that] there is a good candidate for the presidency of Dagestan. I gave his name to the president [Putin], but I will not tell you who it was. I just want to stress that this is my personal opinion.[62]

In the late evening of that same day, there was a closed meeting of Dagestan's State Council at which Magomedov revealed the name of his successor. No official statements were released, and the official mystery was the lead story in all of those weekly newspapers that appear on Fridays. However, this story was followed in each of these publications by unofficial information that Magomedov had recommended, as his successor, Mukhu Aliev, the ethnic Avar speaker of the Dagestani Assembly. The papers reported that, in the absence of two of its members, the State Council had unanimously accepted Magomedov's recommendation. Thereafter Aliev himself was reportedly invited to join the meeting. He formally accepted the chair and thanked the Council for the honor.

On the next day, Friday, February 17, Russian federal envoy Dmitri Kozak arrived in Dagestan. He presided over a joint session of the Dagestani State Council, the Dagestani National Assembly, and Dagestan's Cabinet of Ministers. Kozak convened a discussion of the candidates for the position as head of government. Magomedov immediately proposed Mukhu Aliev with the highest praise, declaring that "[h]e is devoted to Dagestan, Russia, and the Constitution. He is not involved in any faction; no one would be ashamed to nominate him, and no one would be ashamed to vote for him. . . . There is no better candidate."[63]

On Friday, February 17, the central TV channels showed the meeting of Putin with Magomedali and Mukhu Aliev, so that there could be no more doubts about who was the real successor of the outgoing leader of Dagestan. Viewers could see the two of them on either side of the Russian president, they heard Putin offering Magomedali a high position in his administration, and telling Aliev that his "program is completely acceptable."

At a session of the assembly on Monday February 20, Magomedali was bid an honorable farewell, after which Kozak nominated Mukhu Aliev as President Putin's choice for the presidency in Dagestan. After some perfunctory speeches in praise of the candidate, the National Assembly predictably confirmed Aliev by a vote of 101 to 1.[64] Dagestan had its first individual (as opposed to collegial) post-Soviet executive. The same session of the assembly then quickly and without discussion unanimously elected Magomed-Salam Magomedov, the forty-two-year-old son of Magomedali, as the new speaker of the assembly. The election of Magomed-Salam occurred without protest from Amirov or his supporters.

Despite his claims, it is unlikely that Magomedov's resignation was voluntary, or that Moscow's choice of Magomedov's successor was based upon his recommendation. Most likely, he was informed of his dismissal during his Kremlin meeting on February 15, but then persuaded others at the meeting to permit him to announce his "voluntary resignation on medical grounds," and to make a show of nominating his successor. Evidently, Magomedov's proposal of these arrangements was not only consistent with Moscow's objectives, but actually facilitated their plans, since it contributed to the smoothness of the transition. However, it also appeared that Magomedov was able to negotiate a role for his son as speaker of the legislature, perhaps in exchange for his support of the Kremlin's plan to replace him with Aliev. Back home, a similar deal was probably also cut between Aliev and Magomedov.

There were many reasons to believe that the decision to replace Magomedov did not come easily. In the years preceding, Dagestan had eclipsed even Chechnya as the focus of the Kremlin's gravest concerns in the region. Because there were fears that the removal of the long-time leader of the republic would destabilize the situation, the decision was a difficult one. These doubts were compounded by signals deliberately sent to the "top" about the "irreplaceability of Magomedali," about an impending ethnic "conflagration," or a Hobbesian "war of all against all" that might be sparked by Magomedali's departure. When the decision to proceed with Magomedov's replacement was finally made, the Kremlin ensured that the entire procedure was carefully prepared in the strictest confidentiality. Following are some of the key points in its execution:

- The news was kept in complete secrecy up to the moment of Magome-dov's arrival in Dagestan. This avoided the intensive, possibly violent, and potentially destabilizing political maneuvering that otherwise would have preceded a power shift.
- Dagestani society received hints from Magomedali, subsequently con-firmed by Putin, that his long service was warmly appreciated, that he was departing voluntarily as a consequence of considerations arising exclusively from his advanced age and personal health.[65]
- The name of Magomedali's successor was kept secret up to the mo-ment when the uncertainty started to endanger the situation. This pre-vented the formation of factions opposing the appointment of Mukhu Aliev.
- Kremlin anxieties about the outcome ensured that Magomedali retained some bargaining power at the meeting. He was permitted to set some of the terms of his departure, including his nomination of Dagestan's new president, and an executive position for his son. This contributed to the *appearance* that Mukhu Aliev was the natural successor to Magomedov's regime, and not an externally imposed replacement.
- This appearance was further enhanced by the televised coverage of Putin, in the presence of Mukhu Aliev, offering Magomedali a lofty position as head of a department in his Moscow administration. Responsibilities in Moscow could have removed him from Dagestan's political scene (which was no doubt the intent of the offer) while affording him little real power. However, after the transition Magomedov had an office in Makhachkala with, a secretary, an assistant, and personal guards. His title as "honorable chairman of the State Council of the Republic of Dagestan" was probably the result of his own initiative. He spent most of his time in his home, overlooking the Caspian Sea.
- Last but not least, the session of the National Assembly that confirmed Aliev as the first president of Dagestan, also elected Magomedali's son, Magomed-Salam, to the vacant chair of the legislature. Evidently, Ma-gomedali requested Kremlin approval for this, and the Kremlin granted it because they knew that Magomed-Salam's presence would reassure elites with a stake in Magomedov's regime, and would thereby help to prevent clashes between new and old elites.
- The election of Magomed-Salam as chair of the assembly afforded him no real power. Indeed, it meant that he would have less access to the government budget than he did previously, which meant that Magomed-Salam's business interests would probably decline. Magomed-Salam served as a member of the Board of Elbin-Bank and a member of the Working Group for Offshore Oil Resources of the Dagestani Sector of

the Caspian Sea, and he also controlled several local businesses and real estate investments.

- Both budgetary and personnel matters were subsequently controlled by Mukhu Aliev, who evidently followed Moscow's wishes. While he was widely popular, he had never cultivated a factional political base capable of strong, independent action in defiance of the federal center.
- In all of these ways, the Kremlin was careful to avoid a strong negative reaction from Magomedali's supporters who inevitably worried about dramatic changes in wealth and power following the ascendance of a new leader and his team.

Throughout the years, Magomedali Magomedov had proven himself the master of political maneuver. While he lacked Aliev's erudition, he displayed remarkable political intuition. Again and again, he acted quickly and effectively in highly unpredictable situations, and was seemingly capable of any compromise in the name of his main objective: the retention of personal power. He was both the principal architect of, and the central player in, that system of dynamic balancing among pluralistic political forces that structured Dagestani political life for fifteen years after the collapse of the Soviet Union. His political longevity was due to his balancing skills, yielding when necessary, but always combining and recombining diverse political forces to form new coalitions of political allies and supporters. When Moscow started intervening in Dagestani politics, he was the first to recognize it and to appreciate the personal benefits that could be gained. In the 1990s, when he was at the peak of his game, Magomedov was known as "the Chess Player." He played the game on a masterful level, moving his pieces across the board like players upon his political stage.

Yet Magomedov's great political skills were also inevitably his weakness: He lacked the ability to use his power for anything beyond itself. He failed to use his authority for the achievement of social or economic goals, or for any political objective that transcended the simple retention of his influence.

Hence, the political strengths and weaknesses of Magomedov became the political strengths and weaknesses of Dagestan. On the one hand, Magomedov's preservation of his own power through his artful balancing act, had, as its byproduct, preserved Dagestan's stability. Magomedov was a master at recombining political forces, and shifting the political balance in order to preserve the political status quo, and the preservation of this political status quo was also the preservation of Dagestan's political stability. Through a very dangerous and difficult period in its history Dagestan's political stability was preserved, in part, through Magomedov's self-serving efforts to perpetuate his own power. A notable benchmark of this success was that during the years of Magomedov's rule, while the rest of the Russian Federation sank into a profound demographic catastrophe, Dagestan's population steadily rose from 1.8 million to 2.57 million.[66]

Yet this stability was essentially Magomedov's only substantive political achievement. He was never willing, nor perhaps sufficiently visionary (nor perhaps even sufficiently concerned and committed), to stake his power on any sort of socioeconomic, or more broadly and beneficially political, agenda of service to the republic. As a result, Dagestan also languished and gradually deteriorated— economically, socially, morally—under Magomedov's rule. The master of political drama was unable to disguise Dagestan's growing desperation.

Mukhu Aliev was a player of a different stripe. He could not be classified as "a member of Magomedali's team," nor, for that matter, a member of anybody's team. He was an adept and proven manager of any mechanism of power that was functional and predictable in its features. However, he proved much less effective in unpredictable situations and showed no gift for complex political relations. In short, Aliev appeared to be a principled, competent, highly intellectual, and extremely hard working technocrat. He was not a gifted politician.

Judging by this past performance, there was reason to suppose that Aliev would be well suited to the further bureaucratization of Dagestani politics. Insofar as Dagestan's government could rely upon a firmly established and centrally supported bureaucratic structure, then this would be an appropriate stage for Aliev's managerial talents. Moreover, as long as the political situation remained stable and predictable, Aliev was likely to make repairs and improvements to Dagestan's bureaucratic power structure.

An optimistic assessment might conclude that Magomedov was an appropriate leader for Dagestan during a dangerous fifteen years of chaos and uncertainty. This is because his one great achievement was the political stability that followed almost inadvertently from his artful and incessant struggle to preserve his own political power. By extension, this assessment would suggest that insofar as this period of chaos and uncertainty was subsequently superseded by a centrally supported bureaucratic structure, the unstained Aliev was well positioned for a managerial role.

Magomedov used his political skills to retain personal power, and thereby contributed almost incidentally to Dagestan's stability during the tumultuous 1990s; yet Aliev's technocratic approach was more compatible with the centralized bureaucratic administration that Vladimir Putin had subsequently constructed. Aliev made bureaucratic procedure the hallmark of his new regime, restructuring the government, reorganizing budgetary processes, increasing public revenues, and restricting some corrupt officials. He began his tenure with the support of his fellow ethnic Avars, the support of Moscow, and the goodwill of most Dagestanis.

Yet the drama introduced a stark irony: whereas Mukhu Aliev was popular among Dagestanis of all ethnicities, his fastidious avoidance of Dagestan's entrenched factionalism had made him otherwise unelectable as Dagestan's first president. Though Aliev was popular with the people, he had not maneuvered to line up the requisite personal support of intermediate political elites. Hence, he could only have come to power through Kremlin appointment, despite the undemocratic features of this procedure.

A week after the election of Aliev, the new Cabinet of Ministers of Dagestan were appointed. The shakeup featured the replacement of the Kumyk prime minister, Atai Aliev, with another Kumyk named Shamil Zeinalov (b. 1946). Since the president of Dagestan was an Avar, and the chair of the assembly was a Dargin, a Kumyk was chosen to complete the traditional triumvirate.

Like Aliev, Zeinalov had a reputation for holding himself aloof from political factions, and resisting the trend toward personal corruption. With his skills in economic management, he provided a worthy compliment to Aliev's political administration, much as did another Kumyk prime minister, Mirzabekov, in the late 1980s, the last time that Aliev played the leading role. The shakeup altered not only the content but also the structure of Dagestan's government. The number of deputies to the prime minister was reduced from seven to four, and the number of government ministers was reduced from eighteen to fifteen.[67]

In the months following his appointment, Mukhu Aliev embarked upon a largely bureaucratic program to (1) reduce official corruption, (2) reduce nepotism and cronyism, (3) rationalize and ameliorate government appointments, (4) create a meritocratic civil service, (5) rationalize the budgetary process, (6) regulate government expenditures, (7) reduce dependence upon federal subsidies, (8) increase tax revenues with special attention to the small business sector, (9) rationalize (i.e., legalize) the economy, and (10) support small businesses and liberate them from the predations of official corruption.

While each of these reforms was necessary and important, some local critics argued that a more innovative, extra-bureaucratic, approach may have been necessary to jump-start Dagestan's stalled economy. They worried that Aliev had stated his intent to reduce the role of Dagestan's only significant investor— the Kremlin—without specifying plans to increase private investment.

Presumably, Aliev was counting on Zeinalov to formulate a plan for economic development that complemented his program for bureaucratic reform. Yet Zeinalov's greatest previous achievements, like those of Aliev, were under the Soviet system, when local conditions were far more stable and predictable, and when there were no efforts to reduce economic dependence on Moscow. Thus the question was whether these two old Dagestanis could learn new tricks.

8

Conclusion
A Gathering Darkness

Mukhu Aliev's appointment as Dagestan's first president climaxed a six-year process of bureaucratic recentralization that began soon after President Putin's first electoral victory in March 2000. This process of recentralization progressively undermined and replaced the unique democratic system that the Dagestanis had innovated in their 1994 constitution in order to accommodate their ethnic heterogeneity and their ancient traditions of democracy and egalitarianism. Although that democratic system was hampered by endemic problems, it was nonetheless successful in managing the extreme internal tensions and external pressures to which Dagestan was subject in the 1990s. Unlike any of its neighboring territories, Dagestan avoided protracted conflict. Moreover, the constitution initially distributed power pluralistically and established a system of dynamic balancing among a multiplicity of competing interests. Local elections generally were free and fair.[1]

Yet throughout the latter part of the decade, economic and political access gradually contracted. Nepotism and cronyism set the political tone, while corruption became ubiquitous and economic disparities grew. The chair of Dagestan's collegial executive body did not rotate among different ethnic representatives, as the constitution had initially mandated, but instead was monopolized by the ethnic Dargin representative, Magomedali Magomedov. The government failed to resolve any of the republic's chronic problems, including widespread poverty, unemployment, organized crime, drug trade, infrastructural decay, environmental degradation, and near-epidemic levels of infectious diseases such as tuberculosis. The perpetuation of these problems contributed to political alienation, especially in the hopelessly impoverished rural areas that sustained Islamist extremism. Some remote areas were growing so disaffected as to be essentially beyond the control of the Makhachkala administration.

Beginning in 2002, government and law enforcement officials fell under weekly, even daily, attacks. The police responded with a brutal crackdown that contributed to further alienation and extremism. Caught in this vortex of economic collapse, political deterioration, and social despair, some Dagestanis lost confidence in their democratic system. They looked to Moscow for political mediation and welcomed the Kremlin's program of political recentralization.[2]

A New President and a New Bureaucracy

The years immediately following Aliev's accession were characterized by high-profile personnel replacements and widespread disappointment. Not only was the chief executive replaced by Kremlin decree but also the prime minister, his second in government, as well as the chairman of the assembly, who occupied the tertiary power position. Dagestan's previously collegial executive body was entirely eliminated. Half of the ministers and government committee heads were subsequently replaced.

In a move that Aliev rated among his early achievements,[3] the "fourth-ranking" official, the public prosecutor of Dagestan, an ethnic Lezgin named Imam Yaraliev, was also replaced by an interim prosecutor from Moscow. Yaraliev had an unfavorable reputation in the republic, but others with comparable notoriety remained in office. Aliev's immediate dismissals included no one from his own Avar ethnic group.

Most of the republic's prominent elites retained their positions in the government, but, like medieval courtiers, they exercised little real influence over political events. This further focused their attention on their petty rivalries and added new incentives for the physical elimination of their adversaries as one of the few methods of political influence available to them.

Indeed, the centrally bureaucratized political system added new twists to the dark arts of Dagestan's political rivalries. In the case of past rivalries, it was often sufficient for a leader to achieve his political aims simply by demonstrating his armed capabilities. Leaders displayed their real political "credentials" by their capacity to mobilize mass support through the ethnoparties that they led. This option was evident in the numerous armed, but ultimately nonviolent (or low-violence), confrontations that regularly punctuated Dagestan's political development during the 1990s. Yet in the altered political circumstances of 2006, a massive disturbance of this sort could only undermine a leader's standing vis-à-vis the bureaucratic establishment. Hence, Aliev's unexpected appointment created much dismay among local elites who waited passively and patiently to see what the new leader would do.

Yet while local elites adopted a passive approach, the population greeted Aliev's appointment with great enthusiasm and hopes for dramatic improvements. A wide assortment of local publications expressed optimism about Aliev's administration, typically describing him as "an honest leader" who would "bring order," and who deserved public support. Similarly positive anticipations of Aliev's leadership appeared in publications throughout the federation, and particularly in Moscow, including those most critical of the Kremlin. This was a marked contrast to Dagestan's previous administration, which became a target of constant criticism in Dagestan as well as in the central media.

Among the most serious problems facing ordinary citizens was the arbitrary and corrupt Dagestani bureaucracy. The arrival of a leader with a reputation for principle and integrity lent hopes that the situation might improve. As a result of these rising expectations, there was an increase in mass movements protesting local corruption. Quick to take advantage of these were opposition elements, including local leaders and their retinues, certain clans, and even entire djamaats.

While Makhachkala remained relatively quiet, the raions saw mass protests by local groups who were seeking to increase their powers. Local leaders who found themselves on the losing ends of previous power struggles sought to take advantage of Aliev's focus on bureaucratic corruption. Aliev had declared his intent to dismiss corrupt officials who came to power by means of bribes to those above them, and sometimes through brutal force that they applied to those in all other directions. At the same time, populations in the districts were prepared to expel many of their local bosses. Self-seeking and corruption among the latter had resulted in financial stratifications of the sort that most Dagestanis find unbearable in light of their ancient traditions of egalitarianism.

Initially these efforts seemed to produce some results. For example, the head of the Nepaiskii raion, Asan Mamaev, was caught red-handed receiving a bribe in Makhachkala. He was arrested and dismissed from his position. There is no doubt that the incident, bordering on entrapment, was organized by opposition elements in his raion in conjunction with high-ranking law enforcement officials in the capital.

Yet some of the popular protests in the raions were suppressed with a level of brutality previously unprecedented in Dagestan. In the most egregious case, a lawful and peaceful protest that was held on April 25, 2006, in the southern village of Miskindji was put down with stunning violence. (See Appendix.) It was suppressed by two companies of OMON troops that were dispatched from Makhachkala specifically for this purpose. One protester was killed at the scene and two more died in the hospital. Although protestors had gathered substantial evidence of local corruption, neither Moscow nor Makhachkala officials took action against the raion's nepotistic administration. Instead the organizers of the protest were arrested and charged. A similar protest was suppressed only a month before in Dagestan's Kumtorkalinskii raion.

The irony of these events is that Aliev's accession to power, his widespread perception as a principled leader, his early campaign against corruption, all encouraged, or even inspired, the rise of popular resistance to corrupt local bureaucrats. Groups throughout Dagestani society evidently mistook Aliev's appointment as an opportunity to free themselves from local potentates who had propped themselves up through the systematic abuse of their powers. Aliev's replacement of the prime minister along with several other ministers and high-ranking officials gave rise to hopes that a comprehensive political transformation was under way. Without these rising expectations, neither the wave of protests that swept Dagestan in 2006, nor their disappointment and sometimes brutal suppression, nor the sense of horror and heightened political alienation in which they culminated, would have been likely to occur.

Beginning in 2006, when power was bestowed and maintained from above by the centralized bureaucratic order, there was no longer need for popular support. For leaders attuned to this bureaucratization it was of paramount importance to provide for the bureaucrats who sustained them. The bureaucratic dependence of these local leaders was only increased by noisy protests against their local abuses. Thus, the more unpopular a local leader became, the greater the financial leverage that his bureaucratic bosses could wield against him. Abusive local governments favored the financial interests of corrupt bureaucrats, and unpopular local leaders found incentives to increase their abuse of local populations since that provided them with the financial wherewithal to ensure support for their bureaucratic bosses. In short, the new system soon established a vicious cycle that supported abusive local governments. This system was not the inadvertent by-product of otherwise legitimate administrative processes, but was the essence of the new bureaucratic power in Dagestan. Corruption permeated all levels of Dagestani politics and administration.

Any organized opposition to the established powers was viewed as an extrasystemic attempt to change the bureaucratic status quo, and was therefore a threat to personnel throughout the administrative system. Any such popular movement was perceived as a challenge not only to those who were specific targets of opposition movements but also to the entire system of corrupt bureaucratic codependencies. All such challenges were perceived as infractions against the established system.

This self-serving bureaucratic system was incapable of administering the needs of the broader society. Each bureaucratic node sought only for itself and was restricted only by the competence, power, or financial resources that were required by other systemic vertices. Since such a system inevitably stirred popular wrath, its preeminent goals included the perpetuation of its own survival through the suppression of popular discontent.

This mentality was evident in the statement by Putin appointee Dmitri Kozak, the head of the Southern Federal District, following the Miskindji protest: "We are not going to yield to the protesters no matter whether they are right or wrong, since, if we yield, everybody will be protesting and demanding." Similar statements appeared soon thereafter in President Aliev's speeches. During the Miskindji protest, some of the participants carried placards that said: "We Support the President of Dagestan, Mukhu Aliev." Yet it subsequently came to be clear that Aliev viewed such "supporters" as threats to his power. With regard to the Miskindji protesters, Aliev remarked: "Nothing at the protest meeting will ever be considered. There is a court, and they should appeal to the court. Nobody will achieve anything by protest meetings."[4]

Previously, Moscow did not interfere in the struggles among the local clans. Instead the more powerful Dagestani clans struggled among themselves to determine the division of government positions and resources. However, following the appointment of President Aliev, the federal center became the only real player on the Dagestani political scene, whether it dealt directly or through President Aliev. The result was an unresponsively autocratic bureaucracy that managed to cast Dagestan's preceding political arrangements in a flattering light, despite the rampant corruption and chronic inefficacy of Magomedali Magomedov's regime.

Why Is Dagestan Destabilizing?

A careful observer might consider the following tentative conclusions regarding these trends in Dagestani politics:

1. Within the federal bureaucracy, there is a general perception that local officials against whom people protest cannot be dismissed because their removal might start a chain reaction of protest and replacement. Such a chain reaction might feed upon itself exponentially until it destabilized local society. This would be unacceptable.
2. Local elites may be co-opted by the federal bureaucracy, upon which these elites increasingly depend to sustain their political control.
3. In the wake of Russia's recentralization, the federal bureaucracy can be mobilized to undercut local officials whenever the latter cannot be readily co-opted. Ironically, however, this is a prudent recourse only if there have *not* been substantial public protests against the local officials in question.

Since he was at the core of the older cadre of local elites who were not beholden to the federal bureaucracy, Imam Yaraliev, the old prosecutor, had to be replaced by a new one. Moreover, since the new president intended to rule on a basis of bureaucratic power, it was preferable that the new prosecutor be a product of the federal bureaucracy, who lacked a popular political base in Dagestan, and was locally connected only to the president. In this way, the federal bureaucracy extended itself vertically downward into local politics. Local leaders who depended upon the federal bureaucracy found it in their private interest to expand the control of the latter. The result was not the elimination of local corruption, but rather its bureaucratic systemization.

From 2004 to 2006, there was widespread acceptance and support in Dagestani society for the centralization and further bureaucratization of the republic's government under the impetus from the federal center as an alternative to the increasingly corrupt power of local officials. There was considerable confidence in Moscow's leadership, and particularly in the regional bureaucratic structure under the leadership of Dmitri Kozak. However, this confidence was shaken as the local population increasingly found itself in degraded political circumstances. Federal bureaucratization sustained corrupt local elites, while further removing the latter from local accountability.

Dagestani political culture traditionally has been characterized by powerful tendencies toward moderation, accommodation, and endurance. Yet deprived of nearly all mechanisms for political access, accountability, and legitimation, this political culture fell under severe strain. While Islamism, ethnicity, unemployment, poverty, corruption, and criminality were contributing factors to Dagestan's instability, none of them was sufficient to explain it. This was because each of these was also a prominent component of the Dagestani mix throughout the 1990s. During these tumultuous years Dagestan remained stable, even while nationalism, Islamism, poverty, and unemployment were at the root of conflicts that flamed and smoldered in all of the surrounding territories, and that frequently spilled across Dagestan's borders.

So the question was: why did ethnicity, Islamism, poverty, and unemployment become more critically destabilizing factors in the first decade of the twenty-first century than they had been in the last decade of the twentieth century? This question was only the first of three paradoxes arising from Dagestan's growing instability. The second was: why did Dagestan's political stability decline as the institutions of state law enforcement and control were strengthened, and as the power of the federal government returned to the republic following the erratic decentralization of the Yeltsin years? Third, why did Dagestan's stability decrease in a period when economic and political stability were being expanded and consolidated throughout much of Russia? In short, why was Dagestan falling apart, when much of the rest of the Russian Federation seemed to be coming together?

In even in the most optimistic scenario, Dagestan would have encountered some instability in the course of the encompassing economic, social, and political transition that followed the collapse of the Soviet Union. Indeed, for Dagestan, it could never have been simply a transition from one system to another, from the Soviet system to, say, an open system of adversarial democracy and market economics. This is because Dagestan was never more than a superficially Soviet society. Its multicultural mix of indigenous and Eastern traditions ensured that it could never be both an open society and a fully Westernized society, or even a pervasively Slavicized society, at the same time. Any open expression of Dagestani culture and ideals would be at least partially non-Western and non-Slavic and would therefore challenge both Russian and Western models alike. For the same reasons, Dagestan would also inevitably challenge Eastern and Islamist social models.

Thus, Dagestan could never have completed an economic and political transition toward a more open society without also embarking upon a more fundamental and more sweeping social and cultural transformation. The result of a successful transformation would be a Dagestani society that was neither Western, nor Eastern, nor Slavic, but a unique synthesis of the three with Dagestan's own colorful spectrum of cultural traditions.

As Soviet central authority disintegrated in the late 1980s, local groups in Dagestan began to cohere around specific shared agendas. As formal institutions of social order and adjudication became increasingly paralyzed, these groups sought to uphold and advance their interests by retaining or acquiring power and resources, and by protecting their members. While these groups were often characterized as "ethnic" or "clan-based" or "familial," they have been best described as ethnoparties.[5]

For a decade after 1991, the activities of Dagestan's ethnoparties resulted in a fragmented structure of political forces, replete with its own complex of advantages and disadvantages. On the negative side, this fragmentation worked against the alleviation of any of Dagestan's most pressing problems. In addition to political corruption and economic stagnation, these included infrastructural exhaustion, organized crime (especially narco-business), and religious extremism. This was because Dagestan's fragmented political system prevented any of its leaders from consolidating the broad-based support necessary for an innovative, comprehensive, and therefore risky, approach to any major problem. Were any leader to have attempted such a solution, others would have recognized both his immediate vulnerability and his remoter prospects for political ascendancy in the (improbable) event of his program's success. Hence, it would have been in their immediate interest to unite against him. For this reason, there were no serious and concerted attempts to solve Dagestan's major problems.

Yet, on the positive side, this political fragmentation had the benefit of successfully neutralizing the potential energy of the nationalist organizations that sprouted in the Dagestan of the early 1990s, while at the same time pre-

venting the construction of a rigidly hierarchical power structure by avoiding the concentration of power in the hands of any single group. Above all,
these features provided Dagestanis with a unique and indigenous democratic
pluralism, complete with its inherent set of constraints and counterbalances,
that sprang spontaneously from ancient traditions and internal political forces
without need of external imposition. When the power of the federal center
evaporated in the early 1990s, leaving the people of Dagestan without external
management, they drew upon indigenous political traditions in order to innovate viable institutions of executive and representative power that not only
accommodated the tumult of Dagestani society, but derived and sustained its
own dynamic stability out of its incessant flux.

Since this system was innovated locally, without reference to the refine-
ments of developed democracies elsewhere, it involved characteristics that
were regarded by some outside observers as being crude and unruly. For
example, confrontation was the name of the game at all levels of the political
process; the self-serving political maneuvers of Dagestan's elite were often
clumsy and transparent; assassination was among the regular means by which
elites settled disputes with one another; and "vote buying" took a variety of
forms.[6]

Yet elections among Dagestanis[7] were generally free and fair, reliably
determining political winners of competitive races, and bestowing legitimacy
upon the results. The Dagestani media exposed nefarious dealings among
elites, which added to the rough and tumble nature of Dagestani democracy.
Dagestan's National Assembly was the arena of collisions among pluralistic
forces and viewpoints, and decisions were made only as a result of mutual
concessions and compromises suitable to interests of competing parties. This
political system could not function without direct participation of the broader
population, since the strength and authority of ethnoparties substantially depended upon popular support from each particular segment of society.

Dagestan's rough-hewn democracy was neither Western, nor Eastern, nor
Slavic, nor traditional. It conformed neither to the Russian federal constitution
nor to the expectations of Moscow political observers. It met nobody's preconceptions, and satisfied no one's ideals, because it was not just a transition
from one established political model to another, but a full-scale political transformation culminating in an unprecedented system that could not otherwise
have been anticipated precisely because it was both uniquely Dagestani and
uniquely a product of its time. The dynamic and continuing development of
this system enabled Dagestan to negotiate the volatile decade that followed
the collapse of the Soviet Union, and to enter the twenty-first century with a
coherent and stable political structure.

It was at this juncture that Vladimir Putin, while visiting Makhachkala on

New Year's Eve 2000, at the moment of Boris Yeltsin's surprise resignation, declared his "love" for "the Dagestanis," and then embarked upon the re-establishment of a workable political order for the Russian Federation. Yet, it became clear as early as April 2000, just one month after Vladimir Putin's election to the Russian presidency, that his re-establishment of a coherent federal political order would mean the installation of a rigid bureaucratic structure throughout the North Caucasus. Especially fateful for Dagestan were the Kremlin's demands that local institutions should be consistent with the federal constitution and should conform with other governments throughout the federation.

Dagestani officials sought ingeniously, if unsuccessfully, to evade these requirements. Yet by 2002, they had been compelled to amend the republic's constitution at forty-five points where it differed from that of the federation. On July 26, 2003, nine years to the day after the ratification of their democratic constitution, they were forced to accept a new constitution that replaced the State Council with an individual presidency, and revamped the electoral system for the National Assembly. Then on September 13, 2004, in the aftermath of the Beslan hostage massacre, President Putin announced the centralized appointment of regional governors, such as the Dagestani executive, and a new party-based electoral system for State Duma representatives.

It was during this erratic process of federal reforms to Dagestan's indigenous political system, from 2000 to 2006, that destabilizing trends proliferated throughout Dagestani society. What is the relation, if any, between the former and the latter?

Russian observers offered at least two dramatically different answers to this question. Proponents on the one side pointed out that Dagestan's democratic institutions, like all other North Caucasian governments, were mired in corruption and chronic inefficacy. They argued that these institutions had been undermined prior to Putin's election in 2000, and rendered utterly bankrupt by the summer of 2004. They concluded that there was a desperate need for federal intervention in order to prevent greater instability and violence in Dagestan as well as other North Caucasian republics, and that the Kremlin has been responding appropriately, if belatedly, to that need.

Proponents of this view included a number of political observers in Moscow. They placed responsibility for the collapse of North Caucasian democracies upon local officials, and often upon local populations. Sometimes traditional North Caucasian social structures also received a share of the blame. For example, in an article in *Moskovskii Komsomolets,* Julia Kalinina offered the following interpretation of Dmitri Kozak's Southern Federal District Report to the Kremlin, concerning causes of instability in the North Caucasus, that was leaked in July. Note the author's reference to

Dagestan's ethnoparties, as well her implication concerning the desirability of the manipulation of Dagestani politics from the federal center:

> As a matter of fact, Dagestan is ruled by numerous criminal groupings. At present, there is no one among them strong enough to knock down the others. If one such grouping did in fact exist, Dagestan would turn into one of our regular North Caucasian republics like Kabardino-Balkaria or Adygea—subsidized and corrupted, but controllable. As long as such a grouping does not exist, the instability in Dagestan will grow; Wahhabism will become stronger; interethnic confrontations will become more aggravated; and disappointment with the authorities will increase. All this will end in the natural way—civil war, disintegration of Dagestan, and loss of the territories by Russia.[8]

The opposing view of these events was held primarily by political observers in Dagestan. They pointed out that Dagestan remained stable in the 1990s, when it was largely neglected by the federal center. Local instability increased after Putin's first election in direct proportion to federal intervention in Dagestan's political system. On this view, Moscow's efforts to bring Dagestan into political conformity with the rest of the Russian Federation undermined those unique institutions and indigenous social structures through which Dagestan maintained its stability. In their place, the Kremlin entrenched a small group of local elites, who were thereby rewarded for their corruption and incompetence, and who had little interest in accountability to their constituents since their power depended entirely upon Moscow's disposition. The ethnoparties were thereby destroyed, and the dynamic balancing and counterbalancing among these numerous groups that previously had preserved Dagestan's stability was lost.

Which of these two opposing perspectives on the causes of Dagestan's instability is correct? The former view is accurate at least insofar as Russian recentralization introduced Dagestani politics neither to corruption nor to an exclusive and clannish political elite. Corruption was entrenched at all levels of Dagestani government prior to Putin's ascendance, and control of Dagestan's government and economy was already divided among 200 or 300 families. Dagestan's State Council never functioned as intended, since the chair was monopolized from its inception by the Dargin representative, Magomedali Magomedov.

Yet the latter perspective is also correct in that these negative trends were exacerbated and intensified during the period of Russian recentralization. After Dagestan's adoption of a new constitution in 2003, political corruption became even more pervasive. For example, it became impossible to obtain any government position at even the lowest level, to receive any appreciable public service, or even to gain admission to higher education, without paying a substantial bribe. Public officials routinely siphoned the sizable federal subsidies that Dagestan received from Moscow, and, after lining their own pockets, used the funds to extend their personal patronage throughout the republic. At the same time, popular political access steadily contracted as the Kremlin backed a small group of elites. Because these officials came to depend entirely upon Moscow for their power, they were insulated from any need for local accountability.

Liberated from local accountability, Dagestani elites were less concerned than ever before with chronic problems such as poverty, unemployment, public health, infrastructure, environment, and organized crime. Ordinary Dagestanis grew more frustrated by problems such as these, as well as by their lack of political access to contracting circles of elites. Consequently, they grew disillusioned with political and economic reforms, and perceived these as leading only to further disparities of wealth and power. Since they now lacked any other means of political opposition, some turned to radical Islam.

Islam provided the only alternative means of social organization in all of those rural areas where neither the Dagestani government nor the federal government effectively functioned. Because it was thereby placed into a political role, Islam in Dagestan was increasingly politicized, and because this role was parallel with, and often in opposition to the government in Makhachkala, Islam in Dagestan was increasingly radicalized. Throughout Dagestan's rural areas, ordinary villagers, who once looked to democratic institutions for solutions, and to Moscow for support, turned instead to Islamic leaders. Under pressure from the desperate needs of their followers, and for lack of any other alternative, some of these leaders turned toward radicalism.

This trend toward Islamic radicalism gradually overtook the previously moderate outlook of Dagestan's official Islamic (Sufi) administration (DUMD), which was entirely distinct from the intolerantly puritanical, violently expansionist, and highly radicalized ideology of the Wahhabis. After 2002, when Dagestani Wahhabis initiated a series of regular attacks upon government and law enforcement officials, the police response became increasingly brutal, repressive, preemptive, and indiscriminate. Young men were routinely tortured and abused because of suspicions that sometimes were based upon little more than their Islamic affiliations. These abuses radicalized young men who otherwise would not have considered violence. In turn, they exacted their own retribution upon the police, or they gravitated toward Wahhabi leaders, who recruited them for attacks upon officials. Young men attacked the police for reasons of revenge as well as ideology, and the police responded with more brutality. Dagestan spiraled down a vicious cycle of corruption, disparity, poverty, unemployment, frustration, alienation, radicalism, violence, repression, and anger.

To some extent these effects were buffered by Dagestan's traditional culture of political moderation. Dagestanis may have tended toward confrontation, but for the most part they nevertheless sought peaceful solutions and shunned unlimited escalation. There was a minority, perhaps less than 15 percent, that would have supported either violent separatism or an expansionist-Islamist political agenda. Yet it appeared that an overwhelming majority, perhaps more than 80 percent, of the Dagestani people desired to remain within a multiethnic republic as a part of the Russian Federation. They were pragmatic enough to recognize that their aspirations toward security and prosperity would find no place apart from the economic and political space of the Russian Federation. The problem was that apart from these chronically unfulfilled and increasingly frustrated aspirations, some highlanders no longer had good reason to continue as citizens either of Dagestan or of Russia. In some rural areas, the governments of Dagestan and Russia had ceased to function in any other than repressive terms.

So Moscow and Dagestani perspectives on the causes of the republic's growing instability were each partially correct. It was true that prior to April 2000, Dagestan's political system was encountering problems that probably required federal intervention. It was also true that these problems grew worse after that intervention began. Hence, it might have been useful to consider alternative federal strategies.

Had the federal center returned to an active role on Dagestan's political stage by playing the part of an arbitrator or referee in the republic's incessant power struggles, or the part of a guarantor of its democratic procedures, or as an opponent of political corruption, or as an informed and selective investor in local economic projects, then the political system might have grown more stable and its citizens might have grown more loyal to the federal center. Instead, Moscow staked everything upon a narrow group of top-level managers and tolerated their self-serving machinations. The Kremlin made itself an instrument in the struggle between this narrow ruling class and the full range of its local political competitors. It continued to provide substantial financial injections despite the fact that these usually fell into the hands of the ruling groups, thereby exacerbating the disparities of wealth and power that diminished the republic's stability. The stratification of wealth reached extremes that were all but intolerable for most Dagestanis.

In short, the federal center reduced itself to little more than a carrot and a stick. On the one hand, it offered tangible incentives for the fidelity of local potentates, and supplemented these with intangibles such as its blind acquiescence in their flagrant excesses. On the other hand, it punished anything it perceived as infidelity, even when this took the form of legitimate political opposition, or the representation of divergent political interests that is the hallmark of any truly federal system.

There were relatively few opportunities for the political balancing and counter-balancing that once occurred openly and pluralistically through public exposés, legislative debates, coalition building, and other forms of legitimate political opposition. This culminated in the gradual elimination of all ethnoparties from the economic and political life of the republic, other than those that were led by members of the republic's top management. There were more political and economic "losers," who became sullen opponents of the ruling powers in Makhachkala and their sponsors in Moscow. Decreased opportunities for the legitimation of political aspirations led to decreased incentives for the legitimation of economic aspirations. Hence, the economic resources of some of these new outsiders began migrating away from legitimate enterprises toward their shadow and criminal counterparts. Increasingly, networks of connections were established among a wide variety of political outsiders, including those with backgrounds as elites, extremists, and criminals. All such associations were characterized by a common opposition to the ruling authorities.

Beginning in April 2000, as Moscow progressively dismantled Dagestan's innovative democratic political structure, Dagestani political authority gradually diverged from its foundation in Dagestan's traditional social structure. Dagestan's new government reoriented its political focus from the internal "force field" of dynamically competing groups and located its center of gravity outside of the republic at the federal center. Personal political power was no longer based upon internal political conditions, but upon the bureaucratic authority of official functionaries, leaning for power on higher-level administrative organs that were connected ultimately to the Kremlin. As Dagestan's political leaders became increasingly alienated from the surrounding society, they lost the support of local communities.

Thus it should perhaps come as no surprise that when President Aliev in April 2009 announced an effort to amend Dagestan's electoral laws to restore the principle of ethnic proportionality in government institutions, he linked ethnic balance and representation to the government's very legitimacy and the stability of the republic. The move to conform Dagestan's political system with Russia's, even if correct, may have been premature, Aliev suggested. "National feelings just like religious ones are very strong," he said. "Time and patience are needed."[9]

The Russian recentralization drive launched by Vladimir Putin is the latest chapter in a series of struggles that have constituted the history of the North Caucasus over the last two millennia, and it bears similarities to much that has preceded it. In stark contrast to the latitude of the 1990s, Moscow subsequently focused upon the vertical development of bureaucratic control throughout the Russian Federation. It did not offer to compromise with indigenously horizontal North Caucasian social structures, but rather structured its policies around reactions against the compromises of the Yeltsin regime.

Perhaps it was the misfortune of the Putin regime that it began with the invasion of Dagestan in 1999, and was in some ways formed by that experience. In any case, the Kremlin's subsequent approach to most problems in the North Caucasus, and to many problems elsewhere in Russia, was predominantly security oriented and forceful. Often Moscow did not see security measures as paving the way toward a package of compromises with the local peoples that might have been directed toward ameliorating the fundamental problems of the region. Rather it sometimes offered security measures themselves as the solutions to the problems of the region. This approach led Moscow to support corrupt local officials instead of removing them, to undermine and then eliminate local democratic procedures, and to ignore human rights abuses. In this sense, the Islamists have played a role in setting the tone of Kremlin policies, and Moscow has, in some ways, been playing their game.

By all rights, the Islamists should be losing in the North Caucasus. As was once the case with Imam Shamil, Shamil Basaev was waging war against the traditional parochialism of the North Caucasus. That is why he could not be satisfied with a de facto independent Chechnya, and why he invaded Dagestan, Nazran, Beslan, and Nalchik. The ideologies of absolutism and expansionism that have been sequentially propounded by Imam Shamil, Shamil Basaev, and other Islamists are incompatible with the traditionalism, the parochialism, and the pragmatic moderation of North Caucasian cultures.

That is why most North Caucasians looked to Moscow to help them with an absolutist, expansionist, fundamentally uncompromising Islamism. In order to advance the Russian struggle with Islamism, Moscow could have compromised with the traditions and needs of the North Caucasians, in order to give them good reasons to remain Russian citizens.

Once, in the first half of the nineteenth century, and again, in the first half of the twentieth century, the concentration of vertical power issued in a backlash of horizontal disintegration. Is this pattern being repeated in a new century? Many people in Dagestan and across the North Caucasian highlands have grown disillusioned with both Moscow and Islamism. Highland life is collapsing once again into isolated villages headed by local Islamic officials, who are turning their backs upon Islamism and upon Russia, and are finding themselves ominously without any place in the twenty-first century.

Appendix
Miskindji Village Protests

Details of popular protests illustrate the manner in which widespread expectations were disappointed, and political access was restricted, in the months after Mukhu Aliev's February 2006 appointment as Dagestan's first president.

The scene of the most egregious repression was Dokuzparinskii raion, which lies at the southernmost tip of Dagestan, astride some of the highest mountains in the Caucasus range. Although the raion traces its origins to the Soviet era, it did not emerge as a formal administrative unit until the 1990s. At that time, the raion was formed around the union of two historical "free societies" otherwise known as djamaats. Historically, there were three "free societies" in this area of Dagestan: Akhty-para, Dokuz-para, and Alty-para. Akhty-para became the center of the neighboring Akhtynskii raion. In order to form Dokuzparinskii raion, Dokuz-para and Alty-para were combined with the larger town of Miskindji.

Miskindji villagers are the only ethnic Lezgins that follow Shia Islam. By contrast, the Sunni faith embraces all other Lezgins, and indeed all other Dagestani Muslims, apart from the indigenous Azeri population. Historically, this distinction served to separate the Miskindji inhabitants from their neighbors. However, with the declining salience of religious cleavages during the Soviet period, this distinction became relatively inconsequential. The combination of Miskindji with Dokuz-para and Alty-para had produced no previous difficulties. Indeed, religious differences played no overt role in the incidents of 2006, though there was some speculation about the deeper significance of these differences. For example, there were concerns that the brutality of the authorities at the Miskindji protest may have been connected to religious differences.

Dokuzparinskii raion encompasses eight djamaats and two hamlets with an aggregate population of 12,000. Because the main Dokuzparinskii djamaats are high in the mountains, and because there are ancient rivalries among them and their constituent tuhums, none of them was well suited to become the administrative center of the new raion. Hence the administrative center of the raion was established in Usukhchai, in the Samur River valley, just over the border from Azerbaijan. This village was built relatively recently as a way

217

station on the road between Derbent and Akhty and further northwestward to Rutul. Because it is relatively new, Usukhchai is neutral ground among the contending regional tuhums.

On April 25, 2006, lawful protests of the residents of Dokuzparinskii raion against the corruption of the local authorities were brutally suppressed by two companies of OMON that were deployed from Makhachkala specifically for this purpose. One protester was killed at the scene, and two more died soon thereafter in the hospital. These events contrasted starkly with Dagestan's previous protests, which were not met with harsh suppression unless the protesters themselves resorted to violence or other violations of the law. Though Dagestanis have grown somewhat inured to violence, there was widespread shock at this unprecedented response to a peaceful protest by law-abiding citizens.

In an effort to justify their response, the authorities claimed that "obscure oppositional forces were concealed behind the demonstrators." There was an element of truth in this claim. Apparently, local ethnoparties were attempting to overthrow Kerimkhan Abasov (aka Kerimkhan Dokuzparinskii), who headed the powerful and nepotistic Dokuzparinskii clan. The father of Kerimkhan's brother-in-law was the deputy head of Dokuzparinskii raion. Kerimkhan's cousin, Abduragim Aliskerov, was the administrative head of the raion. Kerimkhan's brother, Akimkhan Abasov, was the treasurer for the entire southern region of Dagestan. Kerimkhan's nephew (his sister's son), N. Balasiev, was chairman of the raion's audit committee. Kerimkhan's son was deputy judge of the raion. The list continued.

Yet, despite the monolithic power of this clan, documentation concerning the development of the confrontation in Dokuzparinskii raion suggested that this was Dagestan's first case of an attempt to remove local authorities from power by exclusively lawful means. This time though, it was government agencies, together with the local Abasov administration that demonstrated an unprecedented resistance to the opposition.

In retrospect, it was remarkable that protesting residents of the Dagestani village that is furthest from Makhachkala, and that is among the highest in the mountainous region bordering Azerbaijan, that these people did not turn to the consolations of Islamist ideology, and that they did not opt for methods of political assassination that are traditional in Dagestan. Instead the local opposition leaders, supported by the majority of the population of this region, started an investigation in order to acquire the data necessary to expose the corruption of the local administration. They appealed to appropriate state organs with petitions, complaints, and statements demonstrating the character and degree of the abuse of power by the local authorities.

In early February 2006, the people of this raion sent a petition to Dagestan's chief executive, at the time Magomedali Magomedov. The petition included details and documentation concerning the scale of embezzlement by the head of the raion. The documents showed that during his administration, Abasov had embezzled a total of 115 million rubles, including 16 million rubles in loans for various specific purposes. Twenty-six teachers at the village school in Kaladzhukh wrote to the general prosecutor of the Russian Federation, Vladimir Ustinov, concerning chronic delays in the payment of their salaries even though administrative reports noted no delays.

The people of Dokuz-para wrote to the prosecutor of Dagestan, to the plenipotentiary of Russia's Southern Federal District, and to a range of Dagestani government officials. In response to these petitions, the authorities occasionally dispatched commissions of inspectors to verify the facts, but the work of the inspectors was interrupted by various events, including "natural disasters." Consequently, no findings were reported, no conclusions were drawn, no decisions were made, and no solutions were implemented, either condemning or absolving Abasov.

Only after a petition was sent to President Putin did the residents see the initiation of a serious inspection and a thorough audit of the financial and administrative activities of the authorities of Dokuz-para. Yet even that audit was stalled by bureaucratic obstacles. The first mass protest took place on October 31, 2005. The protesters demanded:

- That the investigative commission include representatives of the local population with access to information regarding the work of the commission.
- That the results of the audit be published in the media.
- That the regulations of the raion be altered to allow for the general election of the head of the raion.
- That there should be "an investigation of the fact of a threatening use of guns against the activists from the village of Mikrakh."
- That, above all else, Magomedali Magomedov should sign Abasov's discharge from his position as head of Dokuzparinskii raion.

Following the protest meeting and the petition to President Putin, it was clear that these demands would not be easily overlooked. Yet the resumption of an investigation was soon followed by a fire that destroyed all of the raion's financial documents. This was despite efforts by the opposition to warn the police that preparations were being made by local officials to torch the archive. Criminal charges were filed regarding the arson, but none of the audits were completed and there was no resolution of the case.

Participants in the October 31 protest meeting had resolved that if the authorities did not act on their complaint, they would hold another meeting in the spring of 2006. The opposition prepared carefully for this meeting, paying special attention to avoid provocation of violence against themselves. They submitted their request for the meeting in due time, stating clearly when, where, why, how long the meeting would last, and who its organizers and leaders were.

Meanwhile, Abasov's supporters also initiated a series of well-organized repressions against the opposition activists. The protesters wrote to the head of the Southern Federal District, Dmitri Kozak, and to the deputy of the general prosecutor of the Russian Federation, Nikolai Shepel. In their letters they stated that "beginning from November 5, the local police, on the order of the prosecutor of the Dokuzparinskii raion, were interrogating, detaining without a warrant, and demanding explanations from the villagers who participated in the meeting." On December 29, 2005, their letter was finally answered by the Office of the General Prosecutor of Dagestan. It stated that "the letters were received and were taken into consideration." In essence, these are the final sentences of the general prosecutor's letter:

> During the investigation, the following documents were collected and sent to the office of the prosecutor of Dagestan:
>
> • On the fact of deliberate destruction of documents concerning the finances of the administration of Dokuzparinskii raion covering the period from 2000 to 2004, given on April 18, 2005 . . . to the archive of the raion for temporary storage.
> • On the fact of embezzlement from the budget of 29,995,000 rubles.
>
> The verification of the above-mentioned facts continues.

Abasov threatened to call upon OMON troops to disperse the protest meeting, a further indication of his lack of support in the raion. The threat was not taken seriously by the residents because there was no precedent in Dagestan for the deployment of OMON against a peaceful protest meeting.

Yet in the intervening months power had shifted in Makhachkala. Instead of Magomedali Magomedov, whose style of leadership and methods for the appointment of key personnel were well known throughout Dagestan, there was now a new leader with a completely different manner. Without question, the arrival of the new leader, committed to the fight against corruption, gave people new hope. Protest meetings became widespread and well-organized with many participants.

On the morning of April 25, 2006, in accord with the request that they had submitted, about 1,000 people gathered by the bridge that leads to the raion's administrative center in the village of Usukhchai. Among them were people from the village of Miskindji. Their intent, as they had stated in the application for a permit, was to march to the central square of Usukhchai, and to hold their meeting in front of the administrative building. However, they were stopped at the bridge by the local police with support from the OMON forces that had arrived from Makhachkala. Protest leaders negotiated with the raion's chief of police, B.A. Akhbarov, for more than an hour in the rain. Chief Akhbarov denied the protestors passage, citing orders from Kerimkhan Abasov. After an hour of fruitless negotiations, the protest leaders asked to meet with Kerimkhan Abasov and the prosecutor for the raion, Firuza Lagmetova. However, Abasov was traveling outside the raion, and Lagmetova declared that the meeting was banned because the venue that the protesters had requested was reserved for a meeting of Abasov's supporters. While the prearranged and lawfully organized meeting was banned, a few of Abasov supporters gathered in the central square for a "spontaneous" meeting.

About noon, the protesters began moving toward the village's center, but were stopped again in front of the building that houses the Prosecutor's Office. There were more negotiations, during which the authorities demanded that the meeting take place in the squalid confines of a nearby cattle yard. Meanwhile, police refused to permit protesters arriving from Miskindji to enter Usukhchai. They were told to organize their own protest meeting in their own village. However, the two groups of protesters started moving toward each other.

From a videotape recording of events that followed, it is clear that as the protesters neared the Cultural Center building, the police began to shove and hit the protesters. The protesters did not respond, but continued moving ahead. Then the OMON troops started to beat the protesters with rubber clubs and the butts of their automatic weapons.

There followed a new round of negotiations. The authorities demanded that the opposition take their protest meeting to Miskindji "to avoid clashes with the supporters of Kerimkhan Abasov." The protesters decided to go to Miskindji. However, it had been raining steadily throughout the day, and many of the protesters had been exposed to the elements for hours. With their ranks diminished by exhaustion, only about 500 protesters arrived in Miskindji.

No one has ever denied that the Miskindji protest meeting was peaceful. No one has ever alleged that provocative statements were made, or that any of the speakers resorted to the rhetoric of Islamist extremism. The only justification for police action was that a road was partially blocked by a pile of stones. There was no clear indication that the stones were connected with the protesters. The protesters claimed that the blockage was not complete, and that cars were driving past the stones without difficulty.

Without warning, at 3:00 PM, the OMON forces surrounded the protesters and advanced on them. The police fired teargas, smoke bombs, and light-and-noise grenades into the crowd, while also firing automatic weapons into the air. There is evidence that members of Abasov's personal guard were among the OMON forces. Many people from various villages recognized them, and were able to give their names. As the protesters started running toward the village center, they were attacked by the OMON troops who beat them with rubber truncheons and butt stocks. Several people were injured by fragments from exploding gas canisters.

At about this point, Murad Nagmetov, a thirty-four-year-old father of two, was killed when a teargas canister was fired directly into his heart from close range. As soon as the meeting was dispersed, a *zachistka* (cleansing action) of the village began, with OMON forces bursting into homes. A. Nasrulaev was wounded by three OMON officers in his own courtyard when a bullet passed near his heart. Another resident of Miskindji, Edman Akhmedkhanov, was seriously wounded when a gas cylinder became lodged in the right side of his chest and began releasing toxic gas internally. Police threw a teargas canister into Vidal Alipanakhov's home, in which children were present. Alidjan Shaidaev was wounded by automatic weapons fire in his own court-yard. The house of Katiriman Abasov was raked by automatic fire. OMON troops indiscriminately grabbed people, beat them, threw them into buses, and delivered them to Usukhchai.

Sixty-seven people were detained in this way. The evidence against them was "dirt on their hands," which was regarded as "proof" that they were throwing stones, according to Dagestani Deputy Interior Minister Izmailov, who led the operation. The detainees endured insults and abuse. Twenty-five of them were left standing outside under a cold rain, and were denied food and water. It was twenty-four hours before a judge arrived at the police station. The first group of detainees was released after thirty hours of detention. The next group was released two days later. Seven people were released after four days of detention. All of those arrested were fined 500 rubles.

These events were followed by a campaign of intimidation aimed at the local inhabitants. Reporters from the weekly *Molodezh Dagestana* came to the village, but could not persuade people to express their views. People refused to talk to them. "Looking around, they were pretending that they did not speak Russian, or that they were not in the village during the protest."

When the Miskindji detainees were interviewed by one of us, they sepa-rately reported that the Dagestani interior minister, Adilgevey Magomedta-girov, had arrived in Usukchai on the first night. When he entered the room where the detainees were held, he asked, "Who are these people?"

"Detainees from the mass disturbance," the chief of police answered.

The interior minister asked, "Why haven't they been shot [*rasstrelyany*] by now?"

"We'll do it right now," said the police chief.

The irony of this exchange was lost on the detainees, who saw it only as a callous display of irresponsibility and disdain for ordinary citizens.

Every one of the detainees and other Miskindji residents who were interviewed for this record claimed that the special forces of OMON had been brought from Makhachkala to the remote Dokuzparinskii raion at the expense of Kerimkhan Abasov for the purpose of suppressing his local opposition. Although there has been no proof of this claim, its widespread acceptance is significant in itself. The facts are that (a) if such a thing happened, it was completely unprecedented in Dagestan and its possibility is widely regarded as horrible; (b) many people believe that this is what happened; so (c) many people believe that something horrible and completely unprecedented occurred.

When reports reached Makhachkala that there had been serious consequences to the violence in Miskindji, particularly the news that a young protester had died, there was alarm and apprehension among the republic's highest ranking officials. Those responsible for decisions in this case tried to justify themselves. Primary responsibility rested, it seemed, in the General Prosecutor's Office, for they were required to investigate the complaints of the people of the raion.

As a result of the events in Dokuzparinskii raion and the concerns that these raised throughout Dagestan, President Mukhu Aliev was compelled to interrupt his visit to Moscow in order to return to Dagestan. Meanwhile Dmitri Kozak rushed to Makhachkala from Rostov-on-Don. On April 27, Kozak met with President Aliev and all of Dagestan's top ministers, including the general prosecutor. Kerimkhan Abasov was present at the meeting, as were A. Mursalov and Gamidullah Esedulaevich Kanberov, who represented the local opposition. After the meeting, Dmitri Kozak told reporters that "the situation is absolutely clear." He explained to reporters that the Miskindji protest "preceded the decision by only one day." Kozak claimed that his meeting had revealed that "based upon the complaints of the citizens and the audit of the raion, decisions were made, and charges were filed against the guilty parties on April 24, but the citizens were not yet informed." Evidently frightened by the gravity of events in Miskindji, bureaucrats in the prosecutors office hastily devised their "decision" regarding Abasov's abuse of power, and backdated it in an effort to cover themselves.

Yet it was only human rights activists who held an investigation, and sought to bring the facts to a broader audience. They published a brochure containing documents, letters, and complaints that exposed the corruption of Abasov's regime. The activists held a press conference in Moscow, but it was attended by few reporters, none of whom asked any questions. When a television monitor malfunctioned, the activists were unable to screen the videotape of the Miskindji protest. *Novaya gazeta* was the only newspaper that published an account of the events. Other media outlets, whether in Russia or the West, did not notice the press conference.

Later, when the first fright had passed and there was no reaction from Moscow, either from the federal authorities or the central media, the bureaucrats in the Prosecutor's Office relaxed. Soon the same bureaucrats who had claimed that a "decision" had been made, and that charges against Abasov had already been filed, were openly declaring that "decisions had not been made and charges had not been filed" in the case of the administration of Dokuz-para, and that such charges would not, and should not, be filed. Instead they began arresting the organizers of the protest meeting. The organizers were charged with four violations of the criminal code. They were charged with violating:

- Article 317: "Encroachment on the Life of an Official of a Law Enforcement Organ"
- Article 318: "Violence Toward a Representative of the Authorities"
- Article 213: "Hooliganism"
- Article 222: "Illegal Possession, Concealing, and Carrying of Weapons"

The Prosecutor's Office did not find any wrongdoing by the local administration toward the participants in the meeting.

As an unprecedented development in Dagestan's post-Soviet history, the incident at Miskindji bears analysis. These events cannot be dismissed as a regrettable mistake or an exception to the rule. Rather these developments illustrate a distinctive pattern. The same kind of corruption and caprice against which the inhabitants of Dokuzparinskii raion were protesting was being consolidated and systematized throughout Dagestan.

Kerimkhan Abasov represented a new type of leader for Dagestan's newly bureaucratized society. He was not akin to the self-made, often charismatic, leaders who emerged in the 1990s to head Dagestan's numerous ethnoparties. Due to their political circumstances, those leaders found it necessary to build support within their djamaats and raions. That political necessity established a fundamental reciprocity between elites and ordinary members of the society that ensured the accountability of the former to the latter. These circumstances restricted overt displays of arbitrariness and blatant abuses of power.

Yet when power was subsequently bestowed and maintained from above by the centralized bureaucratic order, there was no longer need for popular support. For leaders attuned to this bureaucratization it was of paramount importance to provide for the bureaucrats who sustained them. The bureaucratic dependence of these local leaders was only increased by noisy protests against their local abuses. Thus the more unpopular a local leader became, the greater the financial leverage his bureaucratic bosses could wield against him. Abusive local governments favored the financial interests of corrupt bureaucrats, and unpopular local leaders found incentives to increase their abuse of local populations since that provided them with the financial wherewithal to ensure support for their bureaucratic bosses. In short, the new system supported abusive local governments. This system was not the inadvertent by-product of otherwise legitimate administrative processes, but was the essence of power in Dagestan. Corruption permeated all levels of Dagestani politics and administration.

Notes

1. Introduction: Where Mountains Rise

1. In contrast to the incessant, smaller, localized conflicts among the diverse peoples of this region.

2. In 642 AD, Derbent was already more than 3,000 years old.

3. Michael Reynolds, "Myths and Mysticism: A Longitudinal Perspective on Islam and Conflict in the North Caucasus," *Middle Eastern Studies* 41, no. 1 (January 2005): 31–54.

4. Ibid.

5. Ibid., 33.

6. Abu Nasr Al-Farabi lived approximately from 870 to 950.

7. Abu Hamid Muhammad Al-Ghazali lived from 1059 to 1111.

8. "The Basilica of Truth and the Garden of Refinement," in the Manuscript Archive of the Dagestan Scientific Center of the Russian Academy of Science, F3, no. 94.

9. Typically, a Sufi order, or *tariqah,* is named after its founder.

10. Seraffedin Erel, *Dagistan ve Dafestanliar* (Istanbul: Istanbul Matbassi, 1961), 71. Cited in Reynolds, "Myths and Mysticism," 33.

11. Reynolds, "Myths and Mysticism," 33.

12. Hilary Pilkington and Galina Yemelianova, *Islam in Post-Soviet Russia* (London: Routledge, 2003), 28.

13. Ibid.

14. Reynolds, "Myths and Mysticism," 33–34.

15. Erel, *Dagistan ve Dafestanliar,* 58–59. Cited in Reynolds, "Myths and Mysticism," 34.

16. Reynolds, "Myths and Mysticism," 35.

17. Ahmed Cevdet Paşa [Pasha], *Kırım ve Kafkas Tarihçesi* (Kostantiniye: Matbaa-yı Ebüzziya, 1305 [1897]), 54. See also İsmail Berkok, *Tarihte Kafkasya* (Istanbul: n.p., 1958), 13–16. Cited by Reynolds, "Myths and Mysticism," 35.

18. John F. Baddeley, *The Russian Conquest of the Caucasus* (London: Longmans, Green, 1908), xxi–xxii. Cited by Reynolds, "Myths and Mysticism," 35.

19. Reynolds, "Myths and Mysticism," 35.

20. Indeed, in Arabic there is no word for "secularism." See, for example, Oliver Roy, *Globalized Islam* (New York: Columbia University Press, 2004); Oliver Roy and Carol Volk, *The Failure of Political Islam* (Baltimore: Johns Hopkins University Press, 1996); Seyyed Hossein Nasr, *Islam: Religion, History, Civilization* (New York: HarperCollins, 2003); Seyyed Hossein Nasr, *The Heart of Islam* (New York: HarperCollins, 2002).

21. Mohammad's introduction of monotheism inevitably encountered stiff resistance from the pre-Islamic polytheism of the eastern Arabian region, but in the final analysis it was Mohammad's choice to offer political and military responses. He might alternatively

have chosen quiet martyrdom, as did Jesus, or indeed as did Socrates, another inspirational teacher who may have tended toward monotheism, whose persecution resulted, in part, from his heretical transgressions against a polytheistic society.

22. For example, on the contrasts among traditional forms of social organization in Chechnya and Dagestan, see Robert Ware and Enver Kisriev, "Ethnic Parity and Political Stability in Dagestan: A Consociational Approach," *Europe-Asia Studies* 53, January 1, 2001.

23. The statement is intended broadly. Of course, there are also instances of democratic and quasi-democratic organization and impulse throughout much of Russian history.

24. On July 26, 2003, nine years to the day after adoption of its democratic constitution, Dagestani officials yielded to Kremlin pressures by adopting a new constitution that featured a presidential system.

25. Dagestan's State Council has fourteen members, one from each of its principal ethnic groups.

26. Members of Dagestan's State Council were chosen by a Constitutional Assembly whose 242 members were compiled from the 121 members of Dagestan's legislature, plus 121 delegates who were elected from the same legislative districts specifically for purposes of participation in any particular meeting of the Constitutional Assembly. The Constitutional Assembly nominated and elected members of the State Council through a multi-state process that favored candidates with inter-ethnic appeal and successfully avoided ethnic chauvinists.

27. See Ware and Kisriev, "Ethnic Parity and Political Stability in Dagestan."

28. The organization of the Islamic Party of Russia (IPR) was approved by federal authorities, despite Russian federal restrictions on mono-confessional parties. Fearing that this might later become an issue, party leaders changed the party's name to "True Patriots of Russia," playing upon the common Russian acronym. However, in the 2003 Duma election, the IPR campaigned as the "Islamic Party of Russia."

29. Subsequently, Kadyrov was named president in October 2003 and was assassinated on May 9, 2004.

30. Enver Kisriev and Robert Ware, "Irony and Political Islam," *Nationalities Papers* 30, December 4, 2002.

31. As well as with the practices of the communities of Shiites, Christians, and Jews that have long inhabited this region.

32. In 2000, our survey research found that about 90 percent of Dagestanis rejected Wahhabism. See Robert Ware, Enver Kisriev, Werner Patzelt, and Ute Roericht, "Political Islam in Dagestan," *Europe-Asia Studies* 55, March 2, 2003; Kisriev and Ware, "Irony and Political Islam"; Robert Ware and Enver Kisriev, "The Islamic Factor in Dagestan," *Central Asian Survey* 19, June 2, 2000.

2. Murids and Tsars: Islamic Ideology as an Antidote to Russian Colonialism

1. For a brief survey of the historical background see Hilary Pilkington and Galina Yemelianova, *Islam in Post-Soviet Russia* (London: Routledge, 2003), 29.

2. Ibid.

3. Ibid. Also see Alexandre Bennigsen and Marie Broxup, *The Islamic Threat to the Soviet State* (London: Croom Helm, 1983), 34.

4. The name means "to hold" or "to control" the Caucasus.

5. Pilkington and Yemelianova, *Islam in Post-Soviet Russia*, 29.

6. Michael Reynolds, "Myths and Mysticism: A Longitudinal Perspective on Islam and Conflict in the North Caucasus," *Middle Eastern Studies* 41, no. 1 (January 2005): 36.

7. Pilkington and Yemelianova, *Islam in Post-Soviet Russia*, 29. On the one hand, the Cossacks raided the Muslim natives of the region. Yet the Cossacks also interacted closely with the locals on the basis of shared values and norms.

8. Reynolds, "Myths and Mysticism," 36.

9. Ibid., 37.

10. Anna Zelkina, *In Quest of God and Freedom* (London: Hurst, 2000), 66–67.

11. Pilkington and Yemelianova, *Islam in Post-Soviet Russia*, 29.

12. Reynolds, "Myths and Mysticism," 37.

13. See Moshe Gammer, *Muslim Resistance to the Tsar: Shamil and the Conquest of Chechnia and Daghestan* (London: Frank Cass, 1994), 35.

14. For more on *teips* and *tuhums*, see Ware and Kisriev, "Ethnic Parity and Political Stability in Dagestan." See also Ian Chesnov, "Byt' Chechentsem: lichnost i etnicheskie identifikatsii naroda," in *Chechnia i Rossiia: obshchestva i gosudarstva*, ed. D.E. Furman (Moscow: Polinform-Talburi, 1999), 69–71.

15. Reynolds, "Myths and Mysticism," 37.

16. Ibid.

17. Islam does not recognize a divine right in hierarchical social relations. Rather Islamic law and morality require, in the words of M.A. Rodionov, that "All Muslims are brothers, and the nobility of each is measured by his personal piety, and not by his line of predecessors. People are as equal as the teeth of a comb, and there is no advantage of one man over another, apart for that which comes through piety" (Rodionov, *Islam Klassicheskii* [St. Petersburg: Peterburgskoe Vostokovedenie 2001], 35). Whereas Islamic society is also characterized by class structures, these derive from personal qualities without religious legitimation.

18. These famous words are commonly quoted in numerous documents from the period. For example, see A.A. Neverovskii, *O nachele bespokoistv v Severnom i Srednem Dagestane* (St. Petersburg, 1847).

19. Koran 2: 271.

20. F. Bodenstedt, *Narody Kavkaza i ikh osvoboditel'nye voiny protiv Russkikh* (1823–1831) translated from German (Makhachkala: Daggiz–Dagestani Editorial House, 1996), 44. The original edition was published in Berlin in 1847. Four chapters of the book, in which the events of the emergence of Muridism were described were translated into Russian and published in the journal, *Our Dagestan*. In 1996, the same chapters circulated in Dagestan as a pamphlet.

21. *Gazavat* is from the Arabic word for "raid" (ghazwa, ghazawat) and was later adopted by Muslim jurists as a synonym for jihad. Jihad comes from the root meaning "to strive." Thus, when considered in broader contexts, gazavat may actually have stronger martial connotations.

22. This conception may be compared usefully with Western notions of "liberation theology." These refer to claims that people should liberate themselves from social, economic, and political repression in this world, and not wait until the imperfections of this world are corrected in the other world. Doctrines of liberation theology are associated particularly with radical Catholic groups that appeared in Latin America during the 1960s. For example, see T. Louson and G. Harrod, *Sociology A–Z Dictionary* (Moscow: Grand, 2000), 479.

23. A.G. Agaev, *Magomed Yaragskii: musul'manskii filosof, pobornik very, svobody, nravstvennosti.* (Makhachkala, 1996), 85–86.

24. Ibid., 76.

25. During the Crimean War, Britain briefly considered intervention in the Caucasian War on the side of Shamil.

26. The movement of muridism in Dagestan declared "war against adat on behalf of

sharia." Dagestani folklore refers to this period in the struggle against the Russian colonial regime as "the time of sharia."

27. *Shafiya Mazkhab* (one of the four common Islamic judicial interpretations), which is commonly practiced in Dagestan, recognizes decisions that are based upon traditional law—adat—and common sense.

28. In practice, even Shamil was forced to deviate from sharia strictures when these fell too far from traditional Dagestani conceptions of justice.

29. S.G. Rybakov, *Islam in the Russian Empire: Legislation, Descriptions, Statistics* (Moscow: Academkniga, 2001), 267.

30. Pilkington and Yemelianova, *Islam in Post-Soviet Russia*, 31.

31. Including maktabs, or mosque schools, and madrassas.

32. M.O. Kosven, *Study of the History of Dagestan*, vol. 1 (Makhachkala: 1957), 371.

33. Then the capital of Dagestan, this central Dagestani town is now known as Buinaksk.

34. A. Isaev, "Spiritual Literature of the Native Dagestani Languages," in *Islam and Islamic Culture in Dagestan* (Moscow: Nauka, 2001).

35. See Marie Bennigsen Broxup, "The Last *Ghazawat*: The 1920–1921 Uprising," in *The North Caucasus Barrier: The Russian Advance towards the Muslim World,* ed. Marie Bennigsen Broxup et al. (London: C. Hurst, 1992).

36. Andi is a highland village located just to the east of what is now Dagestan's border with Chechnya. Soviet ethnographers classified the Andi people (currently numbering about 30,000) as Avars. While there are genuine ethno-linguistic affiliations between these groups, many Andis regard themselves as a separate ethno-linguistic group.

37. Reynolds, "Myths and Mysticism," 43.

38. Ibid.

39. Ibid.

3. Soviet Rule in the North Caucasus: Betrayal of Islam and Construction of Ethnicity

1. Vedeno, in the mountains of southeastern Chechnya, near the border of Dagestan, was a bastion of the nineteenth-century forces of Imam Shamil, and the home of the late leader of contemporary Chechen militancy, Shamil Basaev.

2. Gail W. Lapidus and Edward W. Walker, "Nationalism, Regionalism, and Federalism: Center-Periphery Relations in Post-Communist Russia," in *The New Russia: Troubled Transformation*, ed. Gail W. Lapidus (Boulder: Westview, 1994).

3. Richard Pipes, *The Formation of the Soviet Union, Communism and Nationalism 1917–1923* (Cambridge, MA: Harvard University Press, 1954).

4. Ualov (A. Avtorkhanov), *Narodoubiistvo v SSSR* (Munich, 1952).

5. Jane Ormrod, "The North Caucasus: Fragmentation or Federation," in *Nations and Politics of the Soviet Successor States*, ed. Ian Bremmer and Ray Taras (Cambridge: Cambridge University Press, 1993).

6. N.G. Volkova and L.I. Lavsov, "Sovremennye ethnicheskie protessy," *Kul'tura i byt narodov Severnogo Kavkaza*, ed. E.P. Prokorov (Moscow, 1968).

7. Victor Zaslavsky, "Success and Collapse: Traditional Soviet Nationality Policy," in Bremmer and Taras, *Nations and Politics of the Soviet Successor States*.

8. Helen Krag and Lars Funch, *The North Caucasus: Minorities at a Crossroads* (London: Minority Rights Group, 1994).

9. Joseph Stalin, *Works*, vol. 4 (Moscow: Politizdat, 1947), 395–96.

10. National committee, or ministry.

11. G.I. Kakagasanov, "Religioznye musul'manskie (primechetskie) shkoly Dagestana," in *Islam i islamskaia kul'tura v Dagestane* (Moscow: *Vostochnaia literatura* Ran, 2001), 132.

12. See G.Sh. Kaimarazov, in ibid.

13. N.P. Samurskii, *Dagestan* (Makhachkala, 1925), 126–27.

14. Kakagasanov.

15. M.O. Kosven, et al., *Ocherki istorii Dagestana,* vol. 2 (Makhachkala, 1957), 212.

16. O. Bobrovnikov, *Musul'mane severnogo Kavakaza* (Moscow: Nauka, 2002), 230.

17. Kakagasanov.

18. This section is drawn largely from Robert Ware's article on "Conflict in the Caucasus: An Historical Context and a Prospect for Peace," *Central Asian Survey* 17, no. 2 (1998): 337–52.

19. Ormrod, "The North Caucasus."

20. Zaslavsky, "Success and Collapse."

21. Lapidus and Walker, "Nationalism, Regionalism, and Federalism."

22. Ibid.

23. See chapter 4.

4. Democratic Dagestan: Ethnic Accommodation in the Constitutional Djamaat

1. This represents an increase of 774,300 people since the last (Soviet) census in 1989. Of this numerical increase, 323,300 were city dwellers, and 451,000 were rural dwellers. The 2002 census showed that the total population had increased in all administrative units of the republic since 1989. Dagestan's population comprised 11.3 percent of the population of the Southern Federal District and 1.8 percent of the whole Russian population. In terms of its total population in 2002, Dagestan occupied the fifth place among all subjects of the Southern Federal District and was twenty-second in the Russian Federation.

2. Daniel Pipes, "Predicting a Majority-Muslim Russia," Weblog, August 6, 2005, www.danielpipes.org/blog/495.

3. Karl Jaspers, 1991, *Smysl i naznachenie istorii* (Moscow: Politicheskaia Literatura), 218.

4. For example, suspected assassins of Representative M. Sulaymanov and former Trade Minister B. Hadjiev were murdered, as was the suspect in the beating of S. Reshulsky.

5. The term "businessman" is a euphemism. Khachilaev acquired much of his initial financial leverage as a loan shark, and his subsequent dealings were sometimes corrupt.

6. Robert Ware and Enver Kisriev, "Ethnic Parity and Political Stability in Dagestan: A Consociational Approach," *Europe-Asia Studies*, 53, January 1, 2001.

7. Dagestanis typically do not use alimi.

8. Robert Ware and Enver Kisriev, "Political Stability and Ethnic Parity: Why Is There Peace in Dagestan," in *Center-Periphery Conflict in Post-Soviet Russia: A Federation Imperiled*, ed. M. Alexseev (New York: St. Martin's Press, 1999); "The Election of Dagestan's Second People's Assembly," *Electoral Studies* 20, September 3, 2001.

9. Officially, Magomedali Magomedov was born June 15, 1930, in the Dargin village of Levashi, the center of Levashinskii raion located in the heart of Dagestan's central foothills. However, there are rumors that he is actually three to five years older. Indeed, during his years in power, there were discrepancies in his official biographies. He graduated from

Levashi High School in 1949. In 1950 he was admitted to the Dagestan Teachers' Institute, where it appears that he studied for as little as a year or a year and a half, although he also appears to have graduated with a pedagogical degree. From 1953 to 1957 he was the head of the Levashinskii raion Department of Education. In 1957 he left the field of education, became the director of one of the kolkhozes in Levashinskii raion, and remained in that position for nine years, until 1966.

10. Born in 1940, Aliev is (at least) ten years younger than Magomedov. In 1957, when the twenty-seven-year-old Magomedov directed a kolkhoz, the seventeen-year-old Aliev graduated from high school with a silver medal, and was admitted to the Dagestan State University with majors in history and philosophy. Just a year before his high school graduation, Aliev had left the high mountain village of Tanusi for Izberbash, where he attended a boarding school. Five years later, in 1962, upon graduating from the university, he went to work as a teacher, and later as a principal in the highland village of Nizhni Gakvari in the Tsumadinskii raion. Two years later, in 1964, he returned to Makhachkala where he worked as a leader of the Komsomol organization at the university. In 1966, he enrolled in a postgraduate course in philosophy, earning his doctorate in 1969. In that same year, at the age of twenty-nine, he was elected to the position that became his springboard to local fame. He became the first secretary of the Makhachkala City Komsomol Committee.

11. At that time, Magomedov (an ethnic Dargin) already had two deputies in the Gossoviet: a Lezgin, Bagautdin Akhmedov, and a Kumyk, Hizri Shikhsaidov. Avars, Dargins, Kumyks, and Lezgins, respectively, are Dagestan's largest ethnic groups. So the addition of an Avar deputy chair would ensure a place for all four of the largest groups in the leadership of the Supreme Soviet.

12. When the Chechens were deported from what is now western Dagestan in 1944, Avars and Laks were forcibly relocated to formerly Chechen villages. This led to territorial disputes when the Chechens returned after their official rehabilitation in 1957.

13. *Novoe delo*, no. 10 (1991).

14. Consociational systems of democracy occur in ethnically and/or religiously segmented societies, such as Dagestan, when political elites from various social segments cooperate through distinctive political institutions. See Ware and Kisriev, "Ethnic Parity and Political Stability in Dagestan: cf n. 6.

15. At that time there were 222 deputies in the Supreme Soviet.

16. As established by the 1994 constitution, Dagestan's National Assembly seated 121 representatives from single-mandate electoral districts.

17. As established by the 1994 constitution, Dagestan's Constitutional Assembly consisted of the 121 National Assembly representatives, plus an equal number selected from the same electoral districts, for a total of 242 members.

18. Arend Lijphart, *Democracy in Plural Societies* (New Haven, CT: Yale University Press, 1977), 5.

19. See Milton Esman, ed., *Ethnic Conflict in the Western World* (Ithaca, NY: Cornell University Press, 1986); Milton Esman, *Ethnic Politics* (Ithaca, NY: Cornell University Press, 1994); Donald Horowitz, "Ethnic Identity," in *Ethnicity: Theory and Experience*, ed. Daniel P. Moynihan and Nathan Glaser (Cambridge, MA: Harvard University Press, 1975); Donald Horowitz, *Ethnic Groups in Conflict* (Berkeley: University of California Press, 1985); Donald Horowitz, "Democracy in Divided Societies," *Journal of Democracy* 4, no. 4 (1993); Will Kymlicka, *Multicultural Citizenship* (Oxford: Clarendon Press, 1995); Lijphart, *Democracy in Plural Societies*; J. Nordlinger, *Conflict Resolution in Divided Societies* (Cambridge, MA: Harvard University Center for International Affairs, 1972).

20. Legislative elections after 2003 did not occur under the 1994 constitution, but under the 2003 constitution, as subsequently explained.

21. See the following discussion of "professional" legislative seats.

22. *Dagestanskaya pravda*, February 2, 1999.

23. Ibid., February 4, 1999.

24. Ware and Kisriev, "Ethnic Parity and Political Stability in Dagestan."

25. Lijphart, *Democracy in Plural Societies*, 41–44.

26. Nordlinger, *Conflict Resolution in Divided Societies*, 32.

27. See Lijphart, *Democracy in Plural Societies*; also D. Dogan and M. Pelassy, *How to Compare Nations* (Chatham, NJ: Chatham House, 1990).

28. See Dogan and Pelassy, *How to Compare Nations*.

29. Arend Lijphart, "Political Theories and the Explanation of Ethnic Conflict in the Western World," in Esman, ed., *Ethnic Conflict in the Western World*, 55–62; Karl Deutsch, *An Interdisciplinary Bibliography on Nationalism, 1935–53* (Cambridge, MA: MIT Press, 1956).

30. Ibid.; see also Hans van Mierlo, "Depolarisation and the Decline of Consociational-ism in the Netherlands: 1970–1985," *West European Politics* 9, no. 1.

31. This is a Dagestani tradition that enables women to prevent violence between men. When a woman steps between two belligerents and removes her headscarf she is exposing herself and thereby shaming the men who have placed her in a position where this became necessary. The men are expected to withdraw from their confrontation in order to prevent further exposure and shame for all concerned. In Dagestan, women are traditional, if not always effective, peacemakers. Though Dagestanis tend to be highly confrontational, they are generally cognizant of long-term consequences, and are some-times open to mediation. Headscarves are often abandoned by Dagestan's urban women, but they continue to be worn by nearly all village women. Urban women wear headscarves when visiting villages, and village women wear headscarves when visiting cities.

32. Who later became mayor of Khasaviurt and the leader of Dagestan's "Northern Alliance" opposition to Magomedov.

33. At the time, the Russian interior minister was Sergei Stepashin.

34. *Dagestanskaya pravda,* June 1, 2001.

35. Enver Kisriev and Robert Ware, "Dagestan's People's Assembly Election 1999," *Electoral Studies*, no. 20 (2001): 463–501.

36. *Molodezh Dagestana*, no. 11, March 12, 1999.

37. By Enver Kisriev.

38. *Moscow Times.com Special Report/Electoral Fraud*, www.themoscowtimes.com/election_fraud.html.

39. Robert Bruce Ware, "Dagestan Demands a Recount," *Moscow Times.com Special Report/ Electoral Fraud*, www.themoscowtimes.com/election_fraud.html.

40. In Russia, thirty-nine subjects of the Federation have only one territorial electoral district for the election in State Duma, including all north Caucasian republics, except Dagestan, which is the most populous republic in the region. The subject with the largest number of territorial districts is Moscow (15), the Moscow region (or oblast with 13), and St. Petersburg (8).

41. Though there were incidents of violence and electoral sabotage during the campaign in the Buinakskii raion it is not clear that these had a substantial effect on the result.

42. For example, while Dagestan's 2002 census was well-organized, there were indica-tions that some local census administrators encouraged inflations of their count in order to meet projections.

43. The first on the list was Klintsevich, the deputy of Kazantsev, the governor of the Southern Federal District of the Russian Federation.

44. Apart from blatant vote buying on many sides and violent incidents in one district.

5. The Islamic Factor: Revival and Radicalism

1. Hilary Pilkington and Galina Yemelianova, *Islam in Post-Soviet Russia* (London: Routledge, 2003), p. 47.

2. Some Muslims and nationalists in the North Caucasus responded to German offers of collaboration. Moscow responded to these limited cases of disloyalty with collective punishments that sometimes approached genocidal proportions. In 1944, all ethnic Chechens, Ingush, Balkars, Karachais, Khamshils, Kurds, Meskhetian Turks, Greeks, Bulgarians, Germans, and Crimean Tatars were hastily transported under brutal conditions to Siberia, Kazakhstan, and Central Asia.

Today Russia faces manifold ethnic and territorial disputes as a result of these dislocations, which in turn resulted in other subsidiary dislocations. For example, Dagestani Avars and Laks were forcibly relocated into villages vacated by the Chechen deportation. The Chechen-Akkins who were deported from this territory have been agitating for its return since 1989. However, the highland villages that the Avars and Laks were forced to vacate have become uninhabitable over the intervening decades. See Pilkington and Yemelianova, *Islam in Post-Soviet Russia*, 47–48.

3. D. Hiro, *Between Marx and Muhammad* (London: HarperCollins, 1994), 33. See Pilkington and Yemelianova, *Islam in Post-Soviet Russia*, 47.

For instance, Valentin Allahiyarovich Emirov (1914–42) was a pilot and hero in World War II. According to official data, he was an ethnic Lezgin, born in the Dagestani highland village of Akhti to the family of a worker. He became a military pilot, and was wounded in the Finnish war. At the beginning of World War II, he was in command of a squadron, and later—as a captain—of a regiment of fighters. In September 1942, near Mozdok, he and another Soviet fighter entered into a "dogfight" with six German fighters. After the other Soviet pilot was downed, Emirov's plane caught fire, but he shot down two German planes and rammed a third. The other three German planes fled. Emirov tried to save his plane, but it was too late to use his parachute. He became a Hero of the Soviet Union posthumously. After the war, he was reburied in Makhachkala.

4. Though many Dagestanis were voluntarily evacuated to Central Asia (under harsh conditions), and though extensive defensive preparations were in place (including antitank trenches around Makhachkala), Dagestan was not invaded by German forces (Pilkington and Yemelianova, *Islam in Post-Soviet Russia*, 49).

5. The Chechen and Ingush ethnic groups were officially rehabilitated in 1957, after which many of their members began to return to their traditional North Caucasian territories from the sites in Central Asia to which they had been brutally deported in 1944.

6. Pilkington and Yemelianova, *Islam in Post-Soviet Russia*, 49, 50.

7. Ibid., 52–53.

8. Ibid., 53.

9. Ibid.

10. Ibid.

11. Ibid.

12. A maktab is a mosque school providing elementary Islamic education.

13. Pilkington and Yemelianova, *Islam in Post-Soviet Russia*, 53.

14. In the history of Sunni Islam, four major schools of *fiqh*, the legal exegesis of

sharia, came to prominence. These four schools (madhabs) are: Hanafi, Maliki, Shafi'i, and Hanbali. The Hanafi madhab originated in Central Asia with the teachings of Imam Abu Hanafa. It was introduced to the Volga Bulgars in the late eighth century by traders from Khazaria and Central Asia, and spread from there to become the dominant form of Islam in all parts of Russia. The exception is Dagestan, where the Shafi'i madhab is predominant.

The Hanafi school appealed to the Turkic peoples of Central Asia, the Volga-Ural region, and the Northwest Caucasus, in part, because it is relatively tolerant of pre-Islamic traditions. The Hanafi madhab is also traditionally tolerant of other faiths, and specifically advocates the coexistence of Muslims and Orthodox Christians. It also adopts a cooperative approach toward political authority, rejecting open rebellion. Hanafi leaders generally support Russia's territorial integrity and secular form of government, accepting the separation of church and state. Yet the passive approach of this school may have also prepared the way for other forms of Islam that call for a more assertive political stance.

15. Sunna is literally "custom" or "example." It consists of examples from the Prophet's life as guidance for every Muslim.

16. Pilkington and Yemelianova, *Islam in Post-Soviet Russia,* 149.

17. Ibid., 151.

18. *Djamaat* used in reference to the political structures traditionally associated with Dagestani village life. *Jamaat* used to designate Islamist organizations.

19. Pilkington and Yemelianova, *Islam in Post-Soviet Russia,* 151.

20. Walter Comins-Richmond, "Legal Pluralism in the Northwest Caucasus: The Role of the Sharia Courts," *Religion, State, and Society* 32, March 1, 2004.

21. Pilkington and Yemelianova, *Islam in Post-Soviet Russia,* 151.

22. Ibid., 154.

23. See Enver Kisriev and Robert Ware, "Irony and Political Islam," *Nationalities Papers* 30, December 4, 2002. See also Pilkington and Yemelianova, *Islam in Post-Soviet Russia,* 104.

24. Ibid., 97–104.

25. Robert Ware and Enver Kisriev, "The Islamic Factor in Dagestan," *Central Asian Survey,* 19, June 2, 2000. Also see Pilkington and Yemelianova, *Islam in Post-Soviet Russia,* 154.

26. Pilkington and Yemelianova, *Islam in Post-Soviet Russia,* 154.

27. It was Raduyev who led the January 9, 1996, raid on the Dagestani city of Kizliar, resulting in his detainment of 350 hostages and a bombardment of the Dagestani village of Pervomayskaya by Russian Federal troops, during which more than 100 of the hostages died.

28. Evidently, the seizure followed a shootout in the streets of Makhachkala between Makhachkala police and the bodyguards of Nadirshah Khachilaev. Nadir, who represented Dagestan in the Russian State Duma, was a prominent Islamic leader who developed ties to radical Islamists in the Karamakhi area as well as in Chechnya. However, his brother Magomed, who joined in the takeover, and who had grown powerful through an early career as a loan shark followed by a lucrative administrative post in the local fishing industry, showed few Islamist tendencies. Though it lasted for twenty-four-hours and threw the entire republic into a state of crisis, the ill-fated seizure seemed to have more to do with tensions among local elites, and with the weakness of the Makhachkala regime, than with Islamist politics. Because of Nadir's role it is possible that the dramatic events in Makhachkala and Karamakhi were coordinated, but it is more likely that his daring simply encouraged the Karamakhi radicals to capitalize opportunistically upon the crisis.

29. *Novoe delo* 28, July 10, 1998.

30. *Dagestanskaya pravda,* August 25, 1998.

31. *Molodezh Dagestana,* no. 34, August 28, 1998.

32. The investigative team included Enver Kisriev of Dagestan Scientific Center along with Werner Patzelt and Ute Roericht of Dresden Technische Universität. The study was supported by the National Council for Eurasian and East European Research and the National Research Council. Preliminary survey research was funded in 1998 by Southern Illinois University, Edwardsville. See "Political Islam in Dagestan," *Europe-Asia Studies* 55, no. 2 March 2, 2003: 287–302. For further details on approach, methodology, and results see "Democratization in Dagestan," paper presented at the annual meeting of the American Political Science Association, San Francisco, September 1, 2001.

33. Ware first learned of the conflict on August 4, 1999, as he was boarding a flight from New York to Moscow with the intent of initiating this study.

34. The lists are compiled by electoral commissions and include all people age eighteen years and older who were officially registered as residing in each area. Random selection from these lists was accomplished according to a "step method." The size of the "step" was determined by dividing the total number of names on any given list by the number of respondents required from that area. As a consequence, the size of the "step" varied, but generally it was greater than twelve. In a case, for example, where the "step" was fourteen, we contacted every fourteenth person on the list. In the event of the unavailability of, or refusal by, one of these selectees, the next person on the list was contacted. Randomizing features of this method generally yielded samples that were proportionate to demographic data with respect to age and gender. However, random sampling in many Dagestani villages, conducted at virtually any time, is likely to lead to overrepresentation of women, as many men go to cities for purposes of employment. Therefore, it was necessary to compensate by sampling in urban areas that were further stratified with respect to gender, so as to balance the number of men in the survey in accord with demographic data. When interpreting the tabular data that follow, it must be borne in mind that data for villages are disproportionately female, and data for towns are disproportionately male. While the overall response rate was 71 percent, some items from completed surveys contain missing values, which are not always randomly distributed.

35. In the tables, data is broken down for Dagestan's most important ethnic groups, since issues of ethnicity are central to every understanding of Dagestan and its cultural features. Because of an extraordinary number of missing cases, valid numbers usually do not add up to the sample size of 1,001; usual case numbers for the different ethnic groups are shown in Table 5.1. Interpretations of survey data are based on comparisons of percentages and means, sometimes on correlation coefficients. Since missing values are not distributed randomly, we tried to avoid missing-sensitive multivariate statistics and calculated percentages regularly on the constant base of the overall sample.

36. Usually, those Dagestanis who see changes for the worse, both in Dagestan's economy (Spearman's rho = -0.12) and political life (Spearman's rho = -0.15), tend slightly to agree with the statement "Wahhabis are extremists behind a religious facade." This corresponds to the conviction expressed in many elite interviews that Wahhabism emerges from Dagestan's transitional problems. Exclusively among Chechens, possibly the least integrated of Dagestan's ethnic groups, Wahhabis are regarded as extremists by those who see both Dagestan's economic situation (Spearman's rho = 0.46) and social and cultural life (Spearman's rho = -0.53) changing for the better. This suggests that even among Dagestan's most alienated group, perceptions of opportunities for economic and cultural improvement undercuts the appeal of Wahhabism.

37. The dependent variable in a logistic regression is coded 0 and 1. A logistic regression defines the relationship between dependent and independent variables in a totally different way from a "regular" regression, where one unit change in the independent variable is connected with a certain change in the dependent variable. Logistic regression uses "odd

ratios" instead, which show the probability for the value one (in the dependent variable) compared with a reference group. The significance column in Table 5.2 indicates statistically significant differences, the standard limit being $p < = 0.05$. The Cox and Snell R^2 is an indicator for the amount of explained variance in the model, comparable to R^2 in the linear regression.

38. See Robert Ware, Enver Kisriev, Werner Patzelt, and Ute Roericht, "Dagestan and Stability in the Caucasus," *Problems of Post-Communism,* 50, no. 2 (March–April 2003), 12–23.

39. See ibid.

40. Since many individuals gave long lists of causal factors, items from several responses had to be attributed to more than one single category.

41. Cf. the following extract from an elite interview: "Earlier we had so-called socialist and capitalist regimes. They tried to maintain an economic, technical, and military balance. Gorbachev, with his perestroika, practically ruined the country, and later Russia found itself on the edge of a crash. I agree that we needed democracy, but not at that speed. Western countries and NATO made all efforts to ruin the USSR and the Warsaw Pact, and later Russia. So they used the religious factor, including Wahhabism. Our country was economically and politically weakened, and it was a good ground for the dissemination of Wahhabism."

6. Conflict and Catharsis: Why Dagestanis Fought to Remain in Russia

1. *Molodezh Dagestana,* no. 17, April 23, 1999.

2. For example, see, Rajan Menon, "Russia's Quagmire: On Ending the Standoff in Chechnya," *Boston Review* (Summer 2004); John B. Dunlop, "The October 2002 Moscow Hostage-Taking Incident," in three parts, Radio Free Europe/Radio Liberty, December 18, 2003, January 8, 2004, and January 15, 2004; David Sattar, *Darkness and Dawn: The Rise of the Russian Criminal State* (New Haven: Yale University Press, 2003); John Sweeny, "Take Care Tony, That Man Has Blood on His Hands: Evidence Shows Secret Police Were Behind 'Terrorist' Bomb," (London) *Observer*, March 12, 2000; Jonathan Steele, "The Ryazan Incident," *Guardian*, March 24, 2000; Jamie Dettmer, "Terrorism: Did Putin's Agents Plant the Bombs?" *Insight on the News*, April 17, 2000.

3. Petra Prokhazkova, *Lidove noviny*, September 9, 1999, 7.

4. Data published in *Novoe delo*, January 9, 2004.

5. Identification with the djamaat is so much weaker than we anticipated as to be inconsistent with anecdotal information that we received from numerous Dagestanis. It is possible that Dagestanis regard identification with djamaati as atavistic, and are therefore less inclined to indicate it in the formal framework of a survey. Conversely, it could also be that anecdotes tend to overplay Dagestani traditions, which are clearly a matter of pride for some individuals. While we regard this as a point for further study, the survey results speak for themselves.

6. The question was: "Dagestan has significantly changed during the past ten years. The changes have significantly affected Dagestani society, economy, and politics. Looking back, what do you think of these changes? These changes turned out to be for (the better [1]; no better, no worse [2]; the worse [3])?"

7. The question was: "In your opinion, on what principles should the Dagestani state be built: (a) on the principles of Islam and Shari'ah (1); (b) on the principles of Western democracies (2); or (c) on the principles of socialism (3)?"

8. The questions was "How would you evaluate the activity of the following state institutions in Dagestan . . . (good [1]; satisfactory [2]; bad [3])."

9. See Robert Ware and Enver Kisriev, "Conflict and Catharsis: A Report on Develop-

ments in Dagestan following the Incursions of August and September 1999," *Nationalities Papers* 28, September 3, 2000; "Political Stability in Dagestan: Ethnic Parity and Religious Polarization," *Problems of Post-Communism* 47, no. 2 (March–April 2000); Robert Ware and enver Kisriev, "Ethnic Parity and Political Stability in Dagestan: A Consociational Approach," *Europe-Asia Studies* 53, January 1, 2001.

10. The question read as follows: "In whom would you place your trust (hope) in the event of an acute crisis in Dagestan? (you may select more than one answer)."

11. The authors, who were present in Russia during the invasions, had the opportunity to observe requests for assistance on the part of Dagestani officials, and the initially fumbling response of the federal government. The extremity of these events may partially account for the strength of this response; yet there is also considerable anecdotal evidence indicating that many Dagestanis look to Moscow to solve the republic's deeper problems.

12. The question was: "What external factors, in your opinion, could threaten the stability of Dagestan? How serious are these threats?" (1) from Russia; (2) from Chechnya; (3) from Western countries; (4) from Eastern countries"; very serious (1); not very serious (2); not serious at all (3).

13. The question was, "In your opinion, how should the relationship of Dagestan and Russia develop?" Dagestan should become even closer to Russia (–1); the present system of relations should continue (0); Dagestan should become more independent (1).

14. *Dagestanskaya pravda*, March 21, 2000.

15. The Decree of the Supreme Council of the Russian Federation on behalf of the Chechen-Akkins for the formation of the Aukhovskii raion of the Autonomous Republic of Dagestan was signed in Moscow in 1944, two weeks prior to the deportation of the Chechens. Its formation was warranted by the concentration of Chechen ethnics in this portion of Dagestan. Interestingly, Stalin often performed favors for individuals just before arranging their imprisonment or execution. The idea seemed to be that of lulling his enemies into a false sense of security before striking them.

16. In the Soviet era, Kremlin policy required that a mass protest would cost the job of a local administrator.

17. See pages 56–57.

18. In 1916, before the Russian Revolution, these territories, including the land of the Aukhovskii Chechens as well as other Chechen territories, were part of the Terskii oblast of the Russian empire. Administrative boundaries rarely matched the traditional borders of ethnic territories. In 1916, Aukh was part of Nozhai-Yurtovskii okrug (district) of the Terskii oblast. The district combined the lands of Chechens, Kumyks, and Avars. For this reason, many Dagestanis do not consider prerevolutionary administrative boundaries as either ethnically or historically justified.

7. Russian Recentralization and Islamic Resistance: Stepping on the Same Rake

1. *Dagestanskaya pravda,* February 2, 1999.

2. Ibid.

3. Enver Kisriev and Robert Ware, "A Summer of Innuendo: Contraction and Competition Among Dagestan's Political Elite," *Central Asian Survey* 20, June 2, 2001.

4. *Dagestanskaya pravda,* February 2, 1999.

5. Dagestan's largest ethnic group, the Avars, account for just over 29 percent of the Republic's population. Thus, all of Dagestan's thirty-four ethno-linguistic groups are technically "minorities." The language of the court is intended to apply to the smaller

ethnic groups, which would not be likely to receive proportionate representation in the absence of ethnic electoral districts.

6. *Dagestanskaya pravda,* February 2, 1999.

7. The situation in Dagestan, which is always complicated, was in fact not especially complicated at that time and was, if anything, likely to be more complicated at a future time. Dagestanis typically employ stalling tactics in order to avoid a dangerous crisis. Often the tactic is successful insofar as it permits the critical situation to cool.

8. An American might describe this in terms of ethnic quotas.

9. Local executive positions with duties comparable to mayors and county managers.

10. *Molodezh Dagestana,* no. 11, March 14, 2003.

11. Leninaul and Kalininaul are the Avar villages from which the residents have refused to move in order to permit rehabitation by Chechen-Akkin residents. The Chechen-Akkins had inhabited these villages prior to their deportation in 1944. At the time the Avars were forcibly transported to these villages, but they have argued that their previous residences are now uninhabitable.

12. It may be worth noting that Chirkey is the residence of one of Dagestan's most respected Sufi sheikhs, Said-afandi of Chirkey.

13. A *kutan* is a summer camp of shepherds high in the mountains, often distant from any village. It is indicative of the extremities that democracy faces in Dagestan that polling stations are established in such remote locations.

14. *Molodezh Dagestana,* no. 12, March 21, 2003.

15. *Molodezh Dagestana,* no. 14, April 4 2003.

16. Ibid.

17. *Dagestanskaya pravda,* May 21, 2003.

18. Due to their newly acquired legislative immunity.

19. G. Abashilov, "The Choice Has Been Made," *Molodezh Dagestana,* no. 12, March 21, 2003.

20. Politicians such as Gadzhi Makhachev, the ethnic Avar Duma representative, Saigidpasha Umakhanov, the Avar mayor of Khasaviurt, who is Magomedov's bitter enemy, and members of Derbent's Kurbanov family, an ethnic Azeri clan that cooperated with Magomedov.

21. Terms that have followed consecutively from the initial two-year transitional term to which he was limited in 1994.

22. Kisriev and Ware, "A Summer of Innuendo: Contraction and Competition Among Dagestan's Political Elite."

23. "Constitution of the Republic of Dagestan," *Dagestanskaya pravda,* June 11, 2003.

24. *Novoe delo,* June 12, 2003.

25. One of his examples was the Avar village of Akhvakh. See below for the ethnic implications of this example.

26. *Novoe delo,* June 12, 2003.

27. Ibid.

28. Ibid.

29. An electromechanical plant.

30. *Novoe delo,* June 12, 2003.

31. Ibid.

32. Ibid.

33. On May 28, 1998, Magomed and Nadir Khachilaev led approximately 200 gunmen when they stormed the main government building in Dagestan, known as the "White House." They departed peacefully the next day, after committing US$1.7 million in dam-

ages. The Khachilaevs claimed to be protesting government corruption in the republic, but appeared to be reacting to a shootout earlier that day between Nadir's entourage and police.

34. *Molodezh Dagestana,* June 12, 2003.

35. Ibid.

36. "Wahhabis Killed Him," *Novoe delo,* August 1, 2003.

37. Ibid.

38. Ibid.

39. "Dagestani Minister Says War on Terror Becoming too Politicized," *Dagestanskaya pravda,* August, 3, 2002.

40. "Car Bomb Driver Detained in Dagestan," Interfax-South, August 28, 2003.

41. Ibid.

42. "Wahhabites Return. Five Policemen Shot in Dagestan," *Izvestia,* October 2, 2003.

43. Rappani Khalilov was killed by Dagestani officials in a shootout on September 18, 2007.

44. "Saving Captain Bekbulatov," *Novoe delo,* October 3, 2003.

45. Ibid.

46. "Wahhabites Return."

47. "Policemen Were Killed as if to Order. Russia's Deputy General Prosecutor Suspects Wahhabites," *Kommersant,* October 1, 2003.

48. "Murder of Dagestani Nationalities Minister Gusaev Blamed on Wahhabites," *Nezavisimaya gazeta,* August 28, 2003.

49. "Official in Caucasus Who Opposed Radical Islamists Is Slain in Blast. Targeted Sect Draws Suspicion in Bombing That Kills a Minister of Russia's Dagestan," *Los Angeles Times,* August 28, 2003.

50. Ibid.

51. "Personal Enemy of Udugov Murdered in Makhachkala," www.utro.ru, August 27, 2003.

52. This is a reference to the central Dagestani villages of Karamakhi, Chabanmakhi, and Kadar, which became an enclave of Wahhabism after the end of 1997, were attacked by Dagestan OMON forces and federal troops during September 1999, and were reconstructed with federal funds distributed by Dagestani officials.

53. "A Unitary State with a Military Bureaucracy," *Nezavisimaya gazeta,* September 14, 2004.

54. See R. Ware, "Who Stole Russia's Election?" *Christian Science Monitor,* October 18, 2000; "Dagestan Demands a Recount," *Moscow Times,* November 12, 2000; Robert Ware and Enver Kisriev, "Ethnic Parity and Political Stability in Dagestan: A Consociational Approach," *Europe-Asia Studies* 53, January 1, 2001; Robert Ware, "Recent Russian Federal Elections in Dagestan: Implications for Proposed Electoral Reforms," *Europe-Asia Studies* 57, June 4, 2005.

55. Zubairu Zubairuev, "Incorrect 'Information,'" *Chernovik,* no. 28, July 22, 2005.

56. The report specifies that sociological studies were conducted by "the service of special communication and information of the Federal Protection Service of the Russian Federation."

57. The power struggle between Dagestan's largest ethnic group, the Avars, and the second largest groups, the Dargins, who controlled Dagestan's chief executive position and the mayor's office in Makhachkala. This changed when Mukhu Aliev, an Avar, was appointed as Dagestan's first president in February 2006.

58. Shikhsaidov left office abruptly and quietly, leading to speculation that he had

finally been compromised by his blatant corruption. Since his corruption had long been common knowledge, in the republic, his sudden departure suggested that he was being sidelined in advance of Dagestan's impending power struggle. This is consistent with his being used as a scapegoat in the report.

59. Aliev was rumored to have paid in excess of US$1 million for the privilege of succeeding Shikhsaidov.

60. "This Is My Final Decision," *Novoe delo,* no. 6, February 17, 2006.

61. Ibid.

62. Ibid.

63. *Novoe delo,* no. 7, February 24, 2006.

64. In Dagestan, there is uncertainty about the identity of the single representative who voted against Aliev. Some say that it was Suleiman Uladiev. However, others insist that Uladiev was absent from this session. It is possible that someone pressed Uladiev's voting button in his absence. It is also possible that someone else still harbored strong feelings against Aliev, or that someone pressed the negative button by mistake.

65. Magomedali, born in 1930, remains vigorous, and there have been no indications of debilitating ailments.

66. *Novoe delo,* no. 6, February 17, 2006.

67. For example, there is now a single Ministry of Industry, Transport, and Communication doing the work of two preceding ministries: the Ministry of Industry and Scientific and Technical Development and the Ministry of Transportation, Road Construction, and Telecommunication Systems. The Ministry of Youth and Tourism was eliminated, along with the Ministry of Melioration and Agricultural Water Supply. The Ministry of Education has now became the Ministry of Education, Science, and Youth Policies. The Ministry of Culture has become the Ministry of Culture and Tourism. The new government features at least five new ministers with proven business skills. Yet it still includes some of those who obtained their high positions, not by their qualifications, but through political appointments.

8. Conclusion: A Gathering Darkness

1. However, there was some evidence of fraud in federal elections. See Ware, "Recent Russian Federal Elections in Dagestan; Robert Ware: "Dagestan Demands a Recount," *Moscow Times,* November 12, 2000. The author has hypothesized that Dagestani officials allowed free local elections among Dagestani candidates, but manipulated federal election results to what they regarded as the benefit of the republic.

2. See E. Kisriev and R. Ware, "Russian Recentralization Arrives in the Republic of Dagestan: Implications for Institutional Integrity and Political Stability," *East European Constitutional Review* 10, no. 1 (Winter 2001); "A Summer of Innuendo: Contraction and Competition Among Dagestan's Political Elite," *Central Asian Survey* 20, June 2, 2001; with Werner Patzelt and Ute Roericht, "Russia and Chechnya from a Dagestani Perspective," *Post-Soviet Affairs* 18, December 4, 2002.

3. See Julia Latynina, "One Day of the President," *Chernovik,* no. 33, August 18, 2006.

4. *Novoe delo,* no. 16, April 28, 2006.

5. See, for example, Robert Ware and Enver Kisriev, "Ethnic Parity and Political Stability in Dagestan: A Consociational Approach," *Europe-Asia Studies* 53, January 1, 2001.

6. In the most blatant cases, people were simply offered cash (occasionally in excess of US$1,500), cans of meat, and the like, in exchange for a vote. In other cases, a candidate would promise to repair roads, install plumbing, and so on, in a village, or even complete such tasks in advance.

7. That is, local elections, or elections to the State Duma from Dagestan's single-member districts, in which all candidates were Dagestanis. In federal presidential and federal party list elections, where there were no Dagestani candidates or where Dagestanis competed with non-Dagestanis there is evidence that Dagestani officials managed the outcomes to benefit both themselves and the republic as a whole. See Ware, "Recent Russian Federal Elections in Dagestan"; Enver Kisriev and Robert Ware, "Dagestan's People's Assembly Election," *Electoral Studies* 20, June 3, 2001; Ware, "Dagestan Demands a Recount."

8. Julia Kalinina, "Clans Are Undermining Russia: In Dagestan, an Actual War Has Been Declared," *Moskovskii Komsomolets,* July 13, 2005.

9. Paul Goble, "Dagestani President Seeks to Stabilize his Republic by Reversing Putin Policy," *Window on Eurasia,* April 23, 2009.

Index

About the Authors

Robert Bruce Ware

Since completing his doctorate at Oxford University, Robert Bruce Ware has conducted field research in the North Caucasus, and has authored numerous articles on the region in scholarly and popular publications. He is a professor of philosophy at Southern Illinois University, Edwardsville.

Enver Kisriev

Enver Kisriev, a Dagestani sociologist, is studying the impact made by traditional institutions of Caucasian communities on the nature of modern political processes. With roots in the Lezgin town of Akhty, he was born in 1947 in Makhachkala, where he graduated from the Dagestan State University majoring in history. In 1972–75 he was a postgraduate in sociology at the Russian Academy of Sciences. After graduation he continued his research work in the Department of Sociology of the Dagestan branch of the Russian Academy of Sciences. In 1979 he defended his thesis titled "National and International in Ethnic and Cultural Processes in Dagestan." In 1988 he became director of the department. In 1994–98, he was an adviser to the chairperson of the Dagestani Parliament while simultaneously continuing his research at the Dagestani Academy of Sciences. In 2001, he moved to Moscow to work at the Moscow branch of the Russian Academy of Sciences and in 2003 he became head of the Sector for Caucasian Studies at the Center for Civilizational and Regional Studies of the Russian Academy of Sciences. He is the author of more than 200 publications.